IMAGING JAPANESE AMERICA

ELENA TAJIMA CREEF

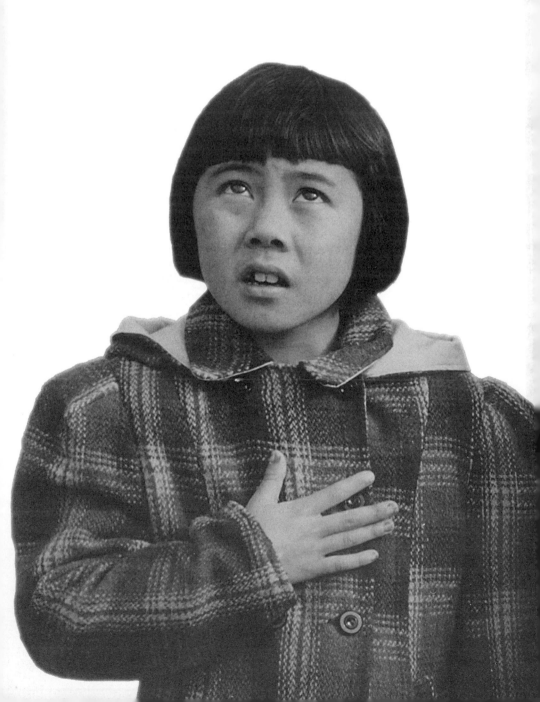

IMAGING JAPANESE AMERICA

THE VISUAL CONSTRUCTION OF CITIZENSHIP, NATION, AND THE BODY

NEW YORK UNIVERSITY PRESS

NEW YORK AND LONDON

NEW YORK UNIVERSITY PRESS
New York and London
www.nyupress.org

Library of Congress Cataloging-in Publication Data
Creef, Elena Tajima.
Imaging Japanese America : the visual construction of citizenship, nation, and the body / Elena Tajima Creef.
p. cm.
Includes bibliographical references and index.
ISBN 0–8147–1621–0 (cloth : alk. paper) —
ISBN 0–8147–1622–9 (pbk. : alk. paper)
1. Japanese Americans in art.   2. Arts, American—20th century.
3. Japanese Americans—Evacuation and relocation, 1942–1945.
4. Japanese Americans—Ethnic identity.   I. Title.
NX652.J37 C74 2004
700'.4529956073—dc22   2003016328

c 10 9 8 7 6 5 4 3 2 1
p 10 9 8 7 6 5 4 3 2 1

CONTENTS

ACKNOWLEDGMENTS

This book emerged from my work in the History of Consciousness program at the University of California at Santa Cruz, and many individuals and institutions have contributed to it in many ways. It is with great pleasure that I am finally able to name and thank all those who enabled me to complete this book.

For their guidance, support, and collective brilliance, I am indebted to Helene Moglen, Akasha Hull, Donna Haraway, Angela Davis, Stephen Heath, Teresa de Lauretis, Hayden White, Michael Cowan, and especially Jim Clifford. Thank you. As my guides and teachers in Santa Cruz, you have all motivated and inspired me more than you will ever know. My deepest gratitude to Sheila Peuse for years of support in all matters great and small and to the Feminist Research Activity Group and the Women's Studies Board—particularly the wisdom and example of Bettina Aptheker.

Renny Christopher, Ellen Hart, Ekua Omosupe, and Miriam Wallace provided invaluable support and friendship. My good friend and colleague Leslie Bow inspired and aided with her dazzling insights, suggestions, and faith in my work. At Wellesley College, I am indebted to the support and friendship of Susan Reverby, Rosanna Hertz, Margaret Centamore, and especially Geeta Patel, for her masterful editing and generous feedback. For their heroic support, I would also like to thank Margaret Ward and Alice Friedman (who inspired the title for this book).

For generously giving me their time and assistance during my research, I wish to thank Tom Crouch at the Smithsonian Institution National Air and Space Museum, the staff at the Eastern California History Museum, the Japanese American National History Museum, the Asian American Studies program at the University of California, Davis (especially Kent A. Ono and Darrell Y. Hamamoto), Bob Williams at the Camera Place in Wellesley, Bill McMorris at the Oakland Museum of California, and Seiko Buckingham. Also, my gratitude to the late Mine Okubo, whose friendship and generosity toward me on my many trips to New York I will always cherish. I am also indebted to the following individuals for allowing me to cite from or reproduce across a range of their creative work: Velina Hasu Houston, Thelma Seto, Ferris Takahashi, Ron Tanaka, Nellie Wong, Kia Asamiya, Asia Carrera, Stan Honda, Archie Miyatake, Renee Tajima-Pena, and Lynn Randolph.

My special thanks to Mitsuye Yamada and Shirley Geok-lin Lim, both of whom have been my role models in courage, teaching, and creativity.

My friends and colleagues—Vicente Diaz, Laura Hyun Yi Kang, Nora Okja Keller, Yuko Matsukawa, Glen Masato Mimura, Marita Sturken, Teresia Teaiwa, Jeni Yamada, Kath Weston, and Holly Uyemoto—for your years of inspiration, shared work, and friendship, I am indebted to you all.

To my students at Wellesley: I have treasured the opportunity to work closely with you over the years. You have been my greatest teachers. I am particularly indebted to Therese Leung, Michelle Cheuk, Mazeda Hossain, Hwasun Lee, and Elena A. Park for their careful research and assistance during the different stages of completing this book.

For their generosity of housing and friendship during my many sojourns back and forth across the country for research, I must thank the following: Yvonne Keller, Meret Keller, Ursula Heise, Melanie Haage, my family, Chiyohi, Art, and Valorie Creef, Dorothy Smith (a.k.a. "Milly"), and Karen Schmidt. I am also grateful for support I received during the writing and research of this book from Wellesley College, the Humanities Research Institute at the University of California, Irvine, and the East-West Center in Honolulu.

At New York University Press, I am indebted to Eric Zinner and Emily Park, who recognized the value of this project and generously shepherded it through the process.

On a personal note, my deepest special thanks to Mark and Skylar Schmidt. To you both I am indebted, past, present, and future, for your love, support, last-minute pinch-hitting as my assistants, and unfailing belief in the best part of me.

Introduction
Carving Japanese American Memory into Place

> In my own journey, the road is a metaphor for the Asian American experience—that is, the exuberant promise of the American landscape, juxtaposed with the loneliness of being considered a foreigner at home. Will we ever truly belong in America? . . . Asian America . . . is a dense, complex landscape—ranging from empirical demographic data to subliminal media messages, romance, public policy, and family legend. Therefore, as metaphor, the road is traveled not only literally in the film. Memory is carved into place, in the subjects and in the past.
>
> —Renee Tajima-Pena, "No Mo Po Mo
> and Other Tales of the Road"

It is not surprising that Japanese American filmmaker Renee Tajima-Pena's first feature-length work, *My America—or Honk if You Love Buddha* (1997), was released just before the turn of the millennium. Crisscrossing the country in search of what she calls "Asian America," her film offers a visual cartography of Asian American identity on the eve of the twenty-first century.[1] In it she literally maps an Asian American presence on the cultural topography of our national historical memory. Her coast-to-coast journey offers us a radical rethinking and revising of the cultural, historical, and political forces that have shaped Asian Americans as citizens of the nation.

The opening image of *My America* consists of a re-creation of a childhood family photograph where the filmmaker poses in front of that unmistakable icon of American identity and nationhood: the

Renee Tajima-Pena as a child of the nation on the road in America. *(Calvin Tajima. Courtesy of Renee Tajima-Pena.)*

Statue of Liberty. This image is accompanied with the following monologue:

> To tell you the truth, I never would have been born if it hadn't been for a mob of Asian haters. You see back in 1906, my grandfather left his family in Japan to start a new life in America. But as soon as he stepped on shore in San Francisco, he was chased down by angry merchant marines. They were battering him with rocks and yelling, "Go home, chink!" So what did grandpa do? Well, he ran for his life and headed south for Los Angeles. And that's how my grandfather just barely missed the great San Francisco earthquake the very next day.

Tajima-Pena's origin story is here self-consciously framed in a narrative of racial hatred, violence, and the ironic, random relationship between Japanese immigration and settlement at the beginning of the twentieth century. Fresh off the boat from Japan, her grandfather steps onto American soil only to be targeted by a confused mob of "Asian haters" who can't tell Chinese apart from Japanese. Just two generations later, the Tajima home movies attest to how well her family has visibly assimilated into the promise of a "new life in America" as second-generation citizens of the nation. Scenes like this remind us of the twentieth-century struggle of Asian Americans to lay claim to the nation even as their individual rights to citizenship were denied or violated. Her film also bears witness to the race-specific consequences of having a body that has been and continues to be subject to scrutiny, misreading, and violence.

The ensuing images from her family's home movies also work to underscore the Tajimas' visible assimilation as fully Americanized *nisei* (second generation) and *sansei* (third generation) whose summer car trips to Mount Rushmore, New York City, and local participation in hometown parades and cowboy pony rides mark their disappearance into what can only be called white Americana. Indeed, Tajima-Pena later reveals that her mother actually "believed that being too Japanese got her sent to the camps," so she and her brothers "were raised to just blend in."

Tajima-Pena herself makes this clear in the recitation of her family biography:

> I was born about two blocks from Wrigley Field. Mom and Dad were the Japanese version of Ozzie and Harriet. Every summer, we piled into the Ford Fairlane and took off for the open road. But I noticed something odd. We'd drive clear across five states and never catch a glimpse of another Asian face.

Her family's visible assimilation into mainstream American culture is rattled only by her growing awareness of the invisibility of Asian Americans across five states. With an ironic sense of humor and an inherent sense of toughness that goes back two generations,

Tajima-Pena recalls, "Whenever I've gotten the same crap as my grandfather, 'go back to where you came from,' I think to myself, what do you mean, Chicago?"

The filmmaker pinpoints the birth of her critical consciousness as a Japanese American to a key moment from her childhood when she interviewed her grandparents about their internment camp experience for a school project. Tajima-Pena recalls:

> My teacher told the class that they were lying. That something like the camps could never happen in America. In that moment I knew it was racism that defined my life and I would never turn the other cheek as my parents had. I'd fight back.

Scenes like this remind us that the repression of historical memory is never accidental but often shaped by the culture of racism. We are also reminded that Japanese American history, particularly the chapter on World War II internment, has been subjected to a very particular mode of late twentieth century repression and erasure.

While *My America* is certainly less about Tajima-Pena's own family history than it is about how Asian Americans have shaped American culture, I invoke the film here in order to extract the filmmaker's strands of Japanese American representation for the larger purposes of this book. If her film tells a story about the multiple ways that Japanese American history and experience have been repressed or erased from dominant view, then her film also demands that Japanese American history be carved back into the topography of places, bodies, and collective and individual historical memory.

There is no better scene in *My America* that illustrates this process than the encounter between legendary activist Yuri Kochiyama and a white Arkansas farmer who meet in the middle of what was once a World War II internment camp in Jerome, Arkansas. In this poignant exchange, memory is carved not only onto the blank physical space of the former camp, but is also stamped onto the bodies of Yuri and the farmer, both of whom remember and retell the story of what happened once in this place. As Bill and Yuri Kochiyama pull up to the site of her former camp, the latter incredulously surveys the flattened landscape and asks, "Wait a minute. That's all that's left?

Where was the camp? What's all that empty space? Is that the camp?" A local white farmer, who has pulled up in a truck, joins the conversation:

> FARMER: I'd taken a bulldozer and buried this thing.
> YURI: You buried what thing?
> FARMER: The camp.
> YURI: Oh, *you* did it?
> FARMER: Oh, yeah. It's buried. A buried city. There was 10,000 of ya'll here. . . . Ya'll wasn't prisoners of war, you was interned . . . for your protection . . . they claimed.

The farmer turns out to be John Ernest Arlington, a local witness to wartime history who remembers when the Japanese Americans were interned in Jerome. In their animated exchange, he tells Yuri that "he fell in love with them" and spent the war years alongside the Japanese Americans. In his recollection of those years, he remembers the great injustice that was done to them and that they "cried just like the white people" over wartime tragedy and loss. In the absence of physical markers signifying Jerome's history, John Ernest Arlington becomes an unexpected living link to camp history and memory as he wistfully observes to an off-screen Tajima-Pena, "Lookee here, girl, all the people that was here is now dead and gone. You're talking about forty years ago and the young folks here don't even know what it's all about." The scene becomes memorable for its double irony: the same farmer who once bulldozed traces of camp memory from the landscape also gives historical testimony through his own sentimental recollections some fifty years later. What remains so unexpected about the scene is that he should have such a simple yet profound grasp on the inherent contradiction between the remembered humanity of the internees and the system of wartime representation that would have marked them as *other* and as enemies. The scene concludes with Yuri snapping a photograph not of the ruined landscape, but of the Arkansas farmer whose body ironically signifies historical memory. She scribbles his name in her notebook so that she can remember their encounter across time in the empty fields of what was once Jerome.

The theme of how Japanese American subjects are looked at and scrutinized under a uniquely American style of representation and how the internment experience is remembered will form the basis for much of this book. Of particular interest are those moments where Japanese Americans have disrupted what performance theorist Peggy Phelan has termed the "psychic and aesthetic economy of the Western gaze," where the "visible image of the *other* necessarily becomes a cipher for the looking self."[2] Such moments of disruption, schism, reversal, or self-articulation and representation expose the mechanics of how highly constructed versions of race, class, gender, and sexuality permeate the visual economy of Japanese American representation.

It is clear throughout *My America* that Tajima-Pena is highly aware of the signifying power of the Asian American body.[3] She fascinates us with her kitschy footage of the unexpected roadside spectacle of an underwater Wiki-Wachi Oriental mermaid show in the South, the hypocrisy of Orange County Chinese American debutantes who parade femininity, heterosexuality, and academic achievement for their parents and Chinese American escorts, the macho posturing of Korean American "Seoul" brothers who are good boys when their parents are around and bad boys when they are alone in front of Tajima-Pena's camera, and the concluding articulations of Mads, the final character in the film, who is highly self-conscious of the infinite signifying power of her own body as a multiracial South Asian "lesbian woman, liberal Indian, and conservative German" now living in the United States. Tajima-Pena's film offers us a thoughtful and provocative examination of what cultural critic Lisa Lowe has elsewhere termed the remarkable "heterogeneity, multiplicity, and hybridity" that marks Asian Americans as a collective body.[4]

This book argues that the visual history of Japanese American representation in the United States has always contained to some degree lessons in the success or failure of how we are supposed to read Asian bodies. Such (mis)readings certainly mark much of the visual representation surrounding Japanese Americans from the internment camps of World War II to the 1992 Winter Olympic games in Albertville, where racial difference is both defined and contained within the framework of enemy aliens, model minorities, and an idealized notion of white American citizenship.

Poet Mitsuye Yamada offers a brilliant grasp of how Asian Americans are scripted outside the visual politics of representation of nation and citizenship. "Mirror Mirror" and "Looking Out" are two excellent examples of what Dorinne Kondo has called "counter-Orientalist" disruptions of the visual economy of representation through the speaker's steadfast refusal to see herself as the Other.[5] Here, identities are literally turned inside out in Yamada's keen understanding of how the politics of the visible are clearly rooted in the politics of one's own positioning and perspective—particularly in the act of looking, writing, or speaking as an American subject.

It must be odd
to be a minority
he was saying.
I looked around
and didn't see any.
So I said
Yeah
it must be.[6]

People keep asking where I come from
says my son.
Trouble is I'm american on the inside
and oriental on the outside
No Kai
Turn that outside in
THIS is what America looks like.[7]

Just exactly "what America looks like" continues to be part of the current crisis in multicultural representation in the United States, where the changing face of its citizenry reflects a national shift in racial demographics.[8] This book seeks to contribute to the new and growing field of Asian American visual and cultural studies in its examination of Japanese American representations in the World War II and postwar years across documentary photography, camp art, film

and video, museum exhibitions, and multimedia and literary representations.[9]

In his book, *Asian/American,* David Palumbo-Liu discusses the
multiple signifying power of the Asian American body in historical
discourse. He writes:

> [By] "Body," I mean both the material, corporeal forms of
> Asian American peoples and the semiotics of those forms—
> that is, both the objective body, with its particular inscriptions
> in material history, and the way that body is semiotically
> deployed in social and cultural discourse.[10]

His description makes clear that he invokes the body as a corporeal
and symbolic construction. *Imaging Japanese America* asks in how
many ways has the Japanese American body been semiotically constructed and inscribed in internment and post-internment representation?

Asian American literary scholars like David Leiwei Li have argued
that the historical process by which the "Oriental" became exclusively racialized as "foreign" is rooted in the late nineteenth and early
twentieth century history of American national formation. Li argues
that the study of Asian American literary production forms another
crucial strand in the "cultural narration of the nation."[11] In particular, his book seeks to illuminate the "repressed relation between the
acts of Asian exclusion and American national formation."[12] He argues that the 1882 Chinese Exclusion Act, the Gentleman's Agreement of 1908, the Immigration Act of 1917, the Immigration Act of
1924, the Tydings-McDuffe Act of 1934, and the Japanese American
internment experience in World War II collectively constitute "direct
expressions of massive American anxiety about the nature of the nation and the contour of the citizenry."[13]

Imaging Japanese America picks up on this latter strand and argues that the representation of the internment experience is worthy
of close critical scrutiny for how it offers a particular visual narration of "massive American anxiety about the nation" through the vehicle of the Japanese American body. This book argues that with respect to twentieth-century Japanese American representation, there

is no single other defining historical event or moment than the mass relocation and internment of 120,000 Japanese Americans during World War II—an event that historian Roger Daniels has argued "remains the central event of Japanese American history."[14] This book positions the visual representation of this historical event as its central subject of critical inquiry. In chapters that specifically examine postwar representations, this book persistently asks what has been the fallout of Executive Order 9066 on the subsequent imaging and imagining of Japanese Americans?

As we have been reminded by the recent national trauma of September 11, 2001, in times of national crisis we take refuge in the visual construction of citizenship in order to imagine ourselves as part of a larger, cohesive, national American community. This book begins by reaching back to another moment of national historical trauma, December 7, 1941, with a simple question: How do wartime photographs create a visual rhetoric signaling "massive American anxiety" about citizenship, loyalty, and obedience to the nation? And how have these images endured throughout the last half of the twentieth century? This book operates on the premise that visual representations can be read on two fundamental levels: (1) as "narratives" that can be subjected to the same kind of critical and theoretical scrutiny, interpretation, and analysis as literary texts, and (2) as symbolic "texts" that instruct us how to "read" the narrative of citizenship and national formation through the lens of race, class, and gender politics.

The book's thesis argues that there is a distinct visual rhetoric in the symbolic and cultural representation of Japanese Americans in the mid- to late twentieth century, where the racist hysteria of World War II unjustly framed this ethnic community as disloyal citizens of the nation. The systematic nature of this racist discourse has had a profound and lasting impact on the visual representation of this marginalized group of Americans. This book offers an interdisciplinary critical analysis of the visual representation of Japanese Americans in the World War II period (1941–1945), then interrogates the ways that American historical memory of World War II continues to shape representations of Japanese Americans, and finally ends with a look at contemporary representations of hybrid multiracial Japanese

Americans as we move into a new century. *Imaging Japanese America* deliberately engages multiple theoretical discourses from women's studies, ethnic studies, and visual culture and uses methodological approaches from feminist theory, semiotics, and literary analysis in its comparative analysis of a wide range of visual and "textual" materials.

In order to begin assessing the visual representation of the relocation and internment experience, we need to chart the lasting impact of this experience in American popular culture and historical consciousness. Chapters 1 and 2 suggest that a point of origin for the visual imaging of this event in Japanese American history begins with its wartime documentation in photography and art by those on both the inside and outside of the experience.

In chapter 1 I argue that the documentary photographs of Ansel Adams, Dorothea Lange, and Toyo Miyatake have remained the most potent images of Japanese Americans behind barbed wire precisely because of their visual power—even fifty years later—to recuperate and transform interned Japanese Americans into loyal American citizens. These photographs are visually striking in contrast to other wartime images of Japanese nationals and "disloyal" Japanese American citizens.

Chapter 2 contrasts the previous body of documentary photography with that of autobiographical self-representations of Japanese American relocation and internment—privileging what art historians like Karin Higa and others have dubbed "the view from within."[15] This chapter offers a brief survey of published collections of camp art before turning its attention to what is perhaps the most widely read but least critically examined work on this subject, artist Mine Okubo's *Citizen 13660*.

Chapter 3 addresses the dramatic lack of representation of Japanese American wartime history in Hollywood film compared to its obsessive treatment in independent Asian American film and video. This chapter then offers a reading and analysis of three films that narrate the Japanese American relocation and internment experience through the spectacle of interracial romance: Steven Okazaki's *Days of Waiting* (1988), Alan Parker's *Come See the Paradise* (1990), and Scott Hicks's *Snow Falling on Cedars* (1999). Each of these films presents us with complex narratives of race, class, and gender subjugation, which, ironically, use Japanese American wartime history as vehicles for the representation of white liberal heroism.

Chapter 4 documents the current representational issues at stake since Congress designated on March 3, 1992, the former site of Manzanar War Relocation Center in Inyo County, California, as a National Historic Site. The designation of Manzanar as a historic site has generated enormous local and national controversy involving the politics of representing a collective public memory of the treatment of Japanese Americans during World War II. This chapter examines the politics of representation at Manzanar in a comparative framework that also includes contemporary exhibitions of internment history at the Smithsonian Institution's American History Museum and the Los Angeles Japanese American National History Museum.

Chapter 5 traces the discomfort of postwar representations of Japanese Americans in popular culture using figure skater Kristi Yamaguchi as a case study. How are contemporary representations of Japanese Americans in popular culture inflected by the politics of historical memory and amnesia from World War II? How does an American style of Orientalist representation continue to conflate Japanese with Japanese Americans in disturbing ways? In particular, this chapter looks at the ways in which Japanese American skater Yamaguchi was visually and rhetorically pitted against Japanese national skater, Midori Ito, in the media coverage of the women's figure skating competition. Chapter 5 offers a gendered analysis of the racist and nationalist nature of the discourse surrounding these Japanese and Japanese American women.

Imaging Japanese America concludes with an Epilogue that looks at the representation of the multiracial Japanese American body at the turn of the millennium. Beginning with multiracial writers and performers who have evinced discomfort with the visual politics of their representation, the Epilogue closes with a series of multiracial Japanese American and Asian American bodies that offer us complex and even pleasurable trajectories for imagining multicultural, multiracial, and multilingual American representation at the beginning of the twenty-first century.

In closing this introduction, I would like to return briefly to the film with which I began. Renee Tajima-Pena's *My America* is filled with memorable episodes and anecdotal accounts of the myriad ways that Asian Americans have had to stake their claim on the nation with force, insistence, and a sense of entitlement that has historically been undermined. Tajima-Pena's film makes clear that as "her America" moves into the twenty-first century, the nation is already indelibly stamped with an Asian American past, present, and future. The opening shot from the film is fashioned after a childhood family photograph of the filmmaker standing before her father's tourist camera. Although the original photograph does not appear in the film, it was used on the video box cover and the poster for the film. The photograph is striking for its juxtaposition of the innocence of Japanese American girlhood standing back to back with that oversized and gendered icon of the nation: the Statue of Liberty.[16] In the photograph, Tajima-Pena is visually stitched into a narrative of the nation as one of its children and as one of its rightful citizen subjects. The image is a striking one for how it positions Japanese American girlhood into a framework of patriotism and citizenship. The visual construction of Japanese American girls as emblems of loyalty and nationhood was originally deployed, as we shall see, over fifty-five years ago by photographer Ansel Adams in his powerful and iconographic photographs of internees at Manzanar. *Imaging Japanese America* begins with an examination of just exactly how we might read such a visual construction of citizenship, nation, and the gendered Japanese American body.

CHAPTER ONE

The Representation of the Japanese American Body in the Documentary Photography of Ansel Adams, Dorothea Lange, and Toyo Miyatake

> This is a face
> (Nisei! Nisei!)
> My face of astigmatic . . .
> Other eyes . . .
> I have no face . . .
> To look the thing I hate and what I am:
> . . . Where is the heart to scour this enemy mask?
> Nailed on my flesh and artifact of my veins?
> Where is the judge of the infernal poll
> Where they vote round eyes honest and mine knave?
> This is a dream,
> These eyes, this face
> . . . Clutched on my twitching plasm like a monstrous growth,
> A twining of hair, of pulp, of teeth . . .
> . . . Tell me this is no face,
> This face of mine—
> It is the face of Angloid eyes who hate.
>
> —Ferris Takahashi, "Nisei! Nisei!" (1946)

Ferris Takahashi's poem "Nisei! Nisei!" speaks to the painful post–World War II legacy of the relationship of the second-generation Japanese American self to the body.[1] Under a hostile Anglo-Orientalist gaze, the Japanese American body is synecdochically broken down into its most visibly different and racially marked constituent parts: eyes, face, teeth, and skin. Within this representation, the Japanese American self becomes almost irreparably distanced from its own body—one which has been rendered not only "Other," but "monstrous" as well. Buried beneath a flesh and blood "enemy mask," the Japanese American self is rendered invisible—and un-readable—on the alienated surface of the body. Published in 1946, on the heels of World War II, the poem offers the reader a moving glimpse into the process of internalized self-hatred—Japanese American-style: "To look the thing I hate and what I am: (Nisei, Nisei!)."

In his 1971 autobiography, Daniel Okimoto rearticulates the phe-nomenon of this schism between the Japanese American body and the self, which he dubs the "American in Disguise" syndrome where "physical characteristics made a kind of mask that prevented the 'others' (as we thought of them) from seeing us as we truly were."[2] He confesses:

> For much of my life, I had struggled with the conviction that I was an American in disguise, a creature part of, yet somehow detached from, the mainstream of American society. This sense of alienation had been a fact of my life from its very beginning, as I was born, the last son of immigrant parents, in the stables of a racetrack in Southern California designated as a transfer point for those Japanese on the West Coast who were being herded into wartime internment camps.[3]

Okimoto gives voice to the origin story behind second-generation Japanese American self-alienation—a moment which he suggests can be traced back to the uprooting and interning of the West Coast Japanese American community during World War II. Certainly one of the most striking and recurrent themes in the Japanese American autobiographies published after the war is that which literary critic Elaine Kim has identified as the "process of self-negation" as writers like Takahashi, Okimoto, Monica Sone (*Nisei Daughter*, 1953), Jeanne Wakatsuki Houston (*Farewell to Manzanar*, 1973) and others chroni-cle an internalized struggle to choose between the (falsely) dichoto-mous poles of a Japanese versus an American identity.[4] The narrator of Sone's *Nisei Daughter* literally feels herself torn asunder under the directive of Executive Order 9066 and describes herself a "despised, pathetic, two-headed freak, a Japanese and an American."[5] Likewise, Houston recounts that her childhood "fear of Oriental faces"—first developed within the Japanese American community on Terminal Island in California—gave way to a fascination with Japanese American faces, bodies, and dress at Manzanar, where she became a captive spectator of exoticism and difference. In the innocence of childhood, it does not occur to her that her own Japanese American face is a smale-scale mirror for that which both repels and intrigues her.

The internalized dilemma between the Japanese American self and body was certainly compounded during the aftermath of the bombing of Pearl Harbor by the seeming inability of white Americans to tell the difference not only between Asians of different ethnicities, but between the faces of the Japanese enemy and that of Japanese American citizens.[6] In a 1943 *Liberty* magazine essay, Mary Oyama speaks to this predicament:

> I used to tell myself in the camp that my only crime was my face. But now, when I look in the mirror, I remember what a friend once said: "When I first met you, Mary, I just couldn't get over the novelty of your Japanese face. Strange that an American like you should look like that. First it was ninety percent strangeness and novelty and maybe ten percent friendly interest. About the second time I saw you, it was fifty percent novelty and fifty percent friendliness. Now I begin to notice less what you *look* like and to know more what you *really are*. Pretty soon I'll forget what you look like altogether. I'll know you only as another fellow American."[7]

In Oyama's account, what is both "strange" and "novel" to her white friend is that her Asian face should appear to be at odds with her identity as an American citizen.

Photographer Emily Medvec also reminds us that outside of the internment camps, in war-hysteric America, "the Japanese face was being engraved on the public mind . . . [through] its exposure to atrocity films, racist headlines and columns and poster campaigns."[8]

She argues that the American public grew to recognize the Japanese face as "dangerous, frightening, and grotesque." Indeed, General John L. DeWitt of the Western Defense Command—one of the strongest forces behind President Franklin D. Roosevelt's signing of Executive Order 9066—forcefully argued that loyal and disloyal Japanese and Japanese Americans could not physically be distinguished from one another with any degree of certainty:

> The Japanese race is an enemy race and while many second and third generation Japanese born on United States soil, possessed of United States citizenship, have become "Americanized" the racial strains are undiluted.

> This population presented a tightly knit racial group. . . . While it was believed that some were loyal, it was known that many were not. To complicate the situation *no ready means existed for determining the loyal and the disloyal with any degree of safety.*[9]

In DeWitt's words, the difference between *loyal* and *disloyal* citizens, which was critical for national security, was also unreadable on the inscrutable Japanese American body; hence, mass migration and incarceration was a more viable solution.[10] In the racist hysteria of post–Pearl Harbor America, not only was the surface of the Japanese American body impossible to read, but DeWitt and others stressed that Japanese treachery was also a biological trait passed on by "undiluted" blood between generations. A *Los Angeles Times* editorial, which appeared just after the bombing of Pearl Harbor, makes a similar argument that Japanese treachery is inherently a matter of blood biology: "A viper is nonetheless a viper wherever the eggs are hatched—so a Japanese American, born of Japanese parents—grows up to be a Japanese, not an American."[11] Within this wartime logic of visual representation and virulent wartime racism, both the Japanese American body and its blood become sites/sights of difference, disloyalty, danger, and degradation that must be appropriately contained, disciplined, and punished for the duration of the war.[12]

Visualizing an Invisible History

Critics like John Welchman have argued that perhaps the two most "controversial and repressed chapters in modern American history [include] the everyday life of blacks in the mid-19th century pre-abolitionist South, and the internment camps that held Americans of Japanese ancestry during World War II."[13] That so little is known about these two historical events—outside the world of specialized scholarship—speaks to our national propensity to render invisible that which is historically too painful to look at and to silence that which still invokes our national shame. And yet it is hardly surprising that the Japanese American internment camp experience has remained so invisible in collective American public memory, given the scarcity of photographic evidence that was allowed to circulate during and immediately after the war. Indeed, critic Marita Sturken has observed that the internment is just one of several "events of World War II that did not produce image-icons" for our national American consciousness.[14] Sturken argues that in contrast to other wartime events involving Americans, there is a corresponding blind spot in the visual history surrounding the camps.

It is no longer a secret that the federal government attempted to control the wartime representation of the Japanese American internment camps through a campaign of visual censorship. In the early days of relocation and internment, cameras and other recording devices in the hands of the internees were strictly banned even as official War Relocation Authority (WRA), Farm Security Administration (FSA), Office of War Information, and military photographers were assigned the task of making a nonpublic visual record of the entire process of evacuation and relocation.[15] In the last twenty-five years, the visual archive of camp representations has noticeably expanded with the new body of work by Asian American filmmakers and video artists who continue to explore the historical trauma of the camps heaped on individuals and families, drawing on official government film footage and illicit home-made movies by internees with 8mm cameras that were smuggled into the camps.[16] Fifty years later, with the visibility and success of the redress and reparations

ment only a decade behind us, and despite the permanent ex-
on the internment camps at the Smithsonian Institution's
rican History Museum, this history remains largely invisible and
ginalized within national American memory and consciousness.

In this chapter I argue that in the twentieth-century history of
Japanese American representation, the mass relocation and internment of some 120,000 Japanese and Japanese Americans continues
to stand as the defining moment of the visual and psychic coloniza-
tion of the Japanese American body that has yet to be fully resolved.
I begin with an examination of the most famous archive of photographic images produced by Ansel Adams, Dorothea Lange, and
Toyo Miyatake. I pose these three photographers together for their
role in producing the most powerful—and arguably iconic—body
of images of Japanese Americans during the war. Their photographs
are also remarkable for the complex ways in which they each attempted to reinscribe the Japanese American face and body with visible signs of American citizenship, loyalty, heroism. The photographic modes of their wartime work are as varied as the photographers themselves and continue to teach us about the visual politics
of representation of race, class, and gender.

"I Do Not Recall One Sullen Face in Manzanar": Documenting the Face of Loyalty in Ansel Adams's Photographs of the Internment

In the opening pages of *Born Free and Equal,* Adams writes, "moved
by the human story unfolding in the encirclement of desert and
mountains and by the wish to identify my photography in some creative way with the tragic momentum of the times, I came to Manzanar with my cameras in the fall of 1943."[17] As a civilian photographer,
Adams was given enormous freedom, over an eighteen-month period, to come and go as he pleased by his friend, camp director
Ralph Palmer Merritt.[18] Indeed, he was given only three official restrictions on what he was not allowed to photograph at Manzanar:
no barbed wire, no armed guards, and no guard towers.[19] Authorized
by the War Relocation Authority, *Born Free and Equal* appeared first
as an exhibit of photographs and as a published text in 1944.[20] It is

unique both as the only political photo-essay to be produced by Adams as well as for its enduring postwar legacy as one of the most celebrated collections of internment camp photographs.

There is no doubt that *Born Free and Equal* is a bold and liberal wartime project laudable for its antiracist agenda during a time when anti-Japanese sentiment was at its peak. Adams himself admits in his introduction that he had two urgent goals at stake in the publication of the book: to "suggest the broad concepts of American citizenship, and of liberal, democratic life the world over" and also to offer visible proof of the loyalty inscribed on the bodies of individual Japanese American citizens unjustly interned. The collection is most striking for its dramatic representation of the relationship of internees to the land, its highly aestheticized images of productive life behind barbed wire, and for its strategic use of the extreme close-up interspersed with vast panoramas of depeopled landscapes. Already explicit in the subtitle of the collection, "photographs of the *loyal* Japanese Americans at Manzanar," Adams not only constructs a visual record of loyalty for a hostile wartime audience but creates powerful wartime counterimages of the Japanese American face. Today, the photographs continue to stand as a fascinating study in the visual politics of Asian American representation, where Japanese Americans are de-Orientalized and refashioned into unambiguously all-American citizen subjects.

If anthropologist and cultural critic Dorinne Kondo is correct that the "face is our primary external, bodily locus of identity," then what is so striking throughout the pages of *Born Free and Equal* is how Adams's photographs work to reappropriate the Japanese American face as an iconographic sign for American citizenship.[21] Critics like Jan Zita Grover have noted that Adams's "use of [extreme] close-ups and strong outdoor lighting produced a visual rhetoric of nothing to hide" and "remorseless scrutiny" that was strategically necessary in his presentation of internees as unjustly incarcerated American citizens.[22] Given the particularly racist nature of U.S. wartime representations of the Japanese, Adams's selection of internees seems calculated to humanize the Japanese Americans at Manzanar for a white American gaze. Not a "sullen face among them," Adams's internees appear to have been handpicked for their

An American school girl.
*(Ansel Adams. Library of Congress,
Prints and Photographs Divisions.)*

"Is her future only a hope
and not an assurance?"
*(Ansel Adams. Library of Congress,
Prints and Photographs Divisions.)*

"The human challenge
rises over all America."
*(Ansel Adams. Library of
Congress, Prints and
Photographs Divisions.)*

photogenic appeal as "solid," "cheerful," and thoroughly "clean" men, women, and children whose distinct style of civilian or military clothing and hairstyles also encodes them as familiar, as non-Other, as Western, indeed as recognizably American—not Asian. Adams's Japanese American subjects are carefully posed, dressed, and aesthetically arranged as if to offer visible proof of their loyalty.

While the majority of Adams's close-up portraits at Manzanar focus on Japanese American men—in civilian or military uniform—it is intriguing that out of some twenty-five photographs, nearly one-fourth are comprised of young Japanese American schoolgirls. Adams disturbs us through his deliberate representation of so many visually harmless and recognizably American children in the camps. Interestingly, there are no corresponding individual close-up images of young Japanese American schoolboys in the collection. The first close-up portrait to confront the reader of *Born Free and Equal* is a head shot of a smiling girl who returns the scrutinizing gaze of Adams's camera with that of her own. Adams's caption gives us no name and instead simply identifies her as an "American school girl." The second and third close-up portraits similarly feature schoolgirls. In each of these and the subsequent portraits, Adams strategically downplays the signs of racial difference mediated through the Japanese American body; instead, the eye is drawn to an American style of feminine clothing and adornment, where Peter Pan collars peek out of cardigan sweaters and pinafores, hair is arranged in pig tails or Shirley Temple ringlets held together with bobby pins, barrettes, or ribbons, and faces are marked by smiles, freckles, and childhood innocence. Adams's careful selection recoups the girls from a visual Orientalist rhetoric of yellow menace, treachery, enemy, alien, and inscrutable Otherness.

The photographs are not only encoded with the recognizable signs of American identity and culture, but Adams marshals sentiment through narrative captions that frame the schoolgirls as good and innocent young citizens of the nation:

> "Is her future only a hope and not an assurance?"
> "The human challenge rises over all America."
> "Americanism is a matter of the mind and heart."

That these docile American bodies are interned in violation of their constitutional rights makes the reader—and by implication the nation—morally culpable for their wartime detention behind barbed wire.

In the absence of any similar close-up representations of schoolboys, Adams's photographs can be read as a kind of visual pedagogy where young Japanese American girls are depicted as educable American subjects who offer the possibility of later producing tractable, cooperative, and loyal citizens of a postwar nation. (Indeed, given the postwar phenomenon of Japanese American women's out-marriage, both the Japanese American body and Japanese American blood will become available to white men in the process of a more complete Americanization.)

Adams's use of submissive Japanese American schoolgirls also thwarts the possibility for a visual memory of Pearl Harbor that the specter of Japanese American schoolboys potentially embodies. Just as the figure of the schoolgirl suggests the potential for motherhood and reproduction of the nation, the figure of the schoolboy leaves open the possibility of adult male militarization and inculcation to war. Indeed, the flip side of the representation of the loyal and heroic Japanese American soldier fighting in the all-nisei segregated units is that of the young *kibei* (U.S. born and educated in Japan) men who denounced their allegiance to a nation bent on their mass relocation and internment. The scant visual archival record of the "No No Boys" forms a counterrepresentation to Adams's photographs of "loyal Japanese Americans at Manzanar."[23]

Perhaps the most striking photographic record of the "disloyal" Japanese American men are the *Life* magazine images taken by photojournalist Carl Mydans on his visit to Tule Lake War Relocation Center in California—the most stigmatized of the ten internment camps for its status as a segregated prison for "disloyal' Japanese and Japanese Americans. In Mydans's photo-essay, he depicts the contrasting body language of young "loyal" Japanese American couples happily awaiting transfer out of Tule Lake to more formidable camps like Manzanar, while those individual men who are identified as "disloyal" prisoners or "Jap troublemakers" slump before his camera in abject, even sullen, self-absorption, or else stand tall and defiant in a photographic lineup, arms crossed or hands pushed deep into pockets, adopting hostile body language in response to the photojournalist's invasive camera.[24]

Adams himself believed that before his arrival at Manzanar, the "dangerous, disloyal individuals [had already] been apprehended and . . . properly dealt with."[25] While there are no individual schoolboys in *Born Free and Equal*, Adams carefully includes close-up images of full-grown Japanese American men, including two uniformed soldiers and one elderly veteran of the Spanish-American War.[26] These men appear, however, subsequent to the parade of schoolgirls who visually set up the conditions for good citizenship and make possible the notion of fully Americanized Japanese American men who take up arms and go to war on behalf of the nation. With the exception of the soldiers, the majority of Adams's close-up portraits of the adult men at Manzanar are not presented with names, but rather are represented as masculine American archetypes of blue- and white-collar wartime workers: the X-ray technician, the student of divinity, the accountant, the electrician, the student of journalism, the garment designer, the welder, the student of diplomacy, the hard-working truck farmer, the tractor mechanic, and the rubber chemist. Called upon to work at Manzanar, these men are productive citizens who clearly pose no danger to the nation.

Adams himself has said that he photographed heads as he would photograph sculpture, where "the head or figure is clearly presented as an object . . . the edge, mass, texture of the skin and general architecture of the face and form is revealed with great intensity."[27] Although Adams's close-up scrutiny attempts to break the stereotypical *inscrutability* of Oriental faces, there is still, ironically, an almost impenetrable, masklike quality to many of his images of adult Japanese American men and women. Consider his photographs of Corporal Jimmie Shohara, Corporal Sato, nurse Aiko Hamaguchi, and Private Margaret Fukuoka, WAC.

Corporal Shohara is perhaps the hardest figure "to read" in this grouping: His upper face is literally half-masked in the contrast between light and shadow. Sandwiched between a U.S. Army hat and uniform, Shohara is visually coded "loyal American soldier." Likewise, the severe close-up of Nurse Hamaguchi is also framed and contained in the starched white linens of her hat and dress as she is transformed into a feminine archetype who is marked and pinned as a loyal American nurse who will fight for, save, and care for the nation during war. In this representation of soldiers, cadets, and nurses, these men and women are no longer visible as Japanese Americans so much as American types of individuals who are reduced by their heavily coded clothing into the essence of an American serviceman and servicewoman. As with the close-up portraits of Japanese American schoolgirls, it is the clothing, not the bodies contained within them, that is most readable. Framed by Adams's close-up camera, clothing functions to signify patriotic and military loyalty.

Corporal Jimmie Shohara. *(Ansel Adams. Library of Congress, Prints and Photographs Divisions.)*

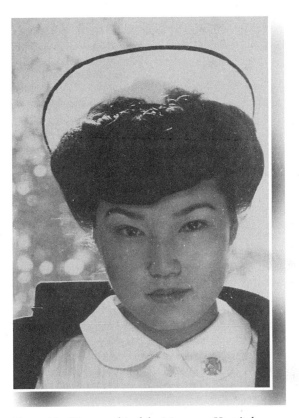

Nurse Aiko Hamaguchi of the Manzanar Hospital.
(Ansel Adams. Library of Congress, Prints and Photographs Divisions.)

Literary critic Elaine Kim has described how highly coded clothing and uniforms participate in the specific racial erasure of minority subjects:

> Fastening on clothes and roles . . . is part of the desire to be
> invisible and acceptable at the same time, just as U.S. Army
> uniforms have made men from minority groups feel more
> "American" and less Asian, Black, or Chicano. Through
> clothes and roles, invisibility can become acceptability, since

attention is drawn not to the person but to the image in the braided uniform or white gown.[28]

According to Kim, one of the most predominant themes running throughout Japanese American literature from World War II through the 1970s is that of "self negation."[29] While there is no question that the *issei* (first-generation immigrants) are fully Japanese—and in fact were barred in 1924 by the Immigration Act from becoming U.S. citizens—their second generation offspring, the nisei, who comprised more than three-fourths of the entire internee population, historically have had to deal with an entirely different identity dilemma. Unlike their issei parents, Kim argues, "[the nisei were] American citizens [who] had no sense of belonging to another country . . .[yet they were] treated by American society as [undesirable aliens]."[30] While their bodies were read as physically Other, the nisei knew who they really were: Americans of Japanese descent.[31] This "twist of physiological irony" is exactly what Daniel Okimoto refers to as the "Americans in disguise" syndrome.[32]

The double alienation of the Japanese Americans results in both what W. E. B. Du Bois and Gloria Anzaldúa have identified as the specific kind of psychological conflict of people of color who are forced to choose where they must fit in between two or more cultures.[33] Under the intense pressure of wartime racism, the Japanese Americans had little choice but to participate in their own racial and cultural erasure in order to prove their loyalty and lay claim to an American identity. In what Kim describes as a "panicked effort to destroy whatever might be construed as evidence of their links to Japan," many Japanese Americans "burned their kimonos, diaries, Japanese language books, letters, photographs, and even their phonograph records and magazines" as they hastily prepared for relocation.[34] It is therefore not surprising that these signs of Japanese culture are absent from so many of Adams's portraits of Manzanar.

Adams's Manzanar portraits were intended for the wartime gaze of a suspicious white American audience that was unused to non-racist or nonstereotypical representations of the Japanese Other. Hence, it was both bold and strategic of Adams to "de-Orientalize" his Manzanar subjects in order to represent them as loyal individual

American citizens. Yet, what begins as a powerful counterhegemonic move backfires: in attempting to strip the Japanese Americans at Manzanar from the racist frame of Orientalist representation, Adams also strips them of the specificity of their cultural and racial identity, thus whitewashing the signs of racial oppression from the context of the camps.

There is already in these photographs a kind of early visual rhetoric of the "model minority" at play: in contrast to Carl Mydans's photographs of internees at Tule Lake, there are only images of loyal, successful, fully assimilated individuals in Adams's portraits. There are no scenes of dissent, or even hints of protest in the camp. In his comments on the people he met at Manzanar, Adams himself observed:

> We are impressed with their solidity of character, their external cheerfulness, and their cleanliness. I have not been aware of any abnormal psychological attitudes, such as one might expect to find in a group which has suffered such severe alterations of its normal life. There is no outward evidence of the "refugee" spirit, no expressed feeling of an endured temporary existence under barrack-life conditions. . . . I do not recall one sullen face in Manzanar.[35]

What remains perhaps most disturbing is how Adams's impression of internee life at Manzanar effaces the physical and psychological violence of relocation that makes possible the forced production of good citizenship in the camps.

If Adams's documentary of life at Manzanar visually reinforces the notion that the camp was a simple study in civil obedience and productivity, then his portraits appear to reinforce his contention that the internees were a "cheerful" lot. His famous head shots of the internees—all shot from below, a photographic technique that deliberately "idealizes and monumentalizes" the subject—have all the familiarity and congeniality of classic American yearbook photos.[36] Adams himself admitted that these photographs implied "a test of true Americanism" and hoped that they might even suggest a photo-documentary approach to the "treatment of other minority

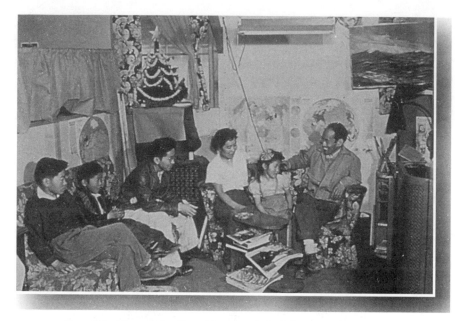

Toyo Miyatake and family at Manzanar War Relocation Center.
(Ansel Adams. Library of Congress, Prints and Photographs Divisions.)

groups."[37] Judging from these photographs, Adams's "test of true Americanism" involves the representation of clean-cut, photogenic, productive, heroic and smiling individuals—all of which one could argue are key ingredients in the construction of the model minority.

One can certainly find all of these ingredients in Adams's portrait of internee photographer Toyo Miyatake and his family. In one portrait, Adams virtually remakes the Miyatakes over into a familiar *Life* magazine mold of the all-American nuclear family happily at home for the holidays.[38] What Adams's camera lens distorts, however, is that "home" is a twenty by twenty-five-foot plywood and tar paper room in a prison camp barracks. Surrounded by chintz chair covers, frilly curtains, miniature Christmas tree, a set of *Encyclopaedia Britannica,* and current copies of *Vogue, The New Yorker,* and a *One World One War* unity map, the Miyatakes are represented as a fully

Americanized nuclear family. In this representation of Manzanar home life, every sign of American culture is stabilized into its proper place, and the family is surrounded by the artifacts that define their lives. Ironically, even as Executive Order 9066 has torn families apart, they are almost obsessively reproduced in Adams's photographs in different versions of their completeness.

Another photograph taken inside the Miyatakes' barracks reveals a domesticated space where Mrs. Miyatake assists her youngest daughter in a crayon drawing while her husband and sons look on. The walls are adorned with the children's art work featuring fantasy images of angels and multiple drawings of the "home" they have left behind.

Adams's portrait of Mr. and Mrs. Dennis Shimizu also represents Manzanar home life in a similar fashion. In this photograph, Mr. and Mrs. Shimizu are carefully posed in the everyday gestures of newlywed domesticity. Mrs. Shimizu smiles demurely, her hands preoccupied with a crochet hook and ball of yarn. At her side, Mr. Shimizu strikes a rather forced casual pose propped up in bed—curiously with shoes still on his feet—pipe in mouth, absorbed in his reading of *Burma Surgeon*.[39] The Shimizu space, like that of the Miyatakes, looks less like a prison barracks than a typical American home filled with all the recognizable signs of domestic comfort: decorative doilies, chenille bedspread, framed pictures, and even a radio (after the difficulties of the first year in the camps, previously contraband objects such as radios and cameras were eventually allowed).

Adams's portrait of the Jive Bombers, Manzanar's most popular jazz dance band, offers still another all-American representation of the internees here cast as a clean-cut, fashionably coifed, bow-tied, music-producing band. According to internee Jeanne Wakatsuki Houston, whose brother played saxophone in this group, the Jive Bombers were seriously devoted to keeping up with the latest hits and could be found playing every weekend in recreation halls packed with bobby-soxed and jitterbugging couples.[40] Bands like the Jive Bombers were crucial in keeping internees smiling and swinging in the flow of then current Americana.

Each group portrait relies for its efficacy upon the unmistakable physical signs of successful American assimilation that work to transform the internees from Japanese Americans into domesticated Americans whose lingering traces of Japanese-ness drop out of the picture. Throughout the pages of *Born Free and Equal,* clothing, hairstyles, domestic props, and broad unself-conscious smiles fully Americanize Adams's internees as his camera repeatedly reconstructs them as loyal American citizen subjects. Adams's portraits at Manzanar consistently work to transform the Japanese American internees into all-American subjects by replacing signs of Otherness with those of sameness. To pass the test of "true Americanism" in Adams's photographs, the Japanese Americans at Manzanar must enact the impossible and be both individual *and* invisible. Represented as individuals, "loyal" Japanese Americans are adaptable, cheerful, strong, and perhaps even heroic under the conditions of relocation.

Adams's insistence on photographing Japanese Americans in individual close-up portraits is reinforced by his insistence that grouping them together as a collective minority community ultimately harms them. He argues that "we must first strive to understand the Japanese Americans, not as an abstract group, but as individuals of fine mental, moral and civic capacities, in other words, people such as you and I."[41] He suggests that the wartime predicament for Japanese Americans is partly self-inflicted due to what he perceived to be the overly strong cultural ties and sense of collective racial identity that characterized their community. His proposed solution involved individual assimilation that would strip Japanese Americans of their collective identity, consciousness, and sense of difference, in favor of a transcendent American individualism:

> One way for minorities to protect themselves is to scatter throughout the country—to avoid concentration in nationalistic groups in towns and rural areas.
>
> The scattering of the loyal Japanese Americans throughout the country is far better for them than reconcentration into racial districts and groups. They wish to prove their worth as indi-

viduals, free to move about the land in pursuit of occupation, education, and recreation.[42]

Adams's perspective on the Japanese Americans was not unique. Indeed, for many of the internees, the experience of displacement in the camps was only the first in a series of deterritorializations inflicted upon them for their own good.[43] Beginning in 1943, the internees were also subjected to loyalty oaths whose purpose was to draft all young eligible men into the military and cut all binding ties to Japan in their complete allegiance to the United States.[44] The unfortunate backlash of the loyalty oaths resulted in the further division and alienation of families and communities. Those who refused to sign the oaths, or who declined to swear allegiance, were separated and sent to Tule Lake under the stigma of "disloyal" internees. By 1944, many internees (predominantly nisei women) were allowed to leave the camps and resettle in the Midwest or East Coast, where they undertook jobs or attended colleges willing to admit them during the war. It was not until after the war that the Japanese and Japanese Americans were allowed to return "home" to the West Coast.[45] Under the ethos of American individualism, internees were encouraged to cut themselves off from Japanese America and resuture themselves into the fabric of the nation as isolated American citizens. Adams's photographs visually reinforce this ethos through his insistence on privileging representations of Japanese Americans as individuals first, and as an interned minority community only second.

In their introductory essay to the *Cultural Critique* special issue on "Minority Discourse," Abdul JanMohamed and David Lloyd state that "the collective nature of all minority discourses . . . derives from the fact that minority individuals are always treated and forced to experience themselves generically."[46] Ansel Adams earnestly attempts to work against the kind of Orientalist reduction that was firmly locked in place under the popular wartime slogan, "A Jap is a Jap," through his emphasis on individualizing the internees. Indeed, the closing pages of *Born Free and Equal* echo JanMohammed and Lloyd, as Adams suggests that it is only when minority subjects are treated as individuals and not as a racial group that discrimination can be overcome:

Treated as individuals, human beings do not present great problems, but when they are treated as arbitrary racial groups, social and international difficulties are created. It is our task to retain the individual as the foundation of society, irrespective of his race, color, or religion.[47]

While there is no question that Adams is sincere in his liberal wartime rallying behind the thousands of unjustly incarcerated Japanese American individuals, his Manzanar photographs remain problematic as visual records of the internment experience. It has been pointed out that because of his insistence on exclusively "understand[ing] the Japanese Americans, not as an abstract group, but as individuals," that "[he] failed to confront them as historical subjects discriminated against collectively"[48] The disturbing subtext of *Born Free and Equal* is the erasure of memory of the physical, constitutional, and psychological violence of the internment experience. Adams's pictorial record of Manzanar speaks to such a forgetting by insisting on a visual rhetoric of "good cheer" which becomes a mandate for the affect of what the good Japanese American citizen—betrayed by the nation state—must publicly display. What the reader (who is presumably constructed as part of a suspicious white, wartime audience) is shown is a visual iconography of Japanese Americans transformed into loyal, unambiguously American citizens who, through a loss of memory, offer an automatic forgiveness of the very people who sanctioned the violence of their forced removal, relocation, and internment in the first place.

Most contemporary readers of internment camp history come to know Ansel Adams's work either through John Armor and Peter Wright's glossy reprint of Adams's internment photographs in *Manzanar* (1988) or else in Emily Medvec's catalog reprint of *Born Free and Equal* (1984).[49] *Manzanar* offers the broadest collection of Adams's camp photographs (including many that he did not use in *Born Free and Equal*), yet it is itself a curious text. The editors make no mention of Adams's narrative text in *Born Free and Equal.* Instead, they surround Adams's photo-text with their own highly critical historical narrative of the camps—much of which visibly contradicts the upbeat tone of Adams's photographs. If Adams's photographs are upbeat representations of cheerful, industrious internees who are fortunate to be interned in the surrounding majesty of the Sierra Nevada mountain range, then Armor and Wright's text is an entirely separate entity filled with an unrelenting sense of bitterness that mirrors and is accentuated by the harsh relationship between internees and environment—a relationship that Adams romanticizes. Armor and Wright oddly make no mention of Medvec's 1984 catalog. Instead, they credit themselves as the first to retrieve Adams's historic images from the archives. Medvec's catalog on the other hand, gives a faithful reproduction of Adams's narrative text; unfortunately, the catalog's reproduction of the photographs is both physically dwarfed and selectively reprinted, giving one a false sense of what Adams originally included.[50]

Ultimately, both Armor and Wright's and Medvec's works continue the curious elision and transformation of Adams's original photo-texual essay on Manzanar. While *Manzanar* expands Adams's notion of the photo-essay, it erases his narrative in *Born Free and Equal*. Conversely, Medvec faithfully reproduces Adams's narrative text, but seriously undermines and edits the visual power of his photographs.

The Relationship of Adams's Internees to the Land

In the tradition of his famous landscape photography, Adams documents the magnificent Sierra Nevada mountain range throughout the pages of *Born Free and Equal*. These mountains form a dramatic and photogenic backdrop for the desert wasteland that is Manzanar. Interspersed with extreme close-up portraits of individual Japanese Americans, the landscape photographs are striking for their almost uniform absence of any human presence; indeed, the representation of Manzanar as a desert "city" populated with ten thousand inhabitants is momentarily lost in these panoramic shots.

Adams's landscape photographs in *Born Free and Equal* are crucial to consider as companion pieces for his study of the Japanese American body at Manzanar. In the opening pages of his text, Adams himself admits that while the internees and their activities are his "chief concern," his visual emphasis on the land is motivated in part by his attempt "to record the influence of the tremendous landscape of Inyo on the life and spirit of thousands of people living by force of circumstance in the Relocation Center of Manzanar."[51] There are several double-page photographs of dramatic, panoramic views of the Inyo and Sierra Nevada mountain ranges that bordered the eastern and western edges of the internment camp. Given the link Adams is intent on making between the internees and the environment, it is ironic that the majority of these landscape photographs contain no discernable trace of a Japanese American presence at Manzanar.

Adams's portrait of the virtual oasis known as Merritt Pleasure Park—one of several recreational sites the internees built—is the only landscape image that marginally includes the presence of internees: its carefully sculpted Japanese rock gardens, reflection pool, hand-hewn foot bridge, and artful arrangement of native plants seem oddly and artificially out of place in the desert setting. If one scans the background, traces of tar-papered barracks and tiny human figures are visible at the edges of the photograph.

By romanticizing the relationship of the internee body to the land, Adams can assert his belief that the "acrid splendor of the desert, ringed with towering mountains, has strengthened the spirit and the people of Manzanar."[52] He admits that not all may be "conscious of this influence, but [he is] sure most have responded, in one way or another, to the resonances of their environment" where "huge vistas and the stern realities of sun and wind and space symbolize the immensity and opportunity of America."[53] In the logic of Adams's narrative, the Japanese Americans are fortunate to have been transported to the desert where they can be transmuted by the landscape and disciplined through the camp's self-sustaining work into productive citizens ready to pursue the "opportunity of America" upon their eventual release.[54]

In Adams's rearticulation, Executive Order 9066 ultimately works to benefit Japanese Americans who must endure internment as a kind of wartime test of loyalty that they must pass if they are to gain full entry as citizens in a postwar America. Working within the limits of polite euphemism, Adams expresses it best in the early pages of *Born Free and Equal*:

> Only a rocky detour on the road of American citizenship, [Manzanar] is a symbol of the whole pattern of relocation—a vast expression of a government working to find suitable haven for its war-dislocated minorities. Manzanar, as a group enterprise in administration and daily life, possesses also the intangibles of spirit and attitude to be found in any well-organized American community, plus a certain intensity and patience born of the shock of enforced exodus.[55]

In this oft-quoted passage, Adams effaces through a kind of pleasant translation, the uprooting, desecration, and subtle violences of "enforced exodus" through his euphemistic depiction of internees as "war-dislocated minorities." This phrase naturalizes, and neutralizes, the forced movement of relocation and moves the violent hand of the government away from any moral responsibility or culpability. Indeed, this hand becomes a benevolent hand, helping out these poor "dislocated minorities." Here, "enforced exodus" has no cause.

If there is any historical trace of violence at Manzanar, Adams suggests that it is the land itself that has been victimized and subjected to harm:

> Into this land, many years ago, reached the tentacles of a water-hungry city: Los Angeles acquired, by fair means and foul, almost total rights to the water of this region. Trees, farms, and enterprises died, homes were cruelly burned, and what had been one of the most charming, self-sufficient, rural regions of the West was left to desolation.[56]

In Adams's mythos, the *relocation* of water, not Japanese American bodies, is the real narrative tragedy of the West. Turn-of-the-century Los Angeles, not Executive Order 9066, is fashioned as the true monster behind the devastation of land and human life in Inyo County.

Interned within this desert wasteland, the Japanese Americans become heroic intercessors reworked through Adams's photo-text as noble rescuers who are able to resurrect life once again from the abandoned, brutalized land:

> There is nothing in the world, perhaps, as poignant as the emergence of crops from harsh and barren land. Out of the desert at Manzanar they have extracted great quantities of nappa . . . squash, potatoes, turnips, and other vegetables. With irrigation—sparse as it is in this land from which most of the water has been appropriated—and with hard work, the men and women of Manzanar have brought forth food from the earth and brought pride of achievement to their hearts.[57]

If Adams's photographs aestheticize the dramatic and stunningly beautiful Sierra Nevada backdrop, they also aestheticize internment.[58] Indeed, in his best-known scenic compositions of Manzanar, Adams presents a harmonic, dust-free, and natural relationship between the landscape and the internees as the latter gather in an early morning circle to burn autumn leaves or else take their places in the orderly rows of potato fields that seem to radiate naturally from the towering Sierra Nevadas. Adams's internees are enobled by their rough environment rather than angered by their own imprisonment. Portraits like those featuring the smiling figures of Richard Kobayashi and Benji Iguchi, surrounded as they are by giant cabbages and towering piles of harvested squash, reinforce the image of the enormous productivity and industry of the model minorities at Manzanar.[59]

From later editors of Adams's work, we are told that "it was his intention to bypass a political study of Manzanar for an independent viewpoint motivated by curiosity and the spirit of discovery."[60] There is no doubt that Adams was "appalled by the injustice of mass internment" and sincerely committed to showing the true loyalty and humanity of Japanese Americans as "a way of easing the discrimination they were likely to face upon leaving the camps."[61] Years later, when asked to reflect upon his work at Manzanar, Adams confessed:

I think that my series of pictures and the text of my book was a rather acceptable interpretation. It did not have the tragic overtones of Lange's work, although there is always a lingering sense of resentment and regret.[62]

Both Adams and Dorothea Lange shared a common outrage over the injustice of internment, as well as a common need to document the experiences of its victims. Nevertheless, the modes of their Japanese American documentation remain distinct from one another. In the case of Adams, Japanese Americans are not so much abject victims as they are loyal individuals who flourish and triumph heroically under conditions of internment. For Lange, however, the Japanese Americans are not heroic, but rather tragic players caught off-guard in the drama of relocation.

Relocating the Japanese American Body in the Documentary Photography of Dorothea Lange

What I photographed was the procedure, the process of processing. I photographed the normal life insofar as I could. . . . I photographed . . . the Japanese quarter of San Francisco, the businesses as they were operating, and the people as they were going to their YWCAs and YMCAs and churches and their Nisei headquarters, all the baffled, bewildered people.
—Dorothea Lange

There goes a "thing" in slacks and she is taking pictures of that old *issei* lady with a baby. She says she is the official photographer, but I think she ought to leave these people alone.
—Charles Kikuchi, *The Kikuchi Diary,* April 30, 1942, Berkeley Central Station

In the spring of 1942, with the solid credential of her Dust Bowl, Depression-era Farm Security Administration (FSA) photographs behind her, Dorothea Lange went to work for the War Relocation Authority (WRA).[63] One of her assignments involved documenting the evacuation and relocation of Japanese Americans in northern California. In contrast to Ansel Adams's photographs of internees at Manzanar, Lange's visual record captures both the impact of the evacuation process on the Japanese Americans as well as their transition into assembly centers and relocation camps. As one of many official WRA photographers, Lange's seven hundred or so photographs make up but a fraction of the much larger visual archive of some 12,500 WRA images. Yet, even fifty years later they continue to stand out as some of the most powerful, even iconic, photographs of the internees.

Photography historians Masie and Richard Conrat have concluded that there are approximately 25,000 photographs in total that depict the different stages of the Japanese American internment experience. They argue that these can be divided into three categories: those that had historical significance but failed as images, those that failed in both respects, and those that have strength both as images and as historical documents.[64] Of the entire visual archive, they argue that there are perhaps no more than one hundred photographs that merit inclusion in the latter category. These photographs are the subject of their 1972 traveling exhibit and published catalog, *Executive Order 9066*. Of the sixty-three photographs they reproduce (from among a dozen photographers), they include twenty-seven of Lange's photographs—and only one by Ansel Adams.[65] According to critic Karin Becker Ohrn, in the late 1960s and early 1970s, Lange's photographs were rediscovered in the WRA archives and were "reinterpreted as providing a 'true' picture of those events." She argues that Lange's photographs—and not Adams's—were the most widely reprinted and exhibited images of the internment experience on its thirty-year anniversary.[66]

As part of her photo assignment, Lange made three brief visits to Manzanar during the relocation camp's earliest days. Scholar Karen Tsujimoto argues that Lange's "photographs evince obvious sympathy with the Japanese Americans" and remain consistent with her liberal political position. In contrast to Adams's monumentalizing close-up portraits of internees—which are shot from below—the majority of Lange's photographs are taken at eye level with her subjects.[67] As a friendly colleague of Adams, Lange was not only aware of his published collection of photographs taken at Manzanar, but she was also known to have said, "He [Adams] never 'got it'. . . never understood what was wrong with the internment."[68] Ohrn has already noted that while Adams had the "full cooperation of his subjects and their overseers" during his visits there, Lange repeatedly had problems getting military clearance, and many of her photographs were censored.[69] When finally allowed inside Manzanar, Lange herself recalled: "It was very difficult. I had a lot of trouble with the Army. I had a man following me all the time."[70]

Karin Becker Ohrn writes that "an Army major working with the Wartime Civil Control Agency went through Lange's photographs and wrote 'impounded' across the many of them—not for release until after the war."[71] Ohrn notes that Dorothea Lange's sympathies with the internees were well known; as a result, she suspected she was being investigated by government officials and was actually called into the War Relocation Authority office twice to "account for alleged misuse" of her internment photographs.[72]

If Adams's photographs are memorable for their aesthetic portrayal of the internment experience and heroic portrayal of the internees, then Lange's photographs are equally noteworthy for their earnest attempt to anchor her subjects to a particular historical and political context.[73] In many ways, one could argue that Lange is one of the few photographers whose work conveys any discernable sense of the tragedy of these events.[74] For Lange, each "photo presented the human condition as it related the individual subject to its social and cultural and geographical environment."[75] For the purposes of my discussion, I will look at those photographs from Lange's WRA collection that focus on the Japanese American body.

During the Depression, Lange and other Farm Security Administration photographers recorded scenes of economic oppression and subsequent migration in the rural areas of the Deep South, the Midwest, and the West Coast.[76] The subject of these photographs consists almost exclusively of poor working-class white and African American sharecroppers and migrant farm workers struggling to make a living under conditions of extreme poverty. Lange's published work on the farm workers during this period does not include any representations of the thousands of Japanese farmers, whose presence before the war was concentrated almost exclusively on the West Coast.[77] Their absence in Lange's work in the 1930s makes their presence in her wartime work all the more interesting given the striking manner in which the representation of the Japanese American body is visually reminiscent of her Farm Security Administration subjects—suggesting a fascinating displacement of race onto class. Indeed, what Erskine Caldwell termed the "tortured face of poverty" among poor white working-class farmers is visually reworked in Lange's WRA photographs as the tortured face of relocation.[78]

Lange's Pre-Evacuation Photographs

Lange's WRA photographs document the process of uprooting and relocation for the northern California Japanese American community in 1942. These images can be divided into pre-evacuation scenes of Japanese American neighborhoods documenting homes, schools, businesses, and community centers on the eve of the mass dispersal, scenes of evacuation at the various gathering stations depicting bewildered crowds of well-dressed individuals and families awaiting travel, and images bearing witness to the early and most difficult days in the assembly centers at fairgrounds and racetracks, and later at the only internment camp Lange visited, Manzanar War Relocation Center.

The pre-evacuation scenes depict a range of last-minute activities of Japanese American families as they prepared for relocation: there are many photographs of the rushed and final harvesting of strawberries, garlic, asparagus, and other crops before they are abandoned, the hasty evacuation sales of furniture and property, and many domestic details overlooked by other photographers, such the last load of laundry that has been washed and hung out to dry, and young Japanese American children playing on the porches of farmhouses in the days just before evacuation.[79]

In many of these photographs, what distinguishes Lange's work from other WRA photographers is not only her habit of getting as close to her subjects as possible—her close-up portraits are often haunting whether individuals choose to return the gaze or not—but also her keen eye for ironic juxtapositions. One of the many sites that Lange visited in the days just before evacuation included the Rafael Weill Elementary School in San Francisco in April. Some of Lange's most striking images as a WRA photographer are from her visit to this school. Two photographs in particular stand out. One was used as the cover shot for the September 1942 issue of *Survey Graphic* magazine featuring an essay by Lange's husband, Paul S. Taylor. Lange and fellow WRA photographer Frances Stewart contributed two pages of images from evacuation and internment for Taylor's essay. Both the essay and captioned photographs remain rare wartime articulations of a critical position on the internment. Lange's cover photograph cleverly juxtaposes the American flag and several Japanese American schoolchildren in a dramatic reappropriation of the symbols of patriotism, citizenship, multiculturalism, and innocence—visual correctives to the wartime discourse casting Japanese Americans as treacherous, disloyal, and un-American. Shot at the eye level of the children, the cover photograph centers on a young Japanese American boy who holds the honorable position of flag bearer in the school's early morning pledge of allegiance. He is flanked on both sides by a veritable rainbow coalition of white, Asian, and African American schoolmates.

The other famous photograph from this series—indeed, one that has arguably attained iconic status—depicts two little Japanese American schoolgirls also engaged in the daily ritual around the flag. The photograph, titled "One Nation Indivisible," remains one of the most reprinted images of the relocation and internment experience for its obvious assertion of American identity, loyalty, and innocence again crafted out of the juxtaposition of the American flag and Japanese American children. The photograph, however, shifts meaning depending on how it has been cropped and reprinted.[80]

In the original photograph, there are two young girls, each dressed in plaid coats, holding their right hands across their hearts while their left hands clutch brown paper sack lunches. The girl on the left bears a baffled expression on her face that is at once serious, even questioning, as she turns her gaze and pledges her allegiance to the off-camera flag. This photograph is most often cropped and

Pledge of allegiance at Rafael Weill Elementary School, a few weeks prior to evacuation, San Francisco, California, 1942. *(Dorothea Lange. Courtesy of the Dorothea Lange Collection, Oakland Museum, 1978.)*

reprinted so that it focuses only on this one serious schoolgirl caught by the camera in a simple gesture of patriotism on the eve of relocation. The young girl on the right smiles unselfconsciously into Lange's camera. Her crooked teeth evoke a poignant visual association with the poor white children from Lange's FSA photographs a decade earlier. Yet her broad smile undercuts the seriousness of the girl standing next to her. The smile of the girl on the right bears no trace of anxiety on the eve of evacuation, no intimation of the tragic consequences that uprooting will bring to her life. Indeed, on the fifty-year anniversary of Executive Order 9066, staff writers for the *San Francisco Examiner,* Mark Constantine and Annie Nakai, looked up several individuals from the best-known photographs of the internment experience.[81] Mary Ann Yahiro is the smiling girl with the crooked teeth—and ironically, she is the one in the photograph whose childhood in the camps will be most deeply touched by tragedy. She was seven years old when Lange took the photograph. Interviewed in Chicago in 1992, Yahiro recalls that she was not only separated from her mother—who was sent to a different camp because she taught Japanese language—but never saw her again. Her mother died from a heart condition one year later. Of the internment, Yahiro says she "isn't bitter, just saddened that her mother died alone." At the close of the interview, Yahiro tells the two journalists that she is "shocked that many people—even her many Caucasian friends and neighbors—still don't know about the camps."

Another of Lange's most frequently reprinted images from the pre-evacuation is a simple portrait of an issei mother standing alongside her son, a nisei soldier, at the edge of a strawberry patch in Florin, California. Lange's notes tell us that the young soldier "was furloughed to help his mother and family prepare for evacuation." The diminutive issei mother stands tall holding a basketful of strawberries. Her well-worn work clothes are topped off with a protective layer of elbow-length gloves, hat, and scarf that she wears to protect herself from the broiling sun. In his U.S. Army uniform, the son appears suspended between dual loyalties to his country and to a family that has been declared the enemy. His rumpled uniform contrasts sharply with Ansel Adams's well-pressed and dressed young men and women in the military at Manzanar. In Lange's portrait, mother

A soldier and his mother in a strawberry field. *(Dorothea Lange. WRA, Florin, California, May 1942.)*

and son are framed together yet stand apart with this apparent sense of irony: enlisted to protect his nation, on the eve of evacuation, he is helpless to protect his own family.

The soldier in the rumpled uniform is Ted Miyata. Journalists Constantine and Nakai also located him in Chicago for a 1992 interview, where Miyata shared with them his deep ambivalence about the camps:

> On the one hand, we had our rights taken away from us . . . on the other, as long as they [his parents] were in camp, I know they were safe. It was very dangerous in those days to be an

Asian. I was worried about my mother being in the centers. But it didn't give America the right to do those things. If it happened, it happened. But you should never forget.

His mother, Mrs. Miyata, died in 1987 at the age of ninety-six, just one year shy of the passage of the Reparation and Redress Bill by Congress. Like other nisei who are dedicated to breaking the silences surrounding the internment experience, Miyata now speaks publicly about the camps. He notes that he is invariably praised "for speaking English so well" and is still asked by strangers where he is from. His standard response has become, "If I'm correct, I'm an American."

Photographs of the Evacuation:
A People "Torn Out by Their Roots"

> As we boarded the bus
> bags on both sides
> (I had never packed
> two bags before
> on a vacation
> lasting forever)
> the *Seattle Times*
> photographer said
> Smile!
> So obediently I smiled
> and the caption the next day
> read:
> Note smiling faces
> a lesson to Tokyo.
> —Mitsuye Yamada, "The Evacuation"

Mitsuye Yamada's poem "The Evacuation" reminds us of the beguiling power of the photograph and its role in historical misrepresentations.[82] Yamada makes it clear how easily the camera can betray the "obedient" body that stands unsuspecting before its gaze. In the WRA archive, and even within Lange's collection, there is certainly a prevalence of evacuees who smile directly into the camera's lens while waiting to be transported, who grin and wave happily to bus-loads of friends and neighbors in the first wave of departure, and who step down out of buses at the assembly centers looking re-lieved and pleased at the offer of assistance from military police and other waiting officials.[83] Certainly, images like these of compliant Japanese Americans were circulated during the war as visual proof of the success and ease of mass relocation and internment.[84] Such photographs are also consistent with the benevolent WRA film footage depicting the civil obedience of Japanese Americans sub-mitting to internment both "for their own good" as well as for "mil-itary necessity."[85]

While Lange documented similar scenes of cooperative, smiling men, women, and children during the evacuation and internment, it is interesting that these images are never reprinted or included in commemorative exhibitions of Executive Order 9066. Instead, it is largely those photographs that capture the sense of Japanese Ameri-can vulnerability, anxiety, and bewilderment that have endured as historical wartime images. Isolated from the rest of the collection, the latter photographs cast the Japanese Americans as tragic players in a historical drama that Lange's camera then reveals as "truthful" counterimages that contradict the notion that the internment was an unfortunate but hardly tragic wartime event. Such a tragic mode of representation is far removed from Ansel Adams's heroic mode of recording the men, women, and children at Manzanar and reminds us that both photographers brought a distinctly different visual rhet-oric to their work. That we continue to be drawn to either Adams's heroic or Lange's tragic modes of visual narrative tells us much about the appeal of such binary poles of representation and its im-pact on the selective nature of our national historical memory.

Since Lange was already well known for her moving photographs of Dust Bowl migrants in the 1930s, it is hardly surprising that her most powerful photographs documenting the evacuation and in-ternment of Japanese Americans are those which visually resemble the look of her earlier Depression-era work on relocation from *An American Exodus: A Record of Human Erosion*.[86] Indeed, her photo-graphs in *Survey Graphic* make the connection between these two groups of uprooted people quite explicit under the title of Paul S. Taylor's essay, "Our Stakes in the Japanese Exodus." If her FSA work is filled with images of downbeaten and dispossessed individuals and families who have found shelter in the dilapidated shacks and tents at pea pickers' camps, her best-known WRA work is filled with photographs—many of which were impounded—of displaced Japanese Americans who try their best to re-create the home in the cramped spaces of hastily converted horse stalls at assembly centers and in the shabby tar-papered barracks at the internment camps.[87] In lieu of the Oklahoma Dust Bowl of the 1930s, Lange records the internment camp dust storms in the 1940s.[88]

Lange's FSA photographs from the 1930s are distinctive for their depiction of white working-class migrants whose bodies and clothing are marked by damage and loss. These signs are visually re-scripted onto the bodies of Japanese Americans who wait passively in long lines during their evacuation, their personal property reduced to what they can carry, their faces lined with the look of the bewilderment and angst that accompanies their displacement and adjustment to life in the camps. Perhaps more than any other WRA photographer, Lange repeatedly focuses her camera onto those most vulnerable to the intrusive gaze of the documentary photographer: women with babies, small children, and the elderly. Her portraits from this group are easily among the most moving, disturbing, and memorable. As a body of historical evidence, these are the only photographs that capture the individual and collective experience of confusion, anxiety, and grief while bearing visual testimony to the psychological pain of abandoning one's home and property before boarding the trains and buses that will take them to an uncertain destination. Sally Stein has written that Lange once admitted to the difficulties of photographing country people in the 1930s who had lost their homes and property during the economic upheaval during the Great Depression. The difficulty lay in photographing people "whose roots were all torn out."[89] As Lange put it, "It's very hard to photograph a proud man against a background like that, because it doesn't show what he's proud about."[90] Certainly, Lange's photographs documenting the Japanese Americans exodus from its beginning stages to the early days of incarceration continue to move us as a stirring record of the loss of homes, of property, and of dignity.

The evacuees were given anywhere between forty-eight hours' and two weeks' notice to settle their affairs and store or liquidate their property. Many were given assurances that their property and possessions would be put into safe government storage for the duration of the war. Yet, through subsequent and widespread theft and vandalism, it has been estimated that nearly $400 million worth of property was lost by evacuees during their incarceration. What remains especially poignant in the photographic record of evacuation is the sight of so many numbered identity tags hanging from the coat lapels and belt loops of well dressed men, women, and children targeted for relocation. Many internees have recalled what it felt like to exchange names for numbers during the relocation process:

> Harry went to the control station to register the family ... [he] came home with twenty tags, all numbered 10170, tags to be attached to each piece of baggage, and one to hang from our coat lapels. From then on, we were known as family #10710. I lost my identity ... I lost my privacy and dignity.[91]

Several of Lange's photographs of tagged and numbered evacuees have become iconic images of the internment.

The photograph of the Mochida family, awaiting the evacuation bus with bags and tags, is one of the most frequently reprinted of Lange's evacuation photographs. Lange's caption to the photograph notes that "identification tags were used to aid in keeping the family unit intact during all phases of evacuation." According to many internees, the impact of evacuation was hardest on families. Many nisei writers recall the severe disruption of normal family life under internment; indeed, some families in the United States and Canada were separated for the duration of the war. Typical of most families on the day of evacuation, the Mochida family is very well dressed for relocation: their hats, caps, bomber jackets, and mock leopard-skin coat collars also signify the acculturation of this large family. Like the portrait of the two girls at the Rafael Weill Elementary School, this photograph is usually cropped with a focus on the two youngest children in the lower left corner of the frame. In this close-up, the emphasis rests squarely on the numbered identity tags hanging from the two girls' coat lapels. The cropped photograph remains a poignant reminder of how the relocation affected the young and innocent.[92] Yet what is lost in the cropping is the interesting range of gazes and small gestures from the original photograph. While a smiling Mr. Mochida looks directly into Lange's camera, his hand resting in paternal fashion on the shoulder of his youngest child, the petite figure of Mrs. Mochida—half hidden behind her son—looks away from the camera either because she is distracted with her own concerns, or as a deliberate response to Lange's intrusion. In any case, Lange's original photograph of the Mochidas remains a rare close-up portrait of an entire family—with bags and tags—uprooted together.

One of Lange's most successful photographs from the evacuation is one which has been consistently overlooked and yet attests to the fact that Japanese American children were often her best subjects. This photograph features a close-up portrait of a little boy dressed up for evacuation in his Boy Scout uniform, his numbered identity tag hanging from a button on his pocket and tucked under his belt. In the background are other tagged children and families. Like Ansel Adams, Lange was certainly aware of the signifying potential of uniform clothing. There is no mistaking the irony of the tag which marks him for expulsion and the uniform that marks him as a boy who has taken the oath of loyalty, patriotism, and honor. One must ask, What gesture is behind the choice of clothing here? Did a parent choose the Scout uniform as a subtle form of protest on evacuation day? The choice of uniform is similar to another photograph taken by Lange of an adult male evacuee who dons his World War I military uniform as an obvious form of silent protest.[93]

The Engendering of Angst

Lange holds a unique place in WRA's visual history as the only woman on the "outside" who officially photographed the Japanese American relocation process. While Lange may not have necessarily

Japanese American Boy Scout dressed for evacuation. *(Dorothea Lange. WRA, 1942.)*

featured more women as subjects in her work than any other WRA photographer, her published photographs of women and children remain distinctive in the archive. While I do not make the claim that her work is particularly "woman-centered," let alone feminist in its perspective, there is a sympathetic consciousness that clearly marks these photographs. Certainly anyone familiar with Lange's work on white working-class migrant mothers from the 1930s cannot help but note the similarity of style that she brings to her wartime portraits of Japanese American women.

If Lange was drawn to portraits of women and children a decade earlier, she certainly was drawn to the same subject in her WRA work. In many of her photographs from the evacuation and assembly centers, her camera singles out anxious mothers with babies as well as lone figures of elderly issei women whose lined, worried faces or clasped hands reveal certain worry. The photographs are remarkable in using such details to evoke and invoke the physical and psychological strain of relocation for so many women. Indeed, Lange's attentive eye, attuned to the smallest gesture, makes her an unusually sensitive representer.

One frequently reprinted photograph depicts a mother and her three children at Turlock Assembly Center. The woman holds a baby in her arms and is flanked on the side by two young daughters and a surrounding crowd of men. One of the young daughters stares blankly into Lange's camera. The woman's eye also catches Lange's camera with noticeable discomfort. In this same Turlock series, Lange's close-up camera isolates an elderly issei woman, dressed up for travel in a hat and coat, whose lined face signifies apprehension and uncertainty.

Lange is also one of the very few WRA photographers who was able to capture a rare glimpse of any outward display of emotion on the part of the evacuees. The Japanese American sense of *gaman* (endurance) is what allowed internees to maintain such a strong exterior sense of dignity in spite of the public spectacle of their dislocation. Two photographs in particular depict the physical outpouring of grief as one woman wipes away her tears as her train prepares to leave Woodland, California. Another is photographed as she collapses with emotion on her way to the trains. The latter image was so unusual that Lange took special care to comment on it in her notes. In several of these portraits, the uncomfortable body language of those being photographed raises profound questions about the role of the outside observer in capturing what one of Lange's critics has termed "the misery exponent" of individuals and families. Lange portrays the intrusiveness of the camera in the discomfort sometimes evinced by her subjects. Her camera recording these nuances becomes the allegory of the eye of the state which literally *over-sees* the events of relocation. In some sense, Lange literally records the violence of the camera as she records the violence of dislocation.

Lange's biographers have consistently noted that her documentary work repeatedly revealed a "preoccupation with the body" as a "site of pain and stigma, of disciplining and sensitivity."[94] According to her biographers, Lange suffered from polio as a young child which left her with a permanently crippled right leg and a "sense of shame."[95] As a young girl growing up in New York City, Lange often had to walk home at night alone through some of the most dangerous neighborhoods. It has been said that out of this experience, she "learned to adopt an expression that would draw no attention to herself, that would make her invisible to the people around her . . . and walk through the worst parts of the city without fear."[96] Lange herself referred to this technique as her "cloak of invisibility," which she claimed enabled her to set up a camera without disturbance to her subjects.[97] Indeed, in an oral history interview with Suzanne Riess, Lange confessed:

> No one who hasn't lived the life of a semi-cripple knows how much that means. I think it perhaps was the most important thing that happened to me, and formed me, guided me . . . helped me, and humiliated me . . . Years afterwards when I was working . . . with people who are strangers to me, where I walk into situations where I am very much an outsider, to be a crippled person, or a disabled person, gives an immense advantage. People are kinder to you. It puts you on a different level than if you go into a situation whole and secure.[98]

Yet, no matter how compassionate—or invisible—Lange may have felt herself to be in relation to her Japanese American subjects, as an Anglo American woman on the outside, the viewpoint of her camera, like Adams's, is based on a limited perspective. In spite of her "cloak of invisibility," she remains what Charles Kikuchi describes in his diary—albeit with sexist irritation—the "thing in slacks," a camera-toting intruder—whose photographs ultimately betray the visibility of the photographic apparatus.[99]

Lange's Representation of Japanese American Masculinity

One of the most consistently unexplored themes of the internment experience has been an examination of the impact of this history on Japanese American masculine identity. *Sansei* writer David Mura is one of the very few to begin exploring the psychosexual fallout of the internment on Japanese American masculinity in his memoir, *Where the Body Meets Memory: An Odyssey of Race, Sexuality, and Identity.*[100] Mura suggests that his own painful history of discomfort with his racial identity and his Asian American body are somehow tied to the "political and historical and cultural silence induced by the camps" which he describes as "a generational wound and amnesia buried in so many of the bodies and psyches of Japanese America."[101] As he makes his own profound connections between his parents' shame and silence surrounding their years in internment, their subsequent assimilation into white middle-class American culture, and his own years of racial and sexual shame and obsession, he writes: "My identity, the most intimate of feelings about my own sexuality, were directly tied to what had happened nearly fifty years ago—the signing of Executive Order 9066 and the internment of the Japanese American community."[102]

There have also been several films which either directly, or obliquely, address the effects of internment history on issei and nisei masculine identity. Filmmakers Janice Tanaka and Loni Ding have begun to explore the internment's impact on Japanese American manhood in their films, *Who's Going to Pay for These Donuts,*

Grandfather and grandchildren awaiting evacuation bus. *(Dorothea Lange. WRA, Hayward, California, May 8, 1942.)*

Anyway? (1992) and *The Color of Honor* (1988). While Tanaka's film tracks the tragic—and personal—story of her father's post-internment institutionalization for mental illness, Ding's film looks at the stories of the Japanese American men who fought in the segregated units during World War II. In addition, John Korty's 1976 television adaptation of Jeanne Wakatsuki's autobiography, *Farewell to Manzanar,* and Alan Parker's feature film, *Come See the Paradise* (1990), also depict the symbolic castration of patriarchal issei fathers who are rendered impotent in their inability to protect both their property and their families. In each film, the issei fathers are imprisoned separately from their families only to return later as broken men who slip into alcoholism, deep depression, and, in the case of the latter film, madness and eventual death.

While the effects of internment on Japanese American masculinity has only recently begun to be addressed, several photographs taken by Lange suggest an early representation of this subject. Although primarily recorded during the most difficult days surrounding the evacuation, these photographs stand in sharp contrast to the portraits taken by Ansel Adams and Toyo Miyatake depicting Japanese American success stories at Manzanar where industrious internees are depicted running businesses, farming the desert land, and finding a broad range of productive roles within camp culture.

The first of Lange's photographs I wish to highlight depicts a Japanese American tenant farmer in Woodland, California, just after his evacuation sale. According to Lange's notes, this man "has just completed settlement of his affairs" and is "packed, ready for evacuation the following morning." Sitting on a makeshift stool, with a cigarette in his hand, the farmer is bent over, his arms resting wearily on his thighs. Frequently reprinted, this photograph remains one of Lange's best-known images capturing the body language of dispossession and defeat even before evacuation has begun.

Another of Lange's evacuation photographs also bears closer examination. Her close-up portrait of an elder issei grandfather and his two young grandsons in Hayward, California, awaiting an evacuation bus has arguably become one of the most famous images from the internment experience. All three figures are tagged and ready for relocation; yet the grandfather sits tall and stiff-lipped as he leans upon his cane and returns the camera's gaze with a solid one of his own. While this photograph is usually read for its show of dignity and strength in the body of Sakutaro Aso, the elder issei grandfather, fifty years later it signifies differently to Jerry Aso, who is one of the grandsons in the photograph. In a 1992 interview, the younger Aso asserted: "When people look at grandfather's face, they see a lot of dignity . . . I see a lot of other feelings . . . pain."[103] Aso speaks to the legacy of silence and damage that the internment experience has left with his family—which did not openly discuss the camps even after the redress checks arrived by mail some forty years later. Asked what lasting impact his childhood experience in the camps has had on him, Aso responds: "A lot of shame, a lot of shame. . . . Sure there was a lot shame for the government, but that's too diffuse. It was shame for me. Even if you're innocent, you're still tainted. It's a part of me. It shaped me." Aso's disclosure, fifty years after Lange snapped his grandfather's portrait, reminds us that the debilitating effects of the internment on individuals and families remain a crucial subtext for reading these historic photographs.

Other photographs include the vulnerable bodies of elderly issei men awaiting relocation. Surrounded by those equally vulnerable bodies of worried mothers with small children and elder women, these men sit passively, their quietness exposing their anguish.

A final close-up portrait that bears closer examination is that of Karl Yoneda, captioned, "Young Man at Manzanar Relocation Center." The caption for this photograph reads, "His Caucasian wife is living with him in the camp, together with their small child." One of the least known facts about the internment is that there were white, Latino, and African American spouses who refused to separate from their husbands and families and were thus also subject to imprisonment for the duration of the war.[104] Compared to Adams's well-groomed heroic close-up subjects, Yoneda's face is less a smooth surface than a heavily lined text inviting a close reading. His face is marked with the same kind of sun-baked, weather-beaten, care-worn look of Lange's and other Depression-era photographers' farm worker subjects. The rumpled hair and unbuttoned wrinkled shirt are details that stand in sharp contrast to Adams's careful portraits at Manzanar. Indeed, critic Karin Becker Ohrn juxtaposes Lange's pho-

tograph of Yoneda with Adams's portrait of Corpora.
Shohara for their similarity in content but radically contra:
sual styles.

Yet, if the representation of racial difference is minimi.
Adams's photographs, so is the representation of race in Lange'.
traits strangely displaced by the category of class. If one compares
Lange's close-up of the young man together with a similar close-up
portrait of the interned grandfather and child, it is not entirely clear
if the squinting eyes of this young man and grandfather are epicanthic folds—those unique racial markers of Asian difference—or
"dust bowl folds." It is the latter which visually prevail in so many of
Lange's Farm Security Administration photographs from the 1930s
in which the faces of her poor white migrant subjects seem to fold in
on themselves as a result of fatigue and sedimentary grit.

The Undercover Eye: Toyo Miyatake's Photographs of Manzanar

> GIRL: Is it against the law to take pictures?
> ZENIHIRO: In here it is.
> GIRL: Then why do you take them?
> ZENIHIRO: Because one day when this is all over, a lot of people
> will want to pretend it never happened. But my pictures
> will not ever let them forget.
> —Scene from *Farewell to Manzanar* (1976)

Toyo Miyatake is perhaps the best-known Japanese American photographer of the internment camp experience. In the 1976 television
film version of *Farewell to Manzanar,* the legendary photographer
was portrayed with heroic zeal as the fictional character Mr. Zenihiro. Played by comic actor Pat Morita, Zenihiro is depicted as a
clever, witty, and heroic undergound chronicler of internment camp
history and experience. He deliberately wears his numbered tags on
his lapels during his three years of confinement as a political statement, and when he is busted by the camp director, for the third
time, the latter relents and allows him to photograph Manzanar
freely for posterity. Writer Cynthia Takano is right when she asserts

that Miyatake holds a "special place in the visual history of the Japanese American internment camps for his role as an underground chronicler of life there."[105] He was a professional photographer from Los Angeles who smuggled a camera lens and film holder into Manzanar at a time when all such recording devices in the hands of Japanese Americans were considered contraband. Using scrap lumber and plumbing fixtures, he was able to fashion a crude undercover camera—which passed as a lunch box—which he was then able to tote inconspicuously while documenting some of the very first internee photographs taken at this camp.[106] After nine months of surreptitious picture taking, he was caught by camp authorities. Manzanar's camp director, Ralph Palmer Merritt, reportedly was sympathetic to Miyatake's argument that "his photographs represented a history he was impelled to record" and allowed him to continue his work albeit with this one concession to military rules: Miyatake could set up his camera and photograph anything he liked, but a white camp worker was required to trip the shutter.[107] Several months later, such strict military regulations were lifted, and by 1943 Miyatake was able to send for his professional equipment from Los Angeles; indeed, he became Manzanar's official in-house photographer until the camp was closed in November 1945.

While there is no doubt that Miyatake's photographs of Manzanar remain one of the most important visual archives from internment camp history, there is a prevalent misrepresentation that all his published work is the result of an illicit photographic gaze, and that his documentary images of the camps are all the more truthful—vis-à-vis the photographs taken by "outsiders" like Ansel Adams and Dorothea Lange—because of his unique position as a chronicler from the "inside."[108]

Graham Howe, Scott Rankin, and Patrick Nagatani, the editors of *Two Views of Manzanar* (1978), which showcases the work of Miyatake alongside that of Adams, write that the interned photographer's "immersion in [the Manzanar] community enabled his success as an *almost omniscient observer* of life in the camps."[109] On the first page of *Two Views of Manzanar*, in extra-large type, the editors preface the collection with an emphasis on Miyatake's surreptitious work: "In 1942, Toyo Miyatake, a Japanese-American photographer, was interned in the Manzanar Relocation Camp where he was impelled to secretly photograph his story." While *Two Views of Manzanar* remains the best published American collection of Miyatake's camp photographs, such a prefatory emphasis on his "secret" documentation is misleading; especially since only one photo out of the thirty-two that are included was actually taken with the infamous "lunch box" camera. (This photograph, "Street Scene of Manzanar" [1943], is reprinted as a mere thumbnail in the back of the book.)[110] The misconception that the bulk of Miyatake's camp photographs were surreptitiously taken has surfaced as recently as 1998, when his images of Manzanar were exhibited alongside those of Adams and Lange at the Ansel Adams Center for Photography in San Francisco. In the official press release for the exhibit, the curators emphasized that Miyatake "secretly photographed the lives of his friends and family, providing an intimate record of life inside the camp."[111] While Miyatake's "lunch box" camera was prominently displayed as a central artifact at this exhibit, curiously none of his photographs on display were those actually taken with it. Nevertheless, Miyatake's undercover camera has become an erroneous frame for reading his body of photographs of Manzanar.

While hardly "omniscient"—or even "almost omniscient"—Miyatake certainly witnessed every stage of Manzanar's development and history from the camp's earliest to its final days as a residential insider. His images record those community events and rituals that would have been difficult to capture on film by an occasional visiting photographer: memorials for the dead, the sending off of male nisei volunteers to the 442nd Regimental Combat Team, camp baseball games, Christmas celebrations complete with a crudely costumed camp Santa, New Year's *mochi* (rice) pounding, scenes of school sports and recreation, victory gardens between barracks, and crowded interiors of the men's barbershops and the women's beauty parlors.[112] These everyday scenes of Manzanar camp life depict the extent to which the internees succeeded in normalizing routine community activities. For the most part, these images—like those of Ansel Adams—virtually and visually reify Japanese Americans at Manzanar as highly industrious, productive, and adaptable model minority subjects of incarceration.

Majorettes at Manzanar. *(Toyo Miyatake. Manzanar War Relocation Center. Used by permission of Archie Miyatake.)*

Because there are scant personal photographs taken by internees themselves that have also been published for public circulation, the documentary work of Adams, Miyatake, Lange, and other War Relocation Authority photographers still stand, over fifty years later, as the dominant visual record chronicling life behind barbed wire.[113] As historical evidence, the work of Adams, and Miyatake in particular, attests to the amazing ability of second-generation Japanese American citizens to overcome adversity and rebound as an unquestionably loyal and resilient American community. Compared to the vast body of literary narratives on internment, the photographs tell us much about the public nature of life in the camps, but very little about the private side of that experience as it impacted over 100,000 individuals. It is not surprising that so many photographs taken during the internment focus on the bodies and faces of those behind barbed wire. Such a close-up scrutiny of the men, women, and children in the camps creates a false visual rhetoric of access, penetration, and documentation of that most internalized notion of a private Japanese American self.

Indeed, the very notion of the private remains highly problematic in any photographic representation of the internment, where individuals were systematically uprooted from their homes and relocated into the public space of the camps that was stripped—like any other prison setting—of any normal sense of private space.

The two photographs by Toyo Miyatake that have generated the most critical discussion are those he took under both relaxed military regulations and official camp scrutiny: the first one, a "Group of Majorettes" (1944), has been singled out by critic John C. Welchman for its ironic composition.[14] The portrait focuses on sixteen bare-legged adolescent girls who belonged to the Manzanar majorette squad. The older girls, standing in the front row, proudly wear their pseudomilitary marching uniforms, their hands at ease resting on drum sticks, while the back row is populated with younger girls in matching pinafores with batons held up at their sides. Welchman notes that Miyatake's photograph seems self-consciously to parody "absurdity as much as it celebrates the achievements of ritualized Americana" as the girls "struggle to retain their camera-induced smiles" while weathering an annoying "dust-blowing wind."[115] He notes that those girls who were "[able] to find or afford them" are wearing the requisite white boots, while others are not. What is most ironic is the image of such a hyper-American and gender-specific activity in the midst of what appears to be the frigid conditions of a desert concentration camp in high winter. Miyatake's majorettes evoke Adams's smiling portraits of docile, innocent schoolgirls dressed up in the clothing and hairstyles that mark them as unambiguously American.

In visual counterpoint to the smiling schoolgirls, Miyatake's portrait of three boys is also worthy of closer critical scrutiny. Of "Children by the Manzanar Security Fence" (1944), Michael Several has noted the sense of despair in the image of the three "sad" and "passive" male figures standing at the barbed wire edge of the camp's

Three boys, barbed wire, and a guard tower. *(Toyo Miyatake. Manzanar War Relocation Center. Used by permission of Archie Miyatake.)*

perimeter, a guard tower looming behind them in the upper right-hand corner of the frame.[116] Beautiful in composition, this photograph is one of the very few unposed portraits of young adolescent boys in the camp. Their body language signals their sense of boredom, longing, and certainly confinement behind the camp's security fence. Most significantly, it remains one of the very few photographs of internment that combines the visually taboo images of barbed wire, guard towers, and internee body language that is less resilient than resigned.

Ironically, what is perhaps Miyatake's best-known photograph of Manzanar—or at least the one that has most frequently been reprinted in books and documentary films is devoid of any actual Japanese American subjects. His stark portrait of one of the camp guard towers, "Watch Tower" (1943), is arguably one of the most powerful documentary images of the camps for its portrayal of a military object that was visually taboo in Adams's and Lange's photographs. The photograph is, initially, visually reminiscent of Adams's scenic Manzanar landscapes of the snow-capped Inyo mountain range in the background, a moon just visible over the low horizon. Yet, a monstrous watch tower looms above the vista like an awkward wooden sculpture—a menacing reminder of the authority of an ever-present military gaze whose gun sights were set on the thousands of internees below its scaffolding. Indeed, this image of the watch tower signifies a pervasive view from above, where armed

The panoptic gaze of the guard tower. *Toyo Miyatake. Manzanar War Relocation Center. Used by permission of Archie Miyatake.)*

A still-life study in citizenship: the interior of the barracks quarters of the Yonemitsu family. *(Ansel Adams. Library of Congress, Prints and Photographs Divisions.)*

sentries kept a panoptic vigil on Japanese American activities below from every barbed-wire corner of Manzanar's one-square-mile perimeter.

While my discussion throughout this chapter has focused primarily on the Japanese American body in internment camp photography, I must point out, with irony, that in addition to Miyatake's "Watch Tower," the two other most arguably iconic images of the relocation and internment experience are similarly devoid of an actual Japanese American presence. I believe that Ansel Adams's most reprinted photograph from Manzanar is a still-life portrait, purportedly shot exactly as he found it, entitled "Top of Radio in Yonemitsu Residence" (1943).[117] In this photograph, a formal portrait of the family's son, Private First Class Robert Yonemitsu, dressed in full military garb, sits atop a radio against a portrait of Jesus Christ, next to a decorated houseplant and festive arrangement of vegetables and recent letters the faithful son and soldier has sent "home" to his sister, Lucy, at Manzanar. This still-life portrait succeeds, in the same manner as Adams's close-up portraits of uniformed individual internees, in conveying an unambiguous image of Japanese Americans re-encoded as patriotic Christian citizen subjects in service to their country. The photograph is striking as an alterlike memorial to family, religion, and patriotism. Even though the son is literally not present, he is remembered through the photograph as an American soldier sent off to war to serve both god and his country.

Likewise, one of Dorothea Lange's best known and most reprinted images of the relocation and internment experience consists of a street-scene photograph of the Japanese American Wanto grocery store in Oakland, California, the day after the bombing of Pearl Harbor, "I am an American" (1942)."[8] One can read Lange's sign as a

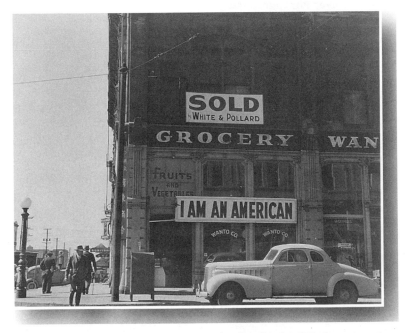

The Wanto grocery store on December 8, the day after Pearl Harbor. *(Dorothea Lange. WRA, Oakland, California, April, 1942. Courtesy of the Dorothea Lange Collection, Oakland Museum, 1978.)*

Japanese American declaration of patriotic American identity; it is, in short, a powerful yet simple de-Othering of the self. The Smithsonian Institution American History Museum has made brilliant use of Lange's photograph by re-creating it as a three-dimensional walk-through stage set in its permanent exhibit on the camps called "A More Perfect Union." In the exhibit, museum goers must literally walk through the life-size re-creation of Lange's street scene—where one can stand in front of the Wanto grocery store and read the actual "Executive Order 9066" sign posted on a nearby lamp pole. Redesigned as a stage set, the visitor is forced to enter the camp exhibit by first walking through Lange's snapshot as if it were a historical time portal where the present is collapsed into the past in a stroke of creative museum staging.[119]

What Is Never Photographed

For anyone who has looked through the War Relocation Authority's archive, it will be readily apparent that the photographic record is incomplete. Indeed, as Sylvia E. Danovitch has correctly noted, one will not find any visual evidence of the harshness or inconvenience of day-to-day living conditions in the camps, or, any signs of the initial internee unrest or protest that went on during the early days.[120] Danovitch speculates that such photographs may have been removed from the official record, or destroyed, or quite simply never recorded in the first place; in any case, she concludes, the War Relocation Authority photographs are "insufficient as historical evidence" and, as a group, are little more than "benign images that tell little or nothing about the injustice inflicted upon this group of Americans."[121] Compared to the autobiographical writings of internees, and visual accounts by interned artists, the photographic record of the camps remains a two-dimensional representation of selectively framed historical snapshots. Critics like Cynthia Takano have pointed out that if Miyatake's body of Manzanar work was one-sided, "his camera's eye was not blind to the reality of barbed wire, but he chose not to dwell on it."[122] Critic Michael Several concurs that while Miyatake was strategic in his photographic choices, he deliberately avoided "divisive and polemical issues and blame of the larger society."[123] Instead, the interned photographer focused on images of the Japanese American community "pulling together and maintaining its collective and individual integrity."[124] Even so, Miyatake's photographs—both those taken surreptitiously as well as those which were later taken in the open atmosphere of relaxed regulations—are somewhat disappointing for their refusal to record almost anything other than upbeat scenes of Japanese American ingenuity and adaptation. Even Archie Miyatake, the photographer's son, has commented that many people have critiqued his father's photographs, arguing that "the people are too dressed up in the pictures, too cheerful."[125] In the final analysis, what remains both fascinating and disturbing is the way in which Miyatake's camera—coded as the undercover eye on internment—promises to take the public on a visual journey into the private, yet delivers only those appropriate images of Japanese American resilience, fortitude, and good cheer that give the good citizen the face she or he is supposed to have.

In Conclusion: Making Visual Reparations

Sansei poet Ron Tanaka forces us to confront the complex politics of positioning surrounding Japanese Americans as visual subjects of World War II history in his poem, "Appendix to *Executive Order*":

> The people who put out that book
> I guess they won a lot of awards.
> It was a very photogenic period
> Of california history, especially
> If you were a white photographer
> With compassion for helpless people.
>
> But the book would have been better,
> I think, or more complete, if they
> Had put in my picture and yours, with

Our hakujin wives, our long hair and
The little signs saying, "remember
Manzanar!" and "never again!" then

On the very last page, a picture of
Our kids. They don't even look like
Japanese. *Mo sunda yo.* After thirty
Years, the picture is now complete.

In his poem, Tanaka addresses the 1972 publication of Maisie and Richard Conrat's powerful collection of photographs in *Executive Order 9066*.[126] Tanaka raises provocative questions about the selective process of representing historical memories and the predominant role of the white photographer as a heroic intercessor, image maker, and witness to minority history. In particular, Tanaka objects to the prevailing mode of representation in this collection that depicts internees as tragic, yet photogenic, objects of history. What the editors have left out, Tanaka suggests, is the photographic evidence of Japanese American agency and political resistance both during the years behind barbed wire and in the postwar years leading up to the successful redress and reparation movement of the 1980s. The last stanza of the poem is a profound reminder that after thirty years of postwar assimilation and interracial out-marriage, post-internment Japanese American children "don't even look like Japanese." Less than one generation later, the Japanese American body has been emptied of all the physical signs of racial difference, thereby undoing the visual rhetoric of difference that underpins World War II representations. This becomes the culmination of the pictorial record.

If there is a single fitting image and icon for the courage of Japanese American self-representation, we must return if not to Toyo Miyatake's photographs, then at least to his "lunchbox" camera. Whether or not one believes Miyatake's representations of Manzanar remain too "dressed up" or "cheerful," the interned photographer's outlaw camera remains a profound symbol for that which was initially—and officially—forbidden: the autonomy of the Japanese American gaze. That Miyatake was allowed by the Manzanar camp director to set up his camera and frame each shot, but had to wait for the authority of a white camp worker to trip the shutter and take the actual picture, raises disturbing and unresolved questions about the ownership of the historical gaze and the power of self-representation.[127]

In 1993, artist Nobuho Nagasawa's bronze replica of Toyo Miyatake's infamous "lunchbox" camera was unveiled on the sidewalk outside the Japanese American National Museum in the downtown area of Los Angeles known as Little Tokyo. It is one of the latest works of public art to commemorate Japanese American history in the Little Tokyo historic district. In addition to *Toyo Miyatake's Camera,* one can also find Jerry Matsukuma's nine-panel photomural *Senzo* (Ancestors) and Sheila Levrant de Bretteville's installation of images and timelines from Japanese American history "embedded in the block-long sidewalk."[128] As art reviewer Michael Several has observed, the street outside the Japanese American museum has become a veritable "street of memory" in recent years as the site of so many public art works unveiled in the post-redress period of the 1990s. These works now make visual reparations in a historic Japanese American neighborhood that has survived upheaval, economic recession, and revitalization in the last one hundred years.[129]

Toyo Miyatake's Camera now stands on behalf of all interned Japanese Americans—and artists from the margins—who have dared to take up the tools of visual representation, whether it was the camera, the sketch pad, or the paintbrush in order to render visible what has been termed elsewhere the "view from within."[130] The triple-sized bronze replica of Miyatake's lunchbox camera now watches over this "street of memory" at the beginning of a new century and remains a potent symbol of what the original itself could not record: the historic moment when a Japanese American photographer stood behind the camera trying to appropriate a forbidden gaze in order to chronicle minority history.

Photographs are, by definition, surface texts. By framing images from the internment experience by noted photographers like Ansel Adams, Dorothea Lange, and Toyo Miyatake in this chapter, we are compelled to read their representations of Japanese Americans as visual texts, where the language of the body lends itself to interpretation in the absence of actual "voice." However, if we want to look below the limited surface of the photograph, perhaps we must look elsewhere—either to the written accounts of internees or to those of other visual artists whose records of life behind barbed wire were not as hampered by censorship or the limits of a camera's gaze. It is with this in mind that the next chapter offers an examination of one of the most famous artistic representations of the interned Japanese American body.

Beyond the Camera and between the Words
Inserting Oneself into the Picture and into
Japanese American (Art) History—Mine Okubo's
Citizen 13660 and the Power of Visual Autobiography

> I am a painter, a very poor talker, very poor. Otherwise I would have
> been a writer. I have lived more than fifty years in the U.S., but do
> not yet speak English well. My Japanese is not good either. So please
> read between the words. We just talk in signs.   —Hisako Hibi

> I paint about three-hundred pictures of camp scenery. At that time,
> we couldn't take a camera, take pictures. All swords, guns, and cam-
> eras prohibited. So I think I paint like I take a picture, you know. I
> have to put in the detail. So just the same as if I took it with a
> camera, these are.   —Charles Mikami

Japanese American artists, Hisako Hibi and Charles Mikami, each
speak to the subversive potential of painting a personal historical
record when other tools of representation are forbidden, unavail-
able, or underdeveloped. In place of language and cameras, both
artists speak to the power of "talking in signs" through painting and
sketching as an alternative system of visual representation that
Japanese Americans were free to use in recording their individual
and collective experiences of relocation and internment.[1]
   Like the photographic archive that documents the wartime experiences of Japanese Americans, the creative body of internee artwork

remains a marginalized visual archive outside of the Asian American community and occasional museum, art gallery, Website exhibitions, and special collections. Two of the most valuable published collections of internee artwork are the 1992 exhibit catalog, *The View from Within: Japanese American Art from the Camps, 1942–1945*, and Deborah Gesensway and Mindy Roseman's 1987 book, *Beyond Words: Images from America's Concentration Camps*.[2] Indeed, *Beyond Words* provides a crucial place to begin an examination of the visual politics of internment-camp art representation. Gesensway and Roseman do a fine job of documenting and reprinting a broad range of work by camp artists, combined with invaluable oral histories. At the same time, the authors raise unsettling questions about the very nature of official historical representations of the camps. A closer look at *Beyond Words* will not only help to frame the politics of internment camp art representation, but will also provide an excellent transition to one of the most multilayered and critically overlooked visual texts from that experience: Mine Okubo's *Citizen 13660*.[3]

Beyond Words: In Search of "Truth" with a Lowercase "T"?

In their preface, Gesensway and Roseman explain how the idea for their book was prompted by the discovery of a box full of camp art, notes, and research materials that once belonged to two former Cornell professors "who had conducted sociological studies in two of the relocation camps, Poston and Manzanar."[4]

> What was it like to be called "enemy alien" in the country of your birth, to prove your loyalty to the United States Constitution by giving up your constitutional rights? What was it like to be suddenly uprooted from everything familiar and corralled behind barbed wire for up to three years? These questions were vividly posed for us . . . on an ordinary spring day in 1980, when we received separate phone calls from Richard Polenberg, a Cornell University professor of American history with whom we had taken a seminar in civil liberties. He told us that many boxes of papers and watercolors had

just been discovered in an attic in Ithaca. The materials seemed to be from the World War II Japanese American relocation camps. Would we be interested in seeing them, that is to say, help carry the boxes to a place where they could be examined?

As we would later learn, these documents belonged to two former Cornell professors of anthropology/sociology— Alexander H. Leighton (also a psychiatrist) and Morris Opler—who had conducted sociological studies in two of the relocation camps, Poston (Arizona) and Manzanar (California). There were biographies, daily reports, minutes of meetings, and notes on all aspects of camp administration and life. But what particularly intrigued us was a series of 130 watercolors . . . which ranged from landscapes to caricatures, [and] were a visual record of the mass incarceration.[5]

The boxes of papers and watercolors, uncovered from the attic in Ithaca, were the partial remnants of official anthropological and sociological studies carried out in the camps by a number of specially appointed groups: the War Relocation Authority's Community Analyst Project (headed by Morris Opler), the Sociology Lab in Poston (headed by Alexander H. Leighton), and the Japanese American Evacuation and Resettlement Study (headed by Dorothy Swain Thomas at the University of California, Berkeley). It has only been in the last twenty years that these official studies have come under intense critical scrutiny from within the Asian American scholarly community. While it is not my intention here to critique these studies, the fact remains that the composite data from this officially sanctioned body of wartime research has formed the basis of much that has been written on internment history. Such a detailed examination and critique of the Japanese American Evacuation and Resettlement Study can be found in Yuji Ichioka's excellent 1989 collection of essays, *Views from Within: The Japanese American Evacuation and Resettlement Study,* as well as in the work of anthropologist Peter T. Suzuki.[6] As one of the most outspoken of these critics, Suzuki has argued that "the camp experience was a corrupting one for those social scientists, who under the pretext of scientific research, undertook such activities as spying, informing, and intelligence work [and] also shows the extent to which the government attempted to manipulate and control the inmates."[7]

Writer and critic Frank Chin is even harsher in his criticism and hypothesizes that if Suzuki is right about the unethical methodology behind these official studies, then "virtually everything in print by an anthropologist/sociologist since the end of the war is suspect."[8] Even the noted internment historian and scholar Roger Daniels has argued that "the role of the community analyst in the [War Relocation Authority] camps . . . was, is, and will probably remain a controversial one."[9] Given the controversy of these projects, it is curious that the editors of *Beyond Words* give an impassioned critique of the internment experience and devote themselves to giving "voice" to the internee artists themselves, yet omit a discussion of the controversial nature of the boxful of artwork and social science research at the center of their work. To their credit, however, both Gesensway and Roseman speak to the politics and limitations of their own positioning with regard to this project:

> From the beginning of our project we were well aware of being outsiders—young and white, interviewing older ethnic Japanese. We did our best to convey our sincerity and break down the barriers, but inevitably we heard what we did because of who we are and who they are. And what we heard was how sensitive and resilient people made the best of, or survived in, or even prospered under adverse conditions. . . . We do not claim truth with a capital "t."[10]

Indeed, armed with grants, a zeal to document the personal "meaning of evacuation," and a book contract from Cornell University Press, Gesensway and Roseman spent the winter of 1982–83 searching the archives for collections of camp art, scouring phone books for names of surviving camp artists, and conducting some twenty-five interviews with former internees, including Mine Okubo. While *Beyond Words* is an invaluable resource book for its rich full-color catalog of camp art and accompanying oral histories, it also remains problematic as an example of internment history prompted by the impulse to "set the record straight" while remaining almost wholly unaware of its own blind spots with regard to what bell hooks terms "the politics of domination."[11] Ironically, the authors began their research on the book at the same time the U.S. Commission on Wartime Relocation and Internment of Civilians was formed in 1980. The absence of any reference to the work of the U.S. Commission is puzzling in *Beyond Words*. As Gesensway and Roseman scrambled to locate and interview internees, the U.S. Commission began holding its series of public hearings across the nation. During these hearings, former internees stood up and gave testimony—many for the first time in their lives. The years 1980–81 thus became a watershed moment where the public breaking of Japanese American silence about the camps became part of national American history and collective memory.

I raise these issues here in order to ask if it makes a difference, in the arena of Japanese American representation, over who is allowed to speak for whom. In my previous chapter, I asked, What difference does it make who represents whom in the visual historical archive? In this chapter, I ask whether it makes a difference whose voice is allowed to stand as the authoritative voice of official history. At whose expense? With only two notable exceptions, why is it that Gesensway and Roseman look primarily to the work of white historians and scholars for the hard data in their research while relying on the oral histories of Japanese Americans as voices of personal experience? What does it mean that their "attic discovery" of work conducted by "officially" sanctioned researchers (anthropologists, sociologists, psychoanalysts)—who were literally placed in the camps as ethnographic data gatherers for government research—is uninterrogated?

To what extent does a work like *Beyond Words* reinscribe the politics of domination, power, and knowledge over internment representation that was set in place some forty years earlier by their distinguished Cornell predecessors? Writer Toni Morrison reminds us that people who belong to any "marginalized category . . . [have seldom been invited] to participate in the discourse even when we were its topic," especially when it comes to writing about their role in history.[12] bell hooks also eloquently addresses the politics of domination that is central to the constructing and defining of minority representations in her essay, "Talking Back":

> As subjects, people have the right to define their own reality and establish their own identities, name their own history. . . . [Every] liberatory struggle initiated by groups of people who have been seen as objects begins with a revolutionary process wherein they assert that they are subjects. . . . Oppressed people resist by identifying themselves as subjects, by defining their reality, shaping their new identity, naming their history, telling their story.[13]

It is especially in light of the highly visible redress and reparation movement of the 1980s and the fifty-year anniversary of the signing of Executive Order 9066 that Japanese Americans have finally begun the process of reclaiming the terrain of history, memory, and authority as they speak out, create, and curate this visual history themselves. This chapter privileges what has been termed the unofficial "view from within" in its look at a 1946 autobiographical art book that, retrospectively, was decades ahead of its time.

Reading Mine Okubo's Visual Autobiography

> Living as we did—on the edge—we developed a particular way of seeing reality. We looked both from the outside in and from the inside out. We focused our attention on the center as well as on the margin. We understood both.
> —bell hooks, from *Margin to Center*

> We were suddenly uprooted—lost everything and treated like a prisoner with soldier guard, dumped behind barbed wire fence. We were in shock. You'd be in shock. You'd be bewildered. You'd be humiliated. You can't believe this is happening to you. To think this could happen in the United States. We were citizens.   —Mine Okubo, from *Beyond Words: Images from America's Concentration Camps*

Published by Columbia University Press in 1946 during a time when "anything Japanese was still rat poison," Mine Okubo's *Citizen 13660* cannot be contained within the narrow confines of either mere visual art or the traditional literary form of autobiography.[14] As "visual autobiography," her hybrid narrative defies the law of genre and as a result is often overlooked in critical discussions of Asian American literature. Indeed, Elaine Kim does not list it in her exhaustive pioneering survey, *Asian American Literature, an Introduction to the Writings and Their Social Context*.[15] It is a unique text—a fusion of pictorial and written storytelling—one where Okubo "talks in signs" both through the convention of literary narrative and through cartoonlike self-portrait sketches. Outside of Asian American literature, the one text that has the most in common with *Citizen 13660* is Art Spiegelman's *Maus: A Survivor's Tale*—another well known cartoon narrative of the World War II concentration camp experience.[16]

Citizen 13660 is the first and arguably the best-known autobiographical narrative of the Japanese American relocation and internment experience.[17] Okubo takes her reader on an uncensored visual tour through some of the most private and public spaces at Tanforan Assembly Center in California and Topaz War Relocation Center in Utah in order to give testimony to the personal and collective effects of relocation and imprisonment. The book's narrative criticizes and subverts the political structures of the internment and stands out for its depiction of the "negative aspects of camp life" compared to other artistic renderings of that experience.[18] Most Japanese American writings were suspended outside the camp communities from 1941 until the early 1950s, particularly on the West Coast. Indeed, Toshio Mori's famous short-story collection, *Yokohama, California*, was originally scheduled for release in 1941, but was postponed for the duration of the Pacific war and not actually published until 1949. *Citizen 13660* is unique in that it was written during the internment years and published immediately afterwards. Indeed, Okubo's book has remained in print for over fifty years, has been translated into multiple languages, and continues to enjoy an international following of readers stretching from the United States to Siberia.[19] It was even honored with an American Book Award in 1984 when it was reissued by the University of Washington Press. Yet, paradoxically, it remains one of the most critically overlooked narratives in Asian American literature by virtue of its refusal to be easily categorized.[20]

In one of the very few literary discussions of *Citizen 13660*, Pamela Stennes Wright correctly observes that Okubo employs two narrative strategies throughout the pages of her book: one involves her use of an overt narrative that documents the "story of a loyal American who returns to the U.S. at the beginning of the war and must come to an understanding of her evacuation and internment."[21] And the other is a covert narrative that suggests "the injustices of those policies through the depiction of massive disruption . . . and changes forced on Japanese Americans."[22] The genius in Okubo's book is the unusual combination of visual and literary narrative that allows her to tell both stories. In the fifty years since its initial publication, *Citizen 13660* remains a groundbreaking work in Japanese American representation for its provocative, and subversive, use of the autobiographical "I" paired with the observational power of her artist's "eye."[23]

Citizen 13660 consists of some two hundred pen-and-ink drawings accompanied by the author/artist's first-person narrative which chronicles her life during the war years.[24] In the prologue, Okubo depicts her experience as a University of California at Berkeley scholarship student traveling in Europe, where she is caught off-guard when England and France declare war on Germany in 1939. Her book thus begins with a story of wartime displacement and the urgent desire to return to the safety of home—especially when she learns that her mother is seriously ill. Okubo tells us that it took her three months to make arrangements to return to France and catch what was literally the last boat home, where she traveled with war-dislocated refugees bound for the United States. These refugees share with her their vivid narratives of uprooting, exile, loss, and longing for freedom—themes that will later reverberate throughout the pages of *Citizen 13660*.

Okubo finally arrives back home in Riverside, California, where she endures the loss of her mother—the first in a series of losses for the artist—and then relocates to northern California, where she rooms with her younger brother and settles into work before her life is forever changed by the events of December 7, 1941. What Okubo does not say in the book is that on her return from Europe she was also hired by the Federal Arts Project, an agency of President Roosevelt's New Deal which commissioned artists to create large monumental works during the Depression. Okubo created numerous frescoes and mosaics throughout the Bay Area for the Project. During this period, she had the opportunity to observe and learn from Diego Rivera, who was also part of the project and who was then painting his 1,800-square-foot mural on the theme of pan-American unity. Even though Okubo never worked directly with Rivera, the painter had an impact on her early work, which used diverse art forms to document injustice.

Citizen 13660 picks up Okubo's story after Pearl Harbor, with the registration and expulsion of people of Japanese ancestry from the West Coast during the spring of 1942. Okubo and her family—and over 100,000 other Japanese Americans—were uprooted from their homes and exiled within their own country, most for the duration of the war, under the authority of Executive Order 9066. Given the complexity of how many large families were transported to different assembly centers and camps, Okubo's family was literally broken apart and scattered across the country: she and her younger brother, Toku, were ultimately sent to Topaz, Utah (where they were reunited with another brother and sister), her eldest sister to Heart Mountain, Wyoming, an older brother was drafted into the army, and other family members were sent to Poston, Arizona. Okubo's father, who was initially arrested by the FBI and shipped to a series of top-security prison camps, was later allowed to join members of his family at Poston.

Armed with rice paper, pens, and other tools of her trade, Okubo devoted her one and half years in the camps at Tanforan and later at Topaz to sketching and painting detailed records of her own daily life and that of her fellow prisoners. According to Okubo, the sketches told "the story of camp life for my many friends, who faithfully sent letters and packages to let us know we were not forgotten."[25] Okubo's camp sketches were originally intended as a personal record assembled for her friends on the outside with an eye for later possible public exhibition:

All my friends on the outside were sending me extra food and crazy gifts to cheer me up. Once I got a box with a whole bunch of worms even. So I decided I would do something for them. I started a series of drawings telling them the story of my camp life. At the time I wasn't thinking of a book; I was thinking of an exhibition, but these drawings later became my book, *Citizen 13660*. So I just kept a record of everything, objective and humorous, without saying much so they could see it all. Humor is the only thing that mellows life, shows life as the circus it is.[26]

As an unofficial record for a private circle of friends, Okubo's sketches of relocation and internment depict the kinds of scenes and images that one will not find in official photographs of the camps.

More than most other camp autobiographies, Okubo positions herself in complex fashion as both an insider and an outsider within the borders of her own community, giving us a rare wartime glimpse of the radical possibility of self-representation from the margins. In virtually every one of her camp sketches, Okubo constructs herself as a participant and observer who holds a multiplicity of complex and shifting positions. Sometimes she depicts herself standing literally inside each frame as a full participant in camp activities (from building furniture, to battling the elements, to throwing her first snowball). In other sketches, she constructs herself as a marginal figure, often standing at a distance on the very edge and border of the frame looking at the crowds of internees as though she herself were an outsider among the exiled. Such a double perspective endows her with a subversive gaze where the artist's "eye" and the writer's "I" are able to look simultaneously from what bell hooks calls "the outside in" and "the inside out."[27] Her written commentary appears on the bottom of each page accompanied by a sketch in which she clearly depicts herself as a witness to wartime history, thus creating a unique, double narrative for storytelling.

Feminist critic Caren Kaplan has argued that as marginalized subjects, women have always been able to move between "the interstices of masculine culture" while using "the dominant language and form of expression" in order to give voice to experiences based on their marginality."[28] In many of her sketches, Okubo depicts herself as lone female figure observing the unique male culture of leader and activities at Tanforan and Topaz. With her sketch pad in he she explores the segregated spaces of the "bachelors' quarters" and bears witness to the effects of boredom and idleness. She also cruises the grandstands, where she observes the spectacle of public sleeping and illegal gambling conducted out of sight of the camp police. In other sketches, Okubo depicts herself making gestures of protest (sticking out her tongue or holding her nose) over the invasive nature of male curfew patrollers, military recruiters, or pro-Japanese leaders in the camp. Many of the women depicted in *Citizen 13660* are shown working hard in gender-specific roles taking care of families, tending to small children, doing laundry, running nursery schools, etc. (Okubo even depicts herself teaching children's art classes at Topaz.)

Okubo's sketches make clear that the camps were run by the male leadership of the Caucasian camp administrators and Japanese American internee volunteers. Her visual representation of the camps is unique for its self-portrayal of an unusually independent, Japanese American female figure who easily traverses the margins and center of both the public, private, and gendered spaces of the camp with her brilliant eye for detail, irony, and critical observation.[29] Writer Gloria Anzaldúa describes this special ability of the writer and artist to shift across positions and perspectives, *la facultad*: "The capacity to see in surface phenomena the meaning of deeper realities, to see the deep structure below the surface."[30] Like Kaplan's "marginalized female subject," Anzaldúa argues that women and others who have experienced dislocation in some form have historically been in a position to develop this remarkable ability:

> Those who do not feel psychologically or physically safe in the world are more apt to develop this sense. Those who are pounced on the most have it the strongest—the females, the homosexuals of all races, the dark-skinned, the outcast, the persecuted, the marginalized, the foreign . . . it's a kind of survival tactic that people caught between the worlds, unknowingly cultivate. It is latent in all of us.[31]

This ability to move between worlds, borders, cultures, and positions is one which enables the subjective and collective experience of the Other to be voiced. It is a skill that Okubo demonstrates with visual mastery in the pages of *Citizen 13660* as a native-born American who has been cast out of citizenship and into a wartime concentration camp.

In one of the first sketches in *Citizen 13660*, Okubo self-consciously constructs herself as the object of a hostile white American gaze as the only Japanese American onboard a public bus directly after the bombing of Pearl Harbor. She is surrounded on all sides by fellow passengers who fix the squirming artist in their collective glare. The accompanying caption says, "The people looked at all of us, both citizens and aliens, with suspicion and mistrust."[32] Okubo's double vision—the ability to see herself as both Japanese and American, as citizen and alien, and as subject and object—is a quality that Elaine Kim argues exists throughout Asian American literature and has a distinct kinship with W. E. B. Du Bois's articulation of "double consciousness" that is unique to people of color.[33] This ability to see oneself through such a double perspective is made possible, Kim argues, "by the writer's biculturalism, which gives them two pairs of eyes through which to see both their communities and their American context without distortion or romanticism."[34] Okubo fully understands the complexity of this double vision in her self-portrait as a Japanese American woman caught in a gaze that is unable to read beyond the surface difference of her skin and recognize her claim to the citizenship that forms part of her book's ironic title.

Okubo is articulate about how her vantage point as an interned artist affords her a particular kind of gaze in her daily observation of life behind barbed wire:

> In the camps, first at Tanforan and then at Topaz in Utah, I had the opportunity to study the human race from the cradle to the grave, and to see what happens to people when reduced to one status and condition. Cameras and photographs were not permitted in the camps, so I recorded everything in sketches, drawings, and paintings.[35]

She uses her sketch pad to record daily scenes in a way that is arguably more fluid and interpretational than the more rigid limitations prescribed by a camera lens. As an independent artist, there were certainly no official camp censors dictating what she was allowed to depict in her representations. Furthermore, Okubo's sketch pad and imagination can freely travel through the public and private spaces of the camp capturing scenes that no photographer would have had access to. Her book is filled with images of internees battling not only the notorious desert dust storms, but also the stench of horse manure, leaky sewage, the invasion of spiders, flies, rats, and mosquitoes, and the personal indignities of dealing with the lack of bathroom or outhouse privacy while living under the ever-present and watchful eye of armed guards, camp police, and nosy neighbors.

Okubo consistently foregrounds almost every camp scene with highly detailed close-up portraits of men, women, and children whose faces reflect the physical diversity of the Japanese American community. Her internees are never homogenized or reduced to recognizable Orientalist stereotypes. While humor is reflected throughout the pages of *Citizen 13660*, what dominates her sketches are the deeply lined faces of internees whose worry, discomfort, irritation, and sadness are inscribed on both male and female bodies. While individual internees are often sketched in close-up form, they are almost always positioned against a distant background teeming with the bodies of hundreds of others in the community, making it virtually and visually impossible to forget the crowded conditions of the camps that were built to house ten-thousand Japanese American prisoners in one square mile. Shirley Sun has argued that compared to Okubo's earlier work in Europe, her wartime sketches are dominated by a "pervasive gloom" where black and white drawings serve as "reflections of stark and somber realities of imprisonment as well as the drab and dusty colors of the desert and earth."[36] In contrast to Okubo's published sketches in *Citizen 13660*, her charcoal drawings from the camps are still darker in their representation of "dejected, helpless Evacuees in despair."[37] Describing these other camp representations by the artist, Sun observes,

The world is seen and felt through these weary adults and children. This is the helpless way we behave under coercion. This is the way we respond behind barbed wire. We huddle together but we don't speak to each other. We wonder why. We become stagnant, unmotivated and pick our teeth. The exaggerated heads, the hunched backs the inward-staring eyes all paint for us a psychological and social reality in the profoundest human terms so that no person seeing them can remain untouched.[38]

Whether she is watching, listening, or recording, Okubo depicts herself as a virtually silent witness to the process of relocation and internment. Indeed, throughout the pages of *Citizen 13660*, she visually depicts herself waiting, eating, sweeping, playing, observing, and sketching; yet, with only one exception, she never depicts herself actually speaking. In the one sketch where she represents herself with her mouth open, engaged in speech, she is fighting with the administrators at Tanforan who are trying to break up what is left of her family. Threatened with separation because of the "lack of family units," Okubo argues in the sketch and in the accompanying captioned text that "my brother and I had come as a family unit of two and . . . we intended to remain that way."[39] Ultimately, Okubo prevails and her "family unit of two" remains in tact through Tanforan and Topaz until her brother eventually leaves for a factory job in Chicago and she is herself approved for resettlement in New York City.

What is remarkable about *Citizen 13660* is Okubo's insistence on combining her peculiar brand of humor together with her critical eye for irony. In her interview with the editors of *Beyond Words*, Okubo illuminates just how exactly the process of internee alienation enabled her creative imagination. She writes:

After being uprooted, everything seemed ridiculous, insane, and stupid. There we were in an unfinished camp, with snow and cold. . . . We had to sing "God Bless America" many times with a flag. Guards all around with shotguns, you're not going to walk out. . . . So many crazy things happened in the camp.

So the joke and humor I saw in the camp was not in a joyful sense, but ridiculous and insane.[40]

As an unofficial record, her autobiographical narrative also doubles as an ethnographic account of the Japanese American community she was incarcerated with. Like a frantic anthropologist, Okubo plunged into her documentation:

> I was always busy. In the daytime I went around sketching. There wasn't any photographing allowed so I decided to record everything. Observing, I went around doing all these minute sketches of people and events. I didn't sleep much.[41]

Anthropologist Dorrine K. Kondo has commented on how the act of writing ethnographic texts "becomes a way of freezing the disturbing flux . . . in order to control it and find meaning in the chaos of lived experience through retrospectively ordering the past."[42] That Okubo worked on her visual record day and night, crafting the daily chaos of life in the camps into a narrative form, speaks to her strategy for maintaining a sense of order, control, and rootedness, in spite of the physical and psychic dislocations that were part of the relocation experience.

In one particular sketch, Okubo makes clear how her role as an artistic observer of camp life was also framed within a complex dynamic of surveillance. Initially, camp authorities spied on internee activities in the different blocks in addition to the twenty-four-hour watch by armed sentries in surrounding watchtowers. Okubo depicts herself spying on one such Caucasian camp policeman who in turn spies on the private activities of internees in their barracks.[43] In this visual exchange, even the gaze of the reader is complicit in the complicated, multilayered panoptic effect of looking and spying among internees, camp police, Okubo herself, and the book's reader.

Okubo was notorious about her need for privacy in the camps and hung a "quarantined" sign on the door, warning intruders to stay away. Preoccupied with documenting the daily details of life behind barbed wire, Okubo tells us that within the crowded atmosphere of the camps she wished mostly to be left alone and managed

The multiple gaze: Okubo spies on a camp spy looking through a spy hole at internee activities. *(Mine Okubo. Used by permission of Seiko Buckingham.)*

it through a witty ruse: "There was absolutely no privacy, so I nailed up a quarantine sign to discourage visitors. I would say I had hoof and mouth disease."[44] For the most part, her trick worked to deter nosy neighbors as well as invasive camp police who routinely conducted searches in the barracks. Yet one of the most playful and subversive sketches in *Citizen 13660* records one such official inspection and positions the artist as a clever trickster who remains one step ahead of the camp police. In this self-portrait, the camp authorities are searching her barracks from "potentially dangerous tools" while a military policeman stands guard.[45] Okubo presents herself as a scissors-happy, but harmless artist. The seizing of contraband during the early months of internment included radios, weapons, tools, Japanese records, literature, and, of course, photographic equipment. While the camera was included in the category of the "dangerous," it is telling that in Okubo's narrative, camp officials and the military ironically allowed art supplies to slip by their immediate inspection. Many camp artists have attested to the surprising ease with which they were able to express themselves freely in their artwork.[46] In this sketch, Okubo undermines the innocence of the artist's tools under the surveillance of an invasive camp and military police search. There are no camp sketches like the ones that ultimately will go into her book that are hanging on her barrack's wall. Instead, the only artwork Okubo leaves lying around in clear view are harmless paper streamers, a horse-head portrait on the wall, a cutout animal by her feet, and a paper snake coiled around her head. Okubo clearly does not represent her barracks as a safe space where the artist can freely exhibit her camp documentations. Yet her point is well made that even under the direct scrutiny of the camp police, the artist's

The artist as trickster during camp police inspection of the barracks.
(*Mine Okubo. Used by permission of Seiko Buckingham.*)

tools of subversion are not only permissible, but invisible to camp authorities.

Several other powerful scenes from *Citizen 13660* remind us of the difference between photographic and artistic representation of the internment experience. Virtually every Japanese American woman's autobiography of the camps includes some description of the personal indignities suffered through lack of privacy in the public toilets and bathrooms. Okubo devotes several pages in her book to giving us what are perhaps the most intimate and detailed representations of these private and gendered spaces in the camps. In one such sketch, her caption tells us that at first, "the women were very self-conscious and timid."[47] Her sketches of the toilets document some of the creative strategies women deployed in partitioning themselves off from one another. In the bathroom, as in the outhouse, there is no room for privacy as the women go about their business.

While Okubo exposes the very personal and intimate day-to-day experiences of life in the camps, she maintains a sense of distance at all times between herself and the other internees as well as between herself and her reader. Okubo is careful to construct herself behind a veil where she remains partially hidden from full view. In one telling sketch of the women's shower stalls, Okubo depicts a long row of undressed women who are busy bathing; yet, the artist draws herself in the far left-hand corner of the frame as a separate, heavily clothed figure whose back is turned away from the scrutinizing gaze of the reader.[48]

Throughout the pages of *Citizen 13660*, we are allowed a glimpse of the personal and the public spaces inside the camp, but we are never allowed any such glimpse into the private space of Okubo's interior self. She may use herself as a reference point from which we may peer voyeuristically into scenes of daily life in the camps, but Okubo does not offer us the same kind of close examination of the intimate details of her own interior life. Whether she is suffering from the death of her mother or the dissolution of her home and nuclear family, Okubo never shows or tells us what she is actually feeling; instead, she gives us a brilliantly detailed—though somewhat detached—record of the internment experience. In her study

The undisclosed self: Okubo records the women in the shower stalls.
(Mine Okubo. Used by permission of Seiko Buckingham.)

of Japanese American women's writing, Traise Yamamoto has said about nisei women's autobiographies that they "are frustratingly unautobiographical, not given to personal disclosure or passages of intimate self-reflection. They are not, to use a pejorative term often applied to those who speak about themselves, self-indulgent."[49]

Throughout the pages of *Citizen 13660*, Okubo gives visual testimony to the outrage over the violation of civil and constitutional rights of American citizens. She documents her disbelief, and that of other nisei, that as American-born citizens they could be subjected to the constitutional violation of rights under Executive Order 9066. (She even notes in one of her sketches the nightly classes in "Americanization" that were offered to issei, who ironically were ineligible by law from ever becoming naturalized American citizens.) In retrospect, Okubo observes: "Time mellows the harsh and the grim. I remember the ridiculous, the insane, and the humorous incidents and aspects of camp life. I was an American citizen, and because of the injustices and contradictions nothing made much sense."[50]

Anthropologist Kamala Visweswaran has discussed the ways in which feminists have been revisioning ethnography at the close of the twentieth century. She states that while "the potential of feminist ethnography . . . has yet to be expressed," she nevertheless envisions that such work might be self-representational and begin by "[locating] the self in the experience of oppression in order to liberate it."[51] If one reads *Citizen 13660* in light of such wishful revisioning, it is possible to see how Okubo's work is clearly ahead of its time as a self-referential, ethnographic wartime record of Japanese American violation and survival. By putting herself literally into the frame of every picture, Okubo not only aligns herself with the collective Japanese American community, but makes herself the subject of her own discourse and, in the process, inserts herself into the text, and into American history. As readers of *Citizen 13660*, Okubo's body becomes a conduit for our own symbolic, virtual journey into the world of the camps. As we reread her account of the Japanese American internment experience, it is now possible over fifty years later to read Okubo's cartoon presence on every page as a kind of magical, historical guide capable of leading us back through time on a virtual, visual tour into the surreal, hellacious, and at times even comical world of wartime relocation and internment.

In one of the final images in *Citizen 13660*, Okubo documents her transformation from interned prisoner to free citizen after she has "[plowed] through red tape" and is approved for release to New York City where a job as an illustrator for *Fortune* magazine and an uncertain future will await her. As an internee on the verge of release, Okubo records the visual process of her assimilation back into mainstream American culture. After attending required classes on "How to Make Friends" and "How to Behave in the Outside World," her body is deemed disciplined and ready for re-entry into the public world. The final pages of *Citizen 13660* document one of the most emotional moments in the book as she undergoes her visual trans-

Disciplined and photographed for release from Topaz War Relocation Camp.
(Mine Okubo. Used by permission of Seiko Buckingham.)

formation from interned prisoner to free citizen and is photographed by the War Relocation Authority and the U.S. Army and released. Traise Yamamoto has observed that "recognition of the manipulation and disciplining of the Japanese American body is nowhere clearer than in internment writing."[52] To this I would add that the visual manipulation and disciplining of the Japanese American body are also central in the visual representations of the internment in art, photography, and film.

Okubo's book continues to stand as a powerful visual representation of the paradoxical relationship of the Japanese American body to citizenship during the racial hysteria of World War II. Like other visual narratives of the internment experience, it captures what Kristine C. Kuramitsu has termed a "confrontation with history."[53] Such visual styles of confrontation have continued to emanate from both within and without the Japanese American community.[54] Chapter 3 will explore the cinematic representation of this episode of history both in independent Asian American film and in Hollywood's big screen imaging of Japanese Americans.

The Gendering of Historical Trauma in Wartime Films and the Disciplining of the Japanese American Body

Anyone studying the filmic representation of the Japanese American internment experience will have to contend with two striking phenomena: the dramatic lack of Hollywood representation of this "central event in Japanese American history" (especially compared to its rich treatment in independent Asian American film) and the semiobsessive depiction of what literary critic Traise Yamamoto has elsewhere termed the "manipulation and disciplining" of the Japanese American body.[1] In order to understand Hollywood's history of relegating this subject to the margins, it is useful to map three distinct waves in the postwar representation of the Japanese American wartime experience in American popular culture and historical consciousness. The first wave begins in 1946, a period immediately after the end of World War II when, as Mine Okubo observed, anything Japanese was still "rat poison."[2] The second wave can be said to span the early 1970s through the late 1980s when, as cultural critic Glen Masato Mimura has argued, "Japanese Americans successfully mobilized as a community to seek redress and reparations for their wrongful internment."[3] The benchmark of this wave is 1981—a year that marked the official "breaking of silence" on the historical trauma of the camps when the U.S. Commission on Wartime Relocation and Internment of Civilians began holding national hearings on the wartime experiences of former internees. These hearings culminated in the passing of the Civil Liberties Act in 1988 which authorized a presidential apology and monetary reparations. And the third and most recent wave of postwar representation can be said to begin in 1992 on the occasion of the fifty-year anniversary of the signing of Executive Order 9066.

In Hollywood's limited imaginary, Japanese American history has certainly been a marginal—if not invisible—subject of representation. In the past fifty years, there have been only five feature films— and one made-for-TV movie—that deal with the experiences of Japanese Americans during World War II. In dramatic contrast, with the prolific production of independent Asian American films and videos since the 1970s, the relocation and internment experience has been one of the most documented and revisited of subjects in what cultural critic Kent A. Ono has elsewhere described as "historical documentaries, fictional dramas, experimental films and videos, and 'found footage' (such as home movies)."[4]

In spite of the tremendous number of films about World War II itself, only three films appeared in the immediate postwar period that represent the plight of Japanese Americans centrally—or even obliquely: *Go for Broke* (1951), *Bad Day at Black Rock* (1954), and *Hell to Eternity* (1960). While these three films are unique for their inclusion of the Japanese American wartime experience, one could argue that all three are centrally structured around the wartime representation of embattled white American masculinity. Indeed, as I will discuss later, white American masculinity has consistently remained the central subject in the only other two feature films to address the Japanese American wartime experience: *Come See the Paradise* (1990) and *Snow Falling on Cedars* (1999).

Since neither *Bad Day at Black Rock* nor *Hell to Eternity* deal centrally with Japanese American characters or history in their storylines, I mention them here only as two unique films that reference the treatment of Japanese Americans during World War II. Directed by John Sturges, *Bad Day at Black Rock* continues to stand as a compelling suspense thriller starring Spencer Tracy as MacReedy, an inquisitive one-armed veteran on a one-man mission to deliver his fallen Japanese American comrade's war medal to his father, Komoko—who we learn has been killed by local vigilantes just after the bombing of Pearl Harbor. While there are no actual Japanese

American actors in the film, there are explicit references throughout to Japanese Americans during World War II. Indeed, *Bad Day at Black Rock* is less about Japanese American history than it is about the violent effects of white racism. In writing about the film, critic Marita Sturken has astutely observed that "the internment camps haunt national memory the way Komoko's death haunts Black Rock, speaking in their absence."[5]

Hell to Eternity (1960) is also worthy of mention as the first Hollywood film to include actual scenes of the Japanese American relocation and internment experience. In spite of its brief depiction of Japanese American history, *Hell to Eternity* is primarily focused on white war hero Guy Gabaldon (played by Jeffrey Hunter). Directed by Phil Karlson, the film chronicles the true story of the homeless, orphaned Gabaldon's adoption into a loving Japanese American family in Los Angeles, where he is raised as one of their own and becomes fluent in Japanese. When Japan bombs Pearl Harbor, Gabaldon's Japanese American family is interned and Guy, as a grown man, rails against the injustice of the U.S. government, joins the Marines, and eventually uses his Japanese-language skills to convince the Japanese civilians and military on Saipan to surrender.[6] Although Guy Gabaldon was a famous World War II Mexican American hero, in *Hell to Eternity* he is racially diluted into a character of mixed-Hispanic origin. The film chronicles the violence of what historian John W. Dower has called the race war in the Pacific, where Gabaldon is dramatically transformed from an honorary Japanese American into a veritable "Jap hating" killing machine and decorated hero.[7]

Of the three earliest Hollywood films to address the Japanese American wartime experience, *Go for Broke* (1951) remains unique as a politically progressive and sympathetic wartime portrayal of the all-nisei 442nd regimental combat team. The film is worthy of mention here for its rare representation of Japanese American masculinity in dramatic juxtaposition to white American masculinity.[8] Furthermore, the film is remarkable for its all-Japanese American casting of the nisei soldiers and for its careful distinction between the Japanese Americans on the mainland ("katonks") and those from

Hawaii ("Buddhaheads"). While the film showcases the heroism of the all-nisei fighting units in World War II, *Go for Broke* actually pivots its main storyline around the racial ambivalence of a physically imposing red-headed redneck from Texas, Lt. Grayson (played by Van Johnson). As a newly commissioned officer, Grayson has just been assigned to lead a platoon of Japanese American soldiers from the 442nd. With a shrewd sense of the irony of his first assignment, he observes, "A guy gets into the war to fight the Japs and ends up fighting with them. It's a hot one, isn't it?"

From the beginning of the film, director Robert Pirosh uses the conventions of physical comedy to pit Grayson's oversized white American masculinity against that of the diminutive, even feminine, Japanese American men. When we first meet Grayson, his extra-tall body is barely contained within the small seat of a U.S. Army jeep driven by a dramatically undersized nisei soldier who escorts him into Camp Shelby. As the jeep drives through the compound, we are visually introduced to the men in the 442nd who, at first glance, appear exotic, comical, and even feminine in their demeanor and size. These Japanese American soldiers not only play the ukulele and gently sway their hips to the hula, but utterly confound Grayson, whose rigid sense of masculinity, American identity, and the Texas color line are immediately threatened by them. The physical comedy that is played out between Grayson and the Japanese American men is nowhere more pronounced than in the scene where Grayson meets Tommy—a nisei orphan from Hawaii whose parents were both killed during the attack at Pearl Harbor. Standing at attention, Tommy is the smallest soldier in the regiment and is literally engulfed like a child in his oversized army uniform. When an angry Grayson asks him why his sleeves are rolled up and his trouser legs are stuffed into inappropriate leggings, Tommy weakly explains, "Sir, that's the smallest size he got, the supply sergeant, sir."

What continues to make the film so compelling to watch is the visual representation of Japanese American masculinity going head to head with white American masculinity and Grayson's determination to transform and discipline the nisei soldiers' bodies into capable men who are ready to go to war. Compared to Grayson's supreme athleticism during the boot camp sequences, the Japanese American men are shown as physically inferior—except when it comes to outsmarting the lieutenant with their clever team effort and a few surprising judo moves. Yet, once the film shifts from basic training at Camp Shelby to the front lines in France and Italy, the men of the 442nd more than rise to the occasion. In a dramatic reversal of masculine power, the 442nd ends up rescuing the helpless Grayson and other white soldiers of the infamous "lost battalion," thereby demonstrating their complete transformation from the physically incompetent, feminized men in combat training to intelligent, dedicated soldiers and war heroes whose battle cry "Go for broke!" has become legendary.

In a concluding series of transformations, Grayson learns to overcome his racist bigotry and comes to respect, even admire, the Japanese American soldiers he has had the privilege of training and working with. Little Tommy also comes full circle: in one of the final shots in the film, a long line of physically imposing but defeated German soldiers march single file under his watchful eye and raised rifle. Tommy may be the smallest soldier in the regiment, but by the film's end, his bravery and heroism are deemed oversized. What's more, he may have been powerless to protect his parents at Pearl Harbor, but he certainly demonstrates his prowess as a defender of the nation in his accomplished role as a loyal citizen soldier.

While *Go for Broke* does not contain any actual scenes of the internment experience, the camps are referred to throughout the film. As one soldier prepares a care package for his family in Poston, Arizona, he dryly refers to their wartime "homestead" as that place of "barracks and barbed-wire." Throughout the film, the nisei characters debate with varying degrees of rage and irony the contradiction of serving a nation that has also unjustly incarcerated their families and communities. Such critical articulations make *Go for Broke* a rare spectacle in the history of early Japanese American representation. Indeed, one must look to the post-redress period for the next Hollywood depiction of Japanese Americans during World War II.

Given such scant cinematic attention to the Japanese American wartime experience during the past fifty years, one is compelled to ask what it is about this chapter in American history that has either been off-limits, or else deemed uninteresting for Hollywood representation. What does it mean that all of the films mentioned above have been crafted by white directors who privilege the representation of white male heroes at the center of their plots? Films like these suggest that Japanese American history has little relevance for white spectators unless the latter can literally see themselves as central players in the script.[9]

In dramatic contrast, if one looks beyond the handful of Hollywood films on the subject, the wartime experiences of Japanese Americans has been one of the most obsessively told stories in contemporary independent Asian American filmmaking since the early 1970s. Some of the most notable independent films that deal with the history of the camps include the early work of Robert Nakamura, such as *Manzanar* (1971), *Wataridori: Birds of Passage* (1976), and *Conversations: Before the War/After the War* (1986), as well as the following flood of films that came out during the peak years of the redress and reparation movement in the 1980s and early 1990s, such as Allie Light and Irving Saraf's *Mitsuye and Nellie: Asian American Poets* (1981), Midi Onodera's *The Displaced View* (1988), Steven Okazaki's *Unfinished Business* (1986) and *Days of Waiting* (1988), Loni Ding's *The Color of Honor* (1988), Lise Yasui's *Family Gathering* (1988), Rea Tajiri's *History and Memory* (1991), and Janice Tanaka's *Memories from the Department of Amnesia* (1991) and *Who's Going to Pay for These Donuts Anyway?* (1992).

The remainder of this chapter will focus on three films from the post-redress and reparation movement period.

The "Breaking of Silence" in the Post-Redress and Reparation Films

One could argue that the silence surrounding the Japanese American internment experience was only officially broken during the powerful public testimonials of internees before the U.S. Commission on Wartime Relocation and Internment of Civilians in 1981–82; yet, in many ways individual as well as collective secrecy surrounding the camps has continued to dominate its filmic representation through the 1990s. Playwright Philip Kan Gotanda speaks to the profound nature of collective internee silence and to its lasting impact on the Japanese American community:

> Even though I wasn't born in Camp and we didn't talk about it much, it's still a very big part of my life. Whether you speak about the Camps or don't speak about them, the experience is passed on generationally . . . it's a psychic scar, almost like an abused-child syndrome.[10]

For many Japanese Americans, the congressional hearings signaled the first occasion where they could finally speak about their experiences. In her poem, "Thirty Years Under," Mitsuye Yamada writes that she was unable to confront her own memories regarding internment until several decades after the fact:

> I had packed up
> my wounds in a cast
> iron box
> sealed it
> labeled it
> do not open . . .
> ever
> and traveled blind
> for thirty years.[11]

Writer Jeanne Wakatsuki Houston echoes a similar observation when asked why she waited some thirty years to break silence in her autobiographical record of the internment, *Farewell to Manzanar* (1973). Before recovering the memories of her family's three and a half years at camp (with the help of her husband and co-author, James Houston), she says she had repressed those years "as if they were a dream."[12] Houston claims that the internment experience operates within internee memory much like posttraumatic shock syndrome does in Vietnam veterans. She recalls that during the public hearings she attended, virtually every man and woman who stood up to give testimony from the war years broke down and cried on the stand.

Houston's autobiography was made into a television movie and first broadcast on March 11, 1976, on NBC. According to film scholar Darrell Y. Hamamoto, it remains a watershed moment in the history of American television not only because it represented the first time ever that a Japanese American family was shown in its full complexity, but also because the internment experience was its central subject of representation.[13] Ironically, Hamamoto observes, this first ever "full-length treatment of an Asian American group" is also "set in a concentration camp rather than in freedom."[14] In spite of the fact that Houston's autobiography has been required reading in public schools since the 1980s, *Farewell to Manzanar* (1976) sadly disappeared from syndicated view for twenty-five years after its initial appearance.[15] It has only recently resurfaced in video form for classroom use.[16]

In Japanese American internment writing and film, the representation of the psychic trauma of camp memory clearly crosses gender lines. Indeed, a worthwhile project, beyond the scope of this chapter, might be to examine the different ways that the stigma of silence and shame has historically shaped representations of male and female experiences in the camps. Glen Masato Mimura has noted that in the privileging of heroic representations of "soldiers, protestors, and No No Boys," the "more commonplace, yet shamefully disavowed, experiences of madness, depression, alcoholism, suicide" and "irrevocable damage" caused by the camps have inadvertently been "displaced and obscured" from storytelling.[17] In the filmic representation of such damage, one can certainly discern a pattern of gendered representation in both contemporary Japanese American literature and independent film where the body signifies the complex process of the dislocation of home, family, and identity. In particular, as I will argue, in post-redress films, the historical trauma of the wartime experience is most powerfully signified through the figure of the Japanese American female body.[18]

Such representations have been central in Japanese American women's writings about the camps. Hisaye Yamamoto's famous short story, "The Legend of Miss Sasagawara," perhaps best encapsulates such an embodied representation of internment trauma through the title character's mental and moral collapse in the camps.[19] Deemed an eccentric artist and dancer, Miss Sasagawara's aberrant behavior crosses the boundary from respectable eccentricity to sexual deviancy during her wartime confinement. Her rage and disgust at confinement give way to a lewd attraction to underage teenage boys, whereupon she is removed from the camps, disciplined, punished, and eventually returned only to descend into madness. Joy Kogawa's masterful novel about Japanese Canadian relocation, *Obasan* (1982), also charts the complex interlocking narratives of the historical trauma of forced removal during the war combined with psychic and sexual abuse that renders two generations of women—both the title character and the novel's primary narrator, Naomi Nakane—numbed into silence and emotional repression. Janice Mirikitani's and Mitsuye Yamada's poetry anthologies, *Shedding Silence* (1987) and *Camp Notes* (1976), also record the traumatic legacy of the internment experience on the female body. Indeed, Mirikitani's poem "Breaking Silence," much of it taken verbatim from her mother's congressional testimonial record, continues to stand as one of the most powerful reclamations of Asian American women's "voice" in contemporary Asian American poetry.

Likewise, many independent Asian American films dealing with the history of the camps also explore the effects of psychic and historical trauma and repressed memory on the bodies of women. Janice Tanaka's experimental *Memories from the Department of Amnesia* (1991) bears closer examination not only for the way the film commemorates the life and death of her mother but reconstructs the latter's life and eventual retreat from family and friends as a series of emotional and physical abuses, abandonments, dislocations, mental breakdown, disease, and disavowals that are acted out upon her body through the official dispossession of her home and property, her internment at Manzanar, her dissolution of a marriage to a spouse officially declared insane, her subsequent passing as "Chinese" as a mode of survival, and finally through a painful rejection by her own mother. While this film is not centrally about the camps but rather about Tanaka's own process of grieving, it is noteworthy for how she stitches together the multiple events from her mother's war years into a broader narrative about what it means to be an alienated Japanese American female subject of history.

The voice-over in *Memories from the Department of Amnesia* consists of shared family memories and storytelling passed down through three generations of women much like the scenes of remembering in Allie Light and Irving Saraf's documentary, *Mitsuye and Nellie: Asian American Poets* (1981), which dramatically stages, among other things, what Gotanda refers to as the intergenerational fallout of Japanese American silence.[20] In one of the most moving moments in the film, poet Mitsuye Yamada's teenage daughter, Hedi, voices how her mother's years of "protective silence" backfired on the children:

> For me, I always felt like I'm so young that nothing like that could ever happen to me. I guess I felt sheltered . . . it was a shock to me when I found out [Mitsuye] was protecting us from something I didn't even know was there. When I was going to school with the other kids—who were all Caucasian—I really had no awareness that I was Japanese. And a little bit later, there was a Korean girl in the class and I felt embarrassed when I saw her and acknowledged that she was different. And then I realized that I was different too. I saw her in a different way than I saw everyone else and now that bothers me.

Cut off from the knowledge of her family's history in the camps, historical erasure and protective silence beget symbolic racial erasure and a sense of shame as Hedi articulates how she had no idea she was not white until the delayed discovery of her own racial difference mirrored uncomfortably back to her in the Asian body of a young Korean classmate.[21]

Rea Tajiri's *History and Memory* (1991) is also situated within a recent wave of independently produced Asian American films that draw upon powerful autobiographical and archival materials in its treatment of the Japanese American internment experience. This film has received perhaps more critical attention than any other contemporary Asian American film for its brilliant examination of what Jun Xing has called its "interweaving multiple voices and texts" and ability to raise "significant questions concerning historical representations, collective memory and the role of an all-encompassing visual media in historical discourse."[22] Indeed, some of the most powerful moments in the film occur as Tajiri screens official wartime footage of the camps for her mother while recording the latter's response on film. In this scene, the jarring disjunctions between an official historical record and fragmented personal recollection are most clearly evident. As the filmmaker screens archival footage from Salinas Assembly Center, her mother responds with incredulity over her own blank memory: "What's this? Canteen? They didn't have a canteen in Salinas Assembly Center. . . . They had one in Poston. I don't remember this. My goodness, I don't remember this." This scene is compelling for how Tajiri records her mother's struggle to recall the lost details from her memory while viewing "official" footage of scenes from her own history. Either her mother has generally forgotten many of the details of camp life, or else the recorded details in the official wartime records do not accurately reflect the truth of individual internee experience.

One of the most frequently cited scenes in *History and Memory* involves Tajiri's mother's narration of a story that embodies the relationship between historical trauma and the female body. She recalls one particular young woman in the camps:

> No, that's the truth I don't remember. . . . When you hear people on television and everything how they felt and everything. I don't remember any of that stuff. All I remember is there was this woman. A beautiful woman. A beautiful young woman who lost her mind . . . and I thought to myself, why did this happen, you know? You can go crazy. You can go out of your mind. So you just put these things out of your mind, you know?

Simultaneous to this story, Tajiri scrolls the following meta-commentary in the margins of the screen: "She tells the story of what she does not remember. But remembers one thing: why she forgot to remember." The logic of her mother's wartime amnesia seems tied to her conscious decision to repress the painful event from her life as a survival tactic. Still, Tajiri suggests, even the post-internment generation of Japanese Americans cannot escape such a fundamental collective trauma. The problem with repressing such traumatic memories is that they resurface intergenerationally:

> I began searching for a history, my own history, because I had known all along that the stories I had heard were not true and parts had been left out. I remember having this feeling growing up that I was haunted by something, that I was living within a family full of ghosts. There was this place that they knew about. I had never been there, yet I had a memory of it. I could remember a time of great sadness before I was born. We had been moved, uprooted. We had lived with a lot of pain. I had no idea where these memories came from, yet I knew the place.

Tajiri suggests that there is a repetition compulsion for Japanese American filmmakers who revisit this chapter in American history that is necessary both in order to exorcise the ghosts in their own family closets and, by extension, our national closet of traumatic wartime memory.

By drawing upon an extensive collection of clips of Hollywood films during World War II, Tajiri weaves together a complex and beautifully multilayered representation of Japanese American wartime experience. What is more, Tajiri also highlights the differential politics of representation between a visual history of internment versus the more photogenic history of the bombing of Pearl Harbor in popular American culture and historical consciousness. The fact that so much original film exists of the attack on Pearl Harbor, and so many more Hollywood films have been devoted to re-creating the events surrounding December 7, 1941, attests to the visual power of remembering its history.[23] Tajiri frames the disparity in the historical representation of these wartime events by foregrounding *History and Memory* in the spectacular power and nature of Hollywood film. Films like *History and Memory* not only define but make clear just who is allowed to be a central subject for Hollywood's selective historical memory and who also traditionally stands outside such a visual economy of representation as both spectator and subject.

One independent Asian American film, however, explores internment camp history from the privileged position of white spectatorship with profound success. In the tradition of Hollywood films about the World War II Japanese American experience, Steven Okazaki's *Days of Waiting* (1988) narrates the history of the relocation and internment through the perspective of a white participant/observer—but with radically different results. Indeed, *Days of Waiting* was rewarded with an Academy Award for best documentary short in 1990 for its depiction of a white woman in the camps who undergoes a profound symbolic metamorphosis that is also bound up in a complex narrative of race, class, and gender subjugation. Films like *Days of Waiting* also grapple, as Kent A. Ono has argued, with the "[profound] question, 'Who is an American?'" and what the "response to this question—caught up with issues of citizenship, loyalty, and betrayal—has meant for Japanese Americans."[24]

"I No Longer Saw Myself as White—as a *Hakujin.* I Was a *Nihonjin*—a Japanese American": The Racial Othering of Estelle Peck Ishigo in Steven Okazaki's *Days of Waiting* (1988)

Film critic Gina Marchetti is right when she observes, "Hollywood favors romances involving white males and Asian females, while Asian men tend to be depicted either as rapists or asexual eunuch figures. By contrast, Asian females are often depicted as sexually available to the white hero."[25] Certainly, postwar, post-redress films like *Come See the Paradise* (1990) and *Snow Falling on Cedars* (1999) clearly follow this formula for big-screen interracial romance and drama. Both films depict Japanese American women as particular objects of desire for white American men. The visual spectacle of white women paired with Asian men is a rarity in both Hollywood and independent film. By choosing to focus on one such relationship, Okazaki breaks new ground and achieves in the process some rather complicated maneuvering involving the representation of racial and gendered difference.

In *Days of Waiting*, the body of Estelle Peck Ishigo comes to signify Japanese American racial difference—an act of symbolic transformation for which she is then subjected to discipline and punishment. Like other interracial spouses unwilling to break up their families, artist Estelle Peck Ishigo voluntarily followed her husband Arthur Shigeharu Ishigo into relocation.[26] While interned at Heart Mountain War Relocation Camp in Wyoming, Ishigo made hundreds of sketches and watercolor paintings and composed the text for her book, *Lone Heart Mountain,* which depicts scenes from the years she and her husband spent in the camps. In contrast to other artistic portrayals of life in the camps, Ishigo's sketches and paintings of extreme weather conditions and ghostly portraitures of what she calls "shabby, shivering people" with patches on their clothes remain among the most haunting images of life behind barbed wire during the war years.[27] Given the initial banning of all cameras and recording devices inside the relocation centers and camps, Ishigo devoted her time, like many other interned artists, to documenting the details of everyday life in order to give testimony through the power of the image.

In the opening pages of *Lone Heart Mountain,* Ishigo identifies herself as a white woman of European ancestry who sought official permission to remain with her Japanese American husband during evacuation and relocation. There are, curiously enough, no sketched self-portraits of her anywhere in *Lone Heart Mountain.*[28] Instead, what begins as an autobiographical account of her life in the camps quickly turns into a meticulous visual record of the physical and spiritual processes of uprooting, relocation, exile, and degeneration of an entire ethnic community within which she quietly aligns herself and then practically disappears from view.[29]

In contrast to Ishigo's visual autobiographical record of her life in the camps, Steven Okazaki not only visually inserts Ishigo back into the historic picture in his film, but is even more explicit about the process of her own symbolic self-erasure as a white woman and her subsequent racial transformation within this exiled community of color. His film is narrated entirely from Ishigo's perspective and testimonial voice in epistolary form while bearing witness to the personal and collective effects of relocation and the postwar diaspora experienced by the Japanese American community.

Like other camp documentaries, the film both begins and ends with a series of shots that focus on derelict, abandoned camp buildings, toppled guard towers, desert landscapes, and the ever present tumbled lines of barbed wire.[30] Such a visual gesture of return to the culture of ruins operates as a metaphor for buried Japanese American history and suggests a kind of archaeology of memory where the filmmaker literally digs up remnants of the past in order to render visible and give voice to histories that have otherwise been erased or silenced in the collective American consciousness. I will discuss how the culture of camp ruins functions in the visual narrative of Japanese American history more fully in chapter 4.[31]

In *Days of Waiting,* Ishigo's stark narrative—much of it gleaned directly from the pages of *Lone Heart Mountain*—is told against sepia-toned archival footage of evacuation and relocation and her own family photographs, sketches, and paintings. Compared to the visual record of internee productivity and adaptability in Ansel Adams's and Toyo Miyatake's famous camp photographs, *Days of Waiting* documents the darker sides of daily life in the camps:

> We lived less than 25 miles from home but it felt like we were in a foreign land. We lived in horse stalls, and cheap shacks, surrounded by barbed wire and machine gun towers. Each day we stood in great long lines to get food. Once inside we ate hastily to make way for the others hungrily peering in. There was rarely enough to eat. Later, we found out that our meat supplies were being diverted from us and sold outside of camp.

Both Ishigo and Okazaki include scenes that touch upon the political and social problems that occurred within the assembly centers and camps such as job blacklisting, news censorship, the corruption within the War Relocation Authority itself (in the wartime black market sales of camp supplies), the breakup of the traditional Japanese structures of family and home life, the problems with youth gangs and unwanted pregnancies, depression, suicide, and even the harsh descent into poverty and homelessness that many of the internees faced in their postwar dispersal.

Yet, what is perhaps most compelling in *Days of Waiting* is Okazaki's deft handling of the gradual process of Estelle Ishigo's symbolic transformation into an honorary Japanese American. From the beginning of the film, Okazaki is careful to mark Ishigo as a white female who is unwanted, outcast, abused, and silenced and who eventually learns to take refuge in a socially transgressive "outsider" identity within a community of color outside of her own. The film documents her movement from runaway, to street adventurer, and ultimately to disowned daughter who falls in love and intermarries during a time when "it was against the law for a Caucasian woman to marry a non-Caucasian man in California." Furthermore, in this film, the process of Othering is specific to gender where Ishigo's female body is repeatedly marked as a site of marginalization, abuse, and exile:

> My parents had not wanted children. They were too old and too busy to take care of a child. I guess I was a mistake. When I was 12, we moved to L.A., and my parents sent me to live with a procession of relatives and strangers. It was an unhappy time. I was raped by one of my guardians who threatened to put me into an institution if I told. Back then, people who caused trouble were put away. After high school I ran away from home. I roamed the streets alone looking for adventure.

Through the process of Othering this white woman in the camps, Okazaki avoids Othering Japanese American camp history and experience for a white American audience. The process is gradual, beginning with her marginalization from her family and white community followed by her first experience of racist discrimination when she loses her job at the Hollywood Art Center after the bombing of Pearl Harbor because of her Japanese name. In her choice to align herself with her Japanese American husband, Ishigo undergoes a psychological and linguistic transformation of consciousness as she moves from an individual to a collective subject position:

> Arthur and I were faced with the choice of separating or going into camps together. I could not desert him. I wanted to stay with him. No matter what happened, no matter where we were sent. We'd been married for thirteen years. Neither of us had ever felt a racial barrier and now society was trying to create one. It seemed like a foul musty thing dug up from the dark ages. . . . We were American citizens, but we were treated as though we were the enemy.

Two-thirds into Okazaki's film, the process of Ishigo's symbolic racial transformation within the margins of her adopted community is complete as she crosses the color line and renounces "whiteness" as a constructed category for race hatred, domination, and power and steps symbolically into a "Japanese American" subject position:

> Strange as it may sound, in this lonely, desolate place, I felt accepted for the first time in my life. The government had declared me a Japanese. And now I no longer saw myself as white—as a *hakujin*. I was a *nihonjin*—a Japanese American. My fellow Heart Mountain residents took me in as one of their own. We all shared the same pain, the same joys, the same hopes, and desires, and I never encountered a single act of prejudice or discrimination.

While Ishigo articulates her symbolic transformation from *hakujin* to *nihonjin*, Okazaki makes clear that this is a political rather than a literal shift in consciousness. His choice of photographs and paintings clearly mark Ishigo as the conspicuous "hakujin with white hair" standing or seated in the company and community of her fellow internees. Yet the trauma of relocation and internment does not end when Ishigo and her husband are released from the camps. The film implies that the couple's descent into poverty and Arthur Ishigo's premature death by cancer are the logical trajectories of the world war and postwar damage that they, like so many others, have been subjected to.

One could argue that *Days of Waiting* ends with at least two dramatic gestures of discovery and recuperation where the white female body stands as a sign of the historically damaged and repressed. We learn that in 1972, fifteen years after the death of her husband, and twenty-seven years after she "had long ago given up hope that [their] story would every be told," Ishigo's art work and manuscript were discovered by the California Historical Society and included in the first show devoted entirely to remembering the internment through the eyes of camp artists. Although Ishigo's body of work was discovered in 1972, Okazaki makes clear that Ishigo's actual body was not discovered and honored until some ten years later. We are told that in 1983 a group of former Heart Mountain internees tracked her down "in a run down basement apartment in Los Angeles where she was living on $5 a week for food and had lost both her legs from gangrene." In the visual rhetoric of the film's final scenes, Ishigo's body, like that of camp ruins, is marked by the passage of time, abandonment, and neglect.[32] By closing the film with footage of the "real" Estelle—elderly, disabled and wheelchair-bound in a convalescent home, her gaze directed off-camera—we can argue that the story of this particular white woman is both rescued and recuperated from history's margins to its center and given "voice" by Okazaki's crew of Asian American filmmakers who forcefully remind us that Japanese American internment history is also a crucial chapter in white American history.[33]

Japanese Americans in the Post-Redress Hollywood Imaginary

> It's not my problem . . . that no American filmmaker has tackled the subject. . . . So I'm suddenly responsible for telling the entire story of the internment of Japanese Americans—as if it's my fault that no one ever touched it before or had the guts to do it. —Alan Parker, director of
> *Come See the Paradise* (1990)

Alan Parker's defensive commentary, quoted above, on the "problem" of making a film on the subject of Japanese American internment is not entirely off the mark.[34] While he may be partially correct that Japanese American wartime history is a subject that most Hollywood directors have avoided, his comment eclipses the substantial body of work on this subject by independent Asian American filmmakers and even John Korty's *Farewell to Manzanar* (1976). *Come See the Paradise* (1990) and *Snow Falling on Cedars* (1999) are unique as the only two Hollywood feature films since World War II that deal explicitly with the Japanese American relocation and internment experience. Both are visually impressive late twentieth century works that belong to the post-redress and reparations period. Both films cast internment as a tragic chapter in American history. And both use this history as a photogenic backdrop for interracial romances between Japanese American women and white American men, who are ultimately impotent in their ability to intervene and rescue their Japanese American women from the effects of Executive Order 9066.[35]

This chapter closes with a brief look at both films for what they might tell us about Hollywood representation of wartime Japanese American history at the close of the twentieth century. What distinguishes these two films from their older postwar counterparts, *Go for Broke* (1951), *Bad Day at Black Rock* (1954), and *Hell to Eternity* (1960) is their visual reliance on the bodies of Japanese American women as sites of desire and difference in narrating the relocation and internment experience. Both *Come See the Paradise* and *Snow Falling on Cedars* present us with what cultural critic Laura Hyun-Yi Kang has identified as stories about racial and gendered difference that are "inscribed on an Asian female body" and "ultimately apprehended by white masculinity."[36] If Kang's thesis is true, then how do Japanese American female bodies not only shore up white American masculinity in these films, but also work to ease guilty historical memory of the camps some fifty years later? If Ansel Adams's wartime photographs at Manzanar once positioned innocent Japanese American schoolgirls into a visual framework of patriotism and citizenship, then are the grown Japanese American women in *Come*

See the Paradise and *Snow Falling on Cedars* the logical end result of that trajectory?

Both films center on heroic white liberal men who each fall in love with a Japanese American woman on the eve of World War II. In *Come See the Paradise,* Irish American labor union activist Jack McGurn (Dennis Quaid) runs away from trouble with the law in New York City and ends up in Los Angeles circa 1937, where he takes a job as a film projectionist at a Japanese movie house in downtown Little Tokyo.[37] There, he quickly meets, falls in love with, and marries his boss's daughter, Lily Kawamura (Tamyln Tomita). The newly-weds settle down in what appears to be domestic bliss in Seattle until the hot-headed Irishman becomes involved again in dangerous union activist work, whereupon Lily takes their small child and goes home to her family in southern California, where their lives are immediately turned upside-down by the events of December 7, 1941. The film is told in flashback form as Lily and her daughter wait at a train station to be reunited with Jack (who is about to be released from wartime imprisonment as an AWOL soldier). Lily proceeds to tell her daughter the story of how she met and married Jack and what they all did during the war years.

In one of the most articulate moments in the film, Lily explains the following to her daughter: "We were in Los Angeles and we were Americans. Or we thought we were Americans. People looked at our faces and we weren't American anymore. We were the enemy." As if to underscore the essential Americanness of Lily and the other nisei in the film, Alan Parker visually renders all of the second-generation Japanese American characters in the film as thoroughly assimilated. Indeed, racial difference is downplayed as we are introduced to a generation of crooning, bobby-soxed, and jitterbugging young men and women whose visual assimilation renders them nonthreatening and familiar—especially compared to their inscrutably old-world Japanese issei parents—where mothers are passive picture-brides and fathers are tyrannical patriarchs.

Literary critic Traise Yamamoto argues that the problem with *Come See the Paradise* is that it "[parades beneath] a present-day ethos of liberal multiculturalism that flouts the reality of 1940s antimiscegenist sentiment and the rarity of Asian-Caucasian marriages" while capitalizing on the "spectacle of interracial sex and a lingering sense of its illicit allure."[38] Considering that this film appeared in 1990, the year before the first reparation checks were sent to the oldest surviving internees, I would like to argue that one might read *Come See the Paradise* as a timely liberal, multicultural spectacle that makes visual reparations for this sad chapter in American wartime history.

In a film laden with strange dialogue, Jack McGurn confesses the following to his Japanese father-in-law as the latter lies helpless in a hospital bed at Manzanar War Relocation Center:

> I feel responsible. I realize I can't help, not one little bit. And I knew this whole terrible thing is my fault. A big part. A little part . . . I just wanted to say, I love you all so much.

Mr. Kawamura's responds to Jack's articulation of white guilt not with a pardon, but with the following directive: "Love Lily. Just love Lily." By the end of the film, the patriarchal center has fallen right out from under the Kawamura nuclear family. Lily's father becomes physically and psychically emasculated and dies in the camp, and her two older brothers disappear from view: one becomes a No No boy and is deported to Japan, and the other joins the 442nd and is killed in action. With the Kawamura men gone, one presumes that Jack will take over as head of the family. In the logic of this reordering, white masculinity replaces the authority of Japanese American masculinity, and love replaces guilt in the new multicultural postwar reconfiguration of the Kawamura-McGurn family.

Both *Come See the Paradise* and *Snow Falling on Cedars* are ultimately about the renewal and redemption of historical consciousness in the post-redress period of the injustices committed against Japanese Americans in the name of Executive Order 9066. In both films, such redemption is made possible through the transcendent love of white American men for Japanese American women. Unlike its immediate predecessor, in *Snow Falling on Cedars* white American masculinity does not usurp or displace Japanese American masculinity. Instead, it is through the benevolent intervention and sacrifice of Ishmael Chambers (Ethan Hawke), the film's white liberal hero, that justice for the Japanese American community is finally served.

Snow Falling on Cedars is essentially a courtroom murder mystery set on fictional San Piedro Island, Washington, in the immediate postwar period. Told in what film critic Kimberly Chun has called an "avalanche of flashbacks and spastic edits," the film reconstructs the anti-Japanese wartime sentiment on the island that continues to impact the 1949 postwar trial of Kazuo Miyamoto (Ruck Yune) for the murder of a white fisherman.[39] At the center of the courtroom intrigue is Ishmael's broken heart and continued desire for Miyamoto's wife, Hatsue (Youki Kudoh), who also happens to be his childhood best friend and first love.[40] As a sleuthing journalist, Ishmael is the one who cracks the case in the murder mystery, and in spite of his jealousy, does the right thing and divulges key information, thereby ensuring justice both for the wronged Kazuo and, by extension, the Japanese American community.

Described by critics as "visually gorgeous" and "somber, velvety," and "haunting," *Snow Falling on Cedars* is a stunning cinematic work, even if it fails in its translation from novel to film.[41] Sadly, the film fails to capture the complexity and interior conflict that Hatsue undergoes in the novel; under Hicks's direction, she is reduced to a one-dimensional character of surface beauty and inscrutable depth. In Guterson's novel, we are given a powerful glimpse below the surface of the same conundrum articulated by Lily Kawamura as Hatsue struggles to position herself between an American and a Japanese identity:

> And what was she anyway? She was of this place and she was not of this place, and though she might desire to be an American it was clear, as her mother said, that she had the face of America's enemy and would always have such a face. She would never feel at home here among the *hakujin*. . . . And then there was Ishmael. He was as much a part of her life as the trees, and he smelled of them and of the clam beaches. And yet he left this hole inside of her. He was not Japanese.[42]

The most lyrical segments of the film are those which show young Ishmael and Hatsue romping on the island's foggy beaches and later experimenting with forbidden love and sexuality in the privacy of their mysterious and secluded cedar grove.

In *Snow Falling on Cedars,* interracial love may be transcendent, but ultimately it also remains taboo and unfulfilled as white masculine desire for Japanese American women is contained and repressed in favor of a higher sacrifice. Ishmael is visually punished for his transgression. During the war, not only does he lose Hatsue (who sends him a "dear John" letter from the camps), but he must also endure the loss of his arm. To make the connection between the violence of his double loss clear, the doubly wounded Ishmael shouts into the camera while undergoing surgery, "Fucking Japanese bitch!" Like Jack McGurn's wartime incarceration as an AWOL soldier, Ishmael Chambers's wartime punishment and loss is rendered more pitiable and tragic than anything the Japanese American families must endure as a result of wartime dispossession, relocation, and internment. While there is no doubt that both films remain highly critical of the injustices perpetrated on Japanese American citizens during World War II, both render white liberal American heroes the true subject of wartime oppression and suffering. Indeed, these post-redress films literally end with an embrace between the Japanese American women and their suffering white lovers—a gesture that literally reverses the presidential apology that was part of the 1988 Civil Liberties Act. In an ironic twist, *Come See the Paradise* and *Snow Falling on Cedars* present us with Japanese American characters who instead apologize to us with their message of tolerance, forgiveness, and redemptive love.

In both films, Japanese American internment history seems, at best, incidental to the central stories of interracial love and the self-tortured angst of its main male heroes. Indeed, Laura Hyun-Yi Kang has noted that in interviews directly after the release of *Come See the Paradise,* director Alan Parker "openly admitted that he did not choose the historical setting to educate or inform the audience about the internment of Japanese Americans during World War II."[43] Given this rather casual inclusion of Japanese American history, it is interesting to consider exactly how Parker and Hicks use the historical representation of the internment camps as visual plot devices in their films.

The most compelling scenes in both films are without a doubt those which depict the evacuation, relocation, and internment of Japanese American characters. Shot in faded, muted color tones to re-create the period look of old photographs, both directors compress the internment experience into a series of flashback sequences.[44] Film critic Stephen Holden maintains that the "strongest scenes" in *Snow Falling on Cedars* "look back to World War II when the island's Japanese-Americans were interrogated, rounded up and sent to internment camps for the duration of the war."[45] Critic Bob Thomas agrees that the film's "most tragic sequence comes when the Japanese are sent to the Manzanar internment center in California after the bombing of Pearl Harbor."[46]

Both films are commendable for their painstakingly detailed representations of the camps. The scenes depicting the procession of thousands of Japanese Americans during evacuation look as though they were carefully re-created from War Relocation Authority photographs. The actual evacuation is deemed so somber an event that both Parker and Hicks film them as virtually silent sequences accompanied only by music and dramatic processional drumbeats. In both films, the camera pans the crowd to pick out the vulnerable figures of elderly issei women in their Sunday best hats and coats and small children sitting alone on piles of luggage. In *Snow Falling on Cedars,* the camera even lingers on an elderly actor and several small children who are dressed up in perfect imitation of Dorothea Lange's famous photograph of Sakutaro Aso and his grandsons.

In *Come See the Paradise,* Jack McGurn marches together with his Japanese American wife and family in the procession. In *Snow Falling on Cedars,* Ishmael Chambers looks on, paralyzed in his helplessness to do anything, as his girlfriend and her family are ironically marched through the town, under a gently flapping giant American flag, and onto a ferry where they begin the arduous physical process of relocation. Film critic Kimberly Chun agrees that the "scenes of the Japanese Americans walking down a dock gangplank to be barged to Manzanar, with tags pinned to their chests and surrounded by luggage, tug at the heart and ironically tap into the same power of images of immigrants arriving at Ellis Island."[47]

Yet in a jarring montage sequence, Scott Hicks turns to archival footage of relocation and internment film and photographs as a narrative device that allows him to compress Japanese American wartime history almost as a visual aside in order to keep the momentum going with the film's central storyline about a murder trial. Alan Parker also attempts a ludicrously compressed representation of the camps in one brief shot where internees arriving at the assembly center at Santa Anita racetrack are literally trotted into their unmucked horse stalls even as giant thoroughbreds are trotted out in the opposite direction. To his credit, however, Parker also manages to slow down and re-create, in a series of beautifully detailed scenes, the look and feel of daily life in the camps once his characters have arrived at Manzanar. There, we are treated to a realistic view of the dust in the barracks, the long lines of people, the morale-building baseball games where even the armed guards in the towers looked on and cheered, the indignity of open rows of toilets and showers, and even a fleeting glimpse of the infamous Manzanar uprising.

It is not surprising that both *Come See the Paradise* and *Snow Falling on Cedars* should choose Manzanar War Relocation Center in Owens Valley, California, as a destination for their Japanese American characters. After all, thanks to the well-circulated photographs of Ansel Adams, Dorothea Lange, and Toyo Miyatake, Manzanar remains the most photogenic and visible of the ten internment camps. In *Come See the Paradise*, Manzanar is described as that place of "the mountains, the cold, and the desert." In *Snow Falling on Cedars*, the bus bearing Hatsue and her family literally drives through a life-size re-creation of Ansel Adams's famous photograph of the camp's front gates. Even though Manzanar was only one of the ten official "war relocation centers," it has been thoroughly iconized through photographs, film, and autobiographical accounts (like *Farewell to Manzanar*). Indeed, in 1992, Congress not only declared it a national historic site, but chose it for restoration as an internment camp education center. What most people don't know is that in the process

Manzanar has become a veritable visual battleground for wartime history and memory. Chapter 4 will examine the contemporary politics of representation at Manzanar National Historic Site as a visually loaded and controversial site/sight for wartime history and deeply contested memories.

Museums, Memory, and Manzanar
Contesting Our National Japanese American Past
through a Politics of Visibility

At the end of the twentieth century, Japanese American internment camp history refuses invisibility. From the desert ruins of the former camps, to the downtown streets of Los Angeles, and through the halls of the Smithsonian Institution's National Museum of American History, the internment experience continues to stake out a visible place in the collective American consciousness that will define how its history will be remembered in the twenty-first century. Currently, its postwar history is not only mapped in multiple mainstream and off-road sights/sites, but also reterritorializes what critics like Lisa Yoneyama have elsewhere called the "cartography of memory" as distinct modes of Japanese American camp history have been and continue to be staged, commemorated, and exhibited in static and moving representations around the country.[1]

This chapter identifies three key sights/sites where the visual politics of internment camp representation reveal much about the contested nature of its national postwar memory and memorialization beginning with the breakthrough 1987 Smithsonian Institution exhibition, "A More Perfect Union: Japanese Americans and the U.S. Constitution," the 1994 Japanese American National Museum exhibition, "America's Concentration Camps: Remembering the Japanese American Experience," and, finally, the unfolding politics of representation now taking place among the desert ruins of Manzanar National Historic Site in Inyo County, California.

Before looking at these sites, let me begin with an important and recent collaboration that engages in serious visual work juxtaposing camp memories together with photographs of camp ruins. Photographer Joan Myers and historian Gary Y. Okihiro's collaborative *Whispered Silences* is perhaps the first work of its kind to suggest an archaeology of memory in its method of literary and visual excavation of internment camp history. Myers's photographs offer mute testament in the form of bold black and white images documenting what might be called the culture of ruins at the ten former internment camp sites. Her images are juxtaposed with Okihiro's personal essay which weaves together his own and other internee voices in a moving polyphonic testimony. In his introduction, Okihiro admits that this visual and literary exercise in internment camp history and self-excavation makes him uneasy, particularly as a traditional historian who is wary of the fine line between "self-inscription and narcissism."[2] Nevertheless, he correctly concedes that their "layered text attempts to make that link between past and present, social relations and individual agency, others and self."[3] Indeed, the book remains one of the most arresting examples of the visual and textual excavation of what Okihiro refers to as "self and history."

Myers is equally articulate in her introductory notes as she narrates her own personal relationship to this project. She discloses how her work began with an inadvertent discovery of the ruins of Manzanar during a 1981 road trip with her family. Educating herself in the history of the camps, Myers spent the next four years methodically traveling to each of the ten former camps in order to photograph the traces of each site's wartime history. In her closing remarks, she writes that it is important to her that this visual work becomes publicly available. She adds that her grandfather happened to be vice-president in the second Roosevelt administration in the early 1940s, and while "he had no direct responsibility for the decision to deprive Japanese Americans of their civil rights," she admits that in some small way she feels "personally accountable" for what happened to the Japanese American community.[4] Rather than paralyzing herself with the burden of white guilt, two generations removed, Myers brings the same aesthetic passion to her photographs of camp ruins that outside photographers like Ansel Adams brought to his liberal documentary study of Manzanar camp life over fifty years ago.

Myers offers a startling and at times microscopic visual tour of the desert wastelands of the camps—those "sacred places" as Okihiro reminds us, that are "littered with remains of ancestors." Her 4 x 5 camera's eye hunts for and turns up the most minute traces of this buried Asian American past, whether in the form of a child's marble or rubber truck literally unearthed from the sun-cracked dirt beneath her tripod's legs, to artifactual remains of medicine bottles, rolls of rusted tin, toppled potato cellar vents, crude home-made signs, pet gravestones, concrete building foundations, and heaps of china shards from the Manzanar camp dump that now stand in ironic juxtaposition to the majestic backdrop of the Sierra Nevada mountain range.

Like so many of the famous photographs by Adams which explored the relationship between the internees and the land, Myers's images excavate the traces of human life and activity that have literally left behind their fingerprints now etched and embedded in these nearly forgotten desert sites. Just as Okihiro's essay testifies to the numerous ways Japanese American lives were uprooted and turned upside-down during the war years, Myers's formal photographic compositions give visual and metaphorical evidence of the debris left behind by so many thousands who were once forced to make these distant desert places their home. Ultimately, Myers's and Okihiro's work reminds us that the ruins of the former camps remain marginalized not only in desolate American landscapes but in our own national memory as well. To revisit this wartime history and these ruins, one must become a kind of determined off-road pilgrim—or tourist.

In her brilliant and probing examination of the embroiled politics of memory surrounding the nuclear devastation of Hiroshima, cultural critic Lisa Yoneyama offers a suggestive approach for how one might rethink the contested nature of remembering other wartime experiences embedded in the visual culture of ruins. She poses these deceptively simple questions at the outset of her study which prove invaluable for revisiting other controversial historical wartime representations: "We must question why and how we remember—for what purpose, for whom, and from which position."[5] My discussion of how we remember the Japanese American internment experience at key museum and memorial sites will be shaped by Yoneyama's cautionary reminder about the politics of positionality and its relation to wartime memory.

For those who remain doubtful of the controversial nature of wartime memory and the camps, I pose the following questions: Over fifty years later, why does the term "concentration camp" continue to disturb when it is used to reference internment camp history?[6] In spite of the evidence left behind by old concrete posts that once anchored armed guard towers, why do some critics still insist that such watchtowers never existed? Why has almost every internment memorial plaque commemorating the history of the camps generated controversy—even defilement? And finally, when the Smithsonian Institution opened its 1987 exhibit on the camps, why were the show's curators accompanied by armed guards?

What remains fascinating is that even fifty years later, invoking World War II memories continues to stir up old wounds, and wartime discourses of loyalty, patriotism, and the inviolability of the nation-state, mostly from those who are old enough to remember those years. In a lecture on contemporary Japan-bashing and the Smithsonian Institution's controversial 1995 exhibition of the *Enola Gay* at the National Space and Air Museum, historian John Dower speculated that the public battle over museum representations of national historical memory may in fact be traced back to the Smithsonian's provocative 1987 exhibit on the camps, curated after all by the same team that would later organize the ill-fated *Enola Gay* exhibit.[7]

With this in mind, let me begin by looking at the first permanent display of internment camp history in that most profoundly symbolic of public storage spaces for national historic memory and identity: the Smithsonian Institution's National Museum of American History.

"A More Perfect Union:
Japanese Americans and the U.S. Constitution"

"A More Perfect Union" was the first large-scale exhibit in the United States to fully explore the Japanese American internment camp experience in all of its complexity. The exhibit first opened in October 1987 and is now permanently installed on the third floor of the National Museum of American History in the east wing between the Armed Forces collection and the display of artifacts from the Vietnam Memorial Wall. Several years in the planning, "A More Perfect Union" was scheduled to mark the museum's two-hundred-year anniversary of the Constitution—a framework that provided the perfect vehicle for "telling the story" of Executive Order 9066.[8] Such a strategic juxtaposition clearly frames the Japanese American internment as one of the most extreme cases of constitutional violation in U.S. history.

The entrance to "A More Perfect Union" is marked by a floor-to-ceiling reproduction of the well-known text from the Constitution superimposed on glass over what I have previously argued is one of the most iconic photographs of the Japanese American internment experience: Dorothea Lange's black and white photograph of two young Japanese American schoolgirls pledging their allegiance to the American flag.[9] Both photograph and text have been blown up and illuminated to fill the entire space of the wall and comprise the first image one sees upon entering the exhibit. The adjacent panel illustrates the ways in which Executive Order 9066 violated the specific amendments, sections, and articles of this national document. Indeed, the recorded voice-over that narrates this portion of the exhibit emphasizes that the American Civil Liberties Union denounced the order as the "single worst violation of civil rights in American history."

One then proceeds through a brief historical display on the pre-war chronology of Japanese immigration (including the issei, picture brides, and plantation life in Hawaii) to some of the earliest anti-Japanese immigration and land-ownership legislation such as the Gentleman's Agreement of 1907 and the California Alien Land Act of

1913 that helps to set the stage for the racist American hysteria that will become unleashed in the aftermath of the Japanese bombing of Pearl Harbor on December 7, 1941.[10] Artifactual paraphernalia remain one of the most intriguing elements of "A More Perfect Union" and are included in each chronological segment of the exhibit. In the section detailing the aftermath of Pearl Harbor, one may see rare wartime posters created and distributed by Douglas Aircraft denouncing "Jap Treachery" with its depiction of ratlike Japanese in mousetraps, as well as badges and ribbons that were proudly worn on the West Coast declaring, "California Jap Hunting License Open Season—no limits."

The core of "A More Perfect Union" centers on the experience of Japanese American dislocation and relocation mandated by Executive Order 9066. Dramatizing the transition into the camp history portion of the exhibit is a life-size Hollywood-style set reconstructed from one of Dorothea Lange's best-known images from the evacuation of Japanese Americans: her photograph of the Wanto grocery store in Oakland, California, with its infamous "I am an American" window sign posted the day after the bombing of Pearl Harbor. Exhibition designer Drew Culbert seized Lange's iconic photograph for its visual power and was the creative force behind transforming the image into a three-dimensional set, where the museum visitor is forced to enter the camp portion of the exhibit by first walking through the photograph as if it were a historical time portal where the present is collapsed into the past.[11]

The Wanto grocery store set literally functions as a gathering and departure point for museum visitors as they enter still deeper into the heart of the exhibit. Beyond the store front, one must walk past a life-size cutout of an armed sentry standing next to a small-scale reproduction of an armed guard tower—like the ones that would have surrounded each of the War Relocation Centers—and under an adobe tile arch that is marked "W.C.C.A Control Station," the historic gathering and departure points for internees outbound for relocation. In the context of the exhibit, the arch becomes a kind of pedestrian gateway into the past.

What is striking throughout the exhibit is the extensive use of historic black and white photographs. While small documentary im-

Dorothea Lange's photograph as a tourist attraction at
the Smithsonian Institution's National American
History Museum. *(Skylar W. W. Schmidt. Used by permission.)*

ages of daily life during evacuation and internment are mounted on
the walls, other photographs of internees lined up awaiting relocation are blown up and cut out as life-size figures inviting present-day
visitors to measure him or herself against these historical images
from the past.

Without doubt, the most striking portion of "A More Perfect
Union" is the meticulous reconstruction of the interior scene of an
actual barracks, relocated from Manzanar to the Smithsonian. Still
marked with its original camp address, "2443," the former home of
the Ozamoto family holds center stage as a fascinating artifact that
has time traveled from wartime America into this contemporary

exhibition. In the reproduction of the Ozamotos' domestic space, the Smithsonian curators have gone to great lengths to ensure that all of the furnishings and artifacts are authentic. Indeed, we are told that everything in the room—designed to hold between four to five family members—was either made or used in the camps, including the crude desk, bunk beds, table and chairs, pot-belly stove, home-made curtains, children's decorative art projects, assorted *Life* magazines, radio and record player, and wads of newspaper stuffed into the drafty cracks of the walls and doorway.

What brings the Ozamoto barracks to life is filmmaker Selma Thomas's clever use of two projected liminal figures—an internee father and his daughter—who stand in the doorway like virtual video ghosts engaged in a series of dialogues about what life was like for those who once lived there. Here the doorway acts as both a screen and time portal for the life-size projection of the father, who recalls that he was eight years old—roughly the same age as his present-day daughter—when he lived in these barracks. Prompted by the endless questions of his young, inquisitive daughter, the father confesses he "forgot how bad it was" as sad memories of camp have given way to pleasant childhood memories of what it was like to make a "decent home in the middle of nowhere."[12]

Indeed, the resilience of internees becomes a recurrent theme in the remainder of the exhibit—both in terms of the video interviews of internee activists and educators like Gordon Hirabayashi, Morgan Yamanaka, Sue Embrey, Mary Tsukamoto, and Nancy K. Araki, as well as in the display of artifacts—such as walking sticks, dressers, bird carvings, furniture, and figurines that attest to the creative talents of those behind barbed wire.[13] One of the final sections of the exhibit focuses on the history and military accomplishments of the 442nd Regimental Combat Team and 100th Infantry Division units of all-nisei Japanese American soldiers as a final statement about nationalism, patriotism, and active duty to uphold the Constitution and democracy.

While "A More Perfect Union" opened in 1987, a formal conclusion to the exhibition was added in 1988 with the passage of the Civil Liberties Act, bringing a kind of narrative closure to the Smithsonian's retelling of the story of the constitutional violation of the rights of Japanese American citizens during the war. Before "A More Perfect Union" officially opened, the museum had received numerous complaints about the proposed exhibit. Predictably, some of the exhibit's harshest critics were World War II veterans for whom any postwar critique of the internment camps has become tied to a critique of the discourse of military necessity—and by extension to their own role as citizen soldiers. The intensity of the criticisms prompted the museum to provide armed guards on the opening day of the exhibit to ensure the personal safety of the show's curators who had received threats. Ironically, once "A More Perfect Union" officially opened, such public criticism ceased. Indeed, the harshest response to the exhibit would come from former internees who complained that, if anything, the representation of camp life appeared too sanitized. Specifically, they complained about the presence of the phonograph player in the barracks and the general coziness of the living quarters. The show's curators countered that the barracks were reconstructed to simulate 1945, and not the earlier period of internment when more restrictions were enforced on the internees. However, embedded in the criticism of former internees are unanswered questions about the limits of using museum representations to re-create the experience of historical trauma. Indeed, most tourists who find their way to the National Museum of American History would rather hunt for Dorothy's red slippers or gaze at the inaugural ball gowns of the nation's First Ladies than study the museum's detailed representation of internment camp history which ultimately asks them to engage in their own self-scrutiny.

There is no question that the years of activist work by Japanese Americans and allies throughout the 1970s and 1980s prepared the way for the Smithsonian's visual revisiting of this chapter in national American history. According to the exhibit's senior curator, Thomas Crouch, "the time was ripe" for the representation of this history; indeed, Roger Kennedy, the Smithsonian Institution museum director at the time, had carefully laid all the necessary political groundwork for this historic exhibit.[14] Considering that the exhibit opened in 1987, and that Congress passed the landmark Civil Liberties Act in 1988, the timing was indeed perfect.

Even though the Japanese American internment experience now holds a permanent place of visibility in one of our national repositories of American history, it is ironic that the camps continue to remain marginalized from mainstream American consciousness. (Indeed, to combat its marginalization, the Smithsonian now sponsors a small-scale exhibit on the camps that travels around the nation on permanent tour.) One of the final questions that the Smithsonian exhibit raises is whether or not a national museum can shape national consciousness of a historical event. Or conversely, does national consciousness determine what can be shown in a national museum? It is with these questions in mind that I turn to another national museum that opened its first internment camp exhibit with an unusual public representation.

The Barracks at the Japanese American National Museum— Another Spectacle on the "Street of Memory"

> This is my boyhood home. . . . Taking back this barracks is taking our whole experience back to California for our children to see.[15] —Tomo Mukai, Citizen #22799 (whose barracks remain on display at the Japanese American National Museum)

Anyone strolling or driving past the northwest corner of 1st Street and Central Avenue in the downtown section of Los Angeles known as Little Tokyo between November 1994 and October 1995 was treated to an unusual spectacle: a sixty-foot stretch of weather-beaten, tar-papered barracks from a World War II internment camp was reconstructed in the empty lot across from the Japanese American National Museum. Given the relative historic invisibility of the internment camps in mainstream American consciousness, these shabby barracks—transported all the way from Heart Mountain, Wyoming—seemed to insist on some acknowledgment from pedestrians and passing drivers who might otherwise be indifferent, or oblivious, to their presence as a ghostly relic from American wartime history.

Heart Mountain barracks on the downtown streets of Los Angeles at the Japanese American National Museum. *(Stan Honda. Used by permission.)*

The Heart Mountain barracks project was conceived as early as 1982 when some of the earliest supporters of the Japanese American National Museum grasped the symbolic significance of the barracks even before they had secured funding to build the museum. According to writer Sharon Yamato, during the earliest planning stages Nancy Araki and John Miyauchi both recognized the artifactual and narrative power that an actual barracks in the museum would have in "telling the story" of the Japanese American internment experience. Indeed, Miyauchi, the designer of the museum, had incorporated sketches of a barracks in his original plan for the building. Efforts to locate surviving remnants of camp barracks were hastened when former internee, Bacon Sakatani, offered invaluable information on the current status and whereabouts of such a historical object. Sakatani had already made several personal trips to Wyoming beginning in 1982 where he determined that of the ten former camps, Heart Mountain had the largest number of original buildings remaining near the site.[16] Ten years later, in September 1994, thirty-two volunteers—nineteen of them former internees—traveled to Wyoming to begin the arduous process of tearing down two donated barracks from Heart Mountain and relocating them by flatbed truck over a thousand miles away to Los Angeles.

Sharon Yamato's self-published essay, *Moving Walls: Preserving the Barracks of America's Concentration Camps* (1998), documents the systematic recovering, dismantling, and rebuilding of these barracks for the museum exhibit. It chronicles—with the help of photographer Stan Honda—how they operate as one of the most powerful artifactual signifiers of the trauma of the internment experience. *Moving Walls* is particularly striking for Yamato's understanding that the barracks operate as a metaphor for collective historical memory and the public and private process of tearing down the walls of silence that have impacted the Japanese American community and families for over fifty years.

What is most compelling in *Moving Walls* is Yamato's story of how the volunteers themselves "reclaim their past" by returning to Heart Mountain, where the physical work of tearing down walls literally unleashes years of repressed memory of familial hardship and shame. For many of the volunteers, the barracks project becomes an intensely personal one. Yamato herself was born in the post-internment years, and like many of the other volunteers, she notes that her parents, now gone, never spoke about the camps. In her meticulous record of the barracks removal project she observes that "somehow, the tattered buildings had a mystifying power to arouse feelings that remained unspoken."[17] One visitor to the barracks, she recalls, was overheard to say, "I don't know why I'm crying." The very existence of the barracks, Yamato writes, "breaks the silence, regardless of whether it leads to dialogue or not."

Transported to Los Angeles, the barracks served as the outdoor exhibit for the museum's first full-scale show on the internment: "America's Concentration Camps: Remembering the Japanese American Experience." The outdoor portion of the exhibit featured a 20 x 60-foot section of an original barracks accompanied by a twenty-six-foot small-scale replica of a guard tower and a World War II–era military jeep.

The volunteer tour guide who is on duty the day I visit is Ike Hatchimonji. Mr. Hatchimonji was fourteen years old during his family's internment. On this day, he wears a button that says, "Ask me about America's concentration camps." After all, not only was he interned at Heart Mountain, but he ironically lived next door to these same barracks, still marked with the family number of its wartime occupants: #22799. As a volunteer tour guide and former internee, he clearly connects camp history through his body and childhood memory of these tattered barracks to the captive circle of pedestrian tourists who gather around him on this hot summer day to listen attentively to his story.

As I wander inside the museum to view the rest of "America's Concentration Camps," it is necessary to first walk past a towering mound of old-fashioned suitcases stacked from floor to ceiling, each marked with a Japanese name and address. This surreal mountain of unclaimed luggage, left behind by internees at a Seattle hotel on the eve of evacuation, has been reclaimed by the museum as an installation art piece called "Common Ground: The Heart of Community." It is clear that this exhibit is meant to be a participatory, even communal, event. The exhibit is designed to introduce a general audience to this history as well as "to engage those who lived through the event in the gathering of artifacts, photographs, and stories."[18] Inside, the museum invites its visitors to "join-in in remembering and understanding" camp history. The exhibit is structured around ten different tables, each one representing one of the ten different camps complete with glass-encased memorabilia, artifacts, and personal items donated by internees. There are multiple ways to participate: if you are an internee or a former camp worker, you can push pin the location of your barracks on the appropriate map; or include your Polaroid picture in one of the camp albums; or write down your wartime stories; or release your memories anonymously into one of the ten different locked boxes. If you were separated during the war from friends or neighbors, there is a lost-and-found bulletin board whose sole purpose is to reconnect you with old wartime friends. If you are not an internee or former camp volunteer, you can simply write down your comments before leaving the museum. I watch as several silver-haired visitors pose for Polaroid pictures that will be added to individual camp albums that are already bulging with the photographs and stories of hundreds of former internees. I wonder what stories will be deposited into the safe anonymity of the locked boxes.

As I leave the exhibit, I note that the simple act of relocating the Heart Mountain barracks from Wyoming to downtown Los Angeles is to insist on a politics of visibility for a late twentieth century memorializing of wartime Japanese American history. The passage of the 1988 Civil Liberties Act was a milestone, the work of decades of activism on the part of the Japanese American community and its allies, but hardly the final act in the public narrative of how we are to remember the historical fallout from Executive Order 9066.

I believe that museum exhibits like the ones now permanently installed at the Smithsonian Institution and the Japanese American National Museum are part of a broader movement identified by media critic Darrell Y. Hamamoto in which Asian American visual artists have begun to radically question the production of historical knowledge through their multiperspectival views and vocal interventions.[19] At the end of the twentieth century, the post-redress Japanese American community continues to make visual reparations even as it grapples with the uncomfortable legacy of intergenerational silence. The public display of barracks at the Japanese American National Museum tells us much about the power of artifactual history removed from its original location and transported to a public site.

The staff at the Japanese American National Museum have reported that ever since they opened their doors in 1992, artifactual objects have continued to pour in. Most are carefully packed and labeled by their donors, while others are left anonymously on the museum's doorstep. One of the greatest artifactual mysteries of the internment experience involves an oil drum filled with stones. At Heart Mountain, a farmer drove his tractor over something hard, buried in the ground. He uncovered an oil drum that was filled with hundreds of smooth stones, each one with a single kanji letter hand-painted onto its flat surface. The Heart Mountain "mystery stones" are now held in the Japanese American National Museum where they are displayed. To date, no one has come forward to claim them, and no one can tell us what they mean and why they were buried there.

If historical memory of the camps is partially embedded in artifactual objects, then what happens when these objects disappear from view? Or when the generation which remembers them has passed on? As historical sites are reclaimed by the desert winds and natural elements, do they also disappear from national historic memory? It is with this final question in mind that I close this chapter with a look at that most visible and controversial culture of camp ruins, Manzanar National Historic Site.

The Controversy Surrounding Manzanar National Historic Site

> Manzanar is a place with layers of pain, a piece of the dark side of American history, not just for its role as a World War II internment camp, but for other sorrows. Native Americans white Americans, and Japanese Americans all have lost something there. And the wounds still have not healed.
> —Carl Nolte, reporter for *The San Francisco Chronicle*,
> April 13, 1997

> In performing acts of remembrance—erecting memorials, testifying, holding public commemorations, or writing autobiographical histories . . . one seeks to reterritorialize the existing cartography of memory.
> —Lisa Yoneyama, *Hiroshima Traces*

On Saturday, April 24, 1993, I traveled up highway 395 from Los Angeles to Owens Valley to participate in the twenty-fourth annual pilgrimage to Manzanar. It was my first visit to this national historic site and a long drive—almost five hours—from L.A. Manzanar is located within a relatively isolated spot on the eastern desert side of the Sierra Nevadas between the towns of Independence and Lone Pine. At its height between 1943–44, at full capacity, it was hailed as the largest city between Reno and Los Angeles. In 1946, a *Los Angeles*

Times headline declared it a "war-born Jap town." During this particular time of year, the desert wildflowers are in full bloom and the range of colors across the desert basin is extremely beautiful.[20] To the west, the snow-capped Sierra Nevada mountain range is magnificent and complements the subtle shades of orange and mauve that adorn the lower Inyo Mountains to the east.

What remains of Manzanar War Relocation Center itself is not hard to find, provided that you know what you are looking for—even though writer James Houston once added, "If you didn't know what to look for, you'd never know who had been there."[21] After the war, with lumber at an all-time premium, the buildings were for the most part disassembled plank by plank, and the rest of the camp was bulldozed or removed until the place was, as one newspaper put it, "flatter than Hiroshima."[22]

And yet, a handful of the original camp structures remain. Two small pagodalike stone buildings, formerly used by the camp police as sentry posts, still stand at what was once the official entryway. And nearby, the barnlike camp auditorium now functions as a storage room for the county. If you walk the perimeter of the camp, littered with gnarled barbed wire, you can find what is left of the toppled concrete foundations that once held up the eight guard towers, as well as the stones marking the old camp flagpole, the camp dump, and the decorative rock gardens that once adorned the housing area for Caucasian personnel. Both the old apple and pear orchards—planted at the beginning of the century by European farmers—as well as the many trees and shrubs which the internees had so carefully arranged and tended have now grown wild and unshapely from years of neglect. National Park Service archaeologists, who have now spent three seasons surveying the site, have discovered hundreds of names and dates written by internees in the concrete foundations of the camp hospital, laundries, and reservoir.[23]

A map provided by the National Park Service makes it easy to walk about the one square mile of the camp's perimeter and feel the presence of the thousands of Japanese Americans who lived here from 1942 to 1945. It is with the aid of this map that I am able to find my way to what is left of Merritt Park—one of the impressive formal Japanese gardens built by internees and rendered immortal in Ansel

Adams's photographs—and the Children's Village, a happy euphemism for the notorious camp orphanage that housed just over one hundred children, some as young as six months old, some who were a mere one-eighth Japanese.[24]

Even without a map, you can still make your way around the camp, following the contours of the old deeply rutted roads, and pick out the concrete foundations that mark where washrooms and communal toilets once stood on each block, walk up stone steps that led to the camp hospital, and find thousands of small rock gardens and cairns that have been left behind to mark the entryway to someone's home. Abandoned by the War Relocation Authority over fifty years ago and reclaimed by the National Park Service and the sage brush flats of the Owens Valley desert, Manzanar now holds historical fascination as a culture of ruins, as a kind of Japanese American ghost town and archaeological dig. One thing remains certain: even though thousands of visitors trek annually into this desert site, Manzanar continues to be a place on the American map that many would still like to forget.

The Annual Pilgrimage of Memory

> What is this memorial about?
> We recall the painful injustice
> What is the injustice?
> The unconstitutional removal of Japanese Americans and their
> parents into concentration camps by the United States
>   government.
> What do we remember?
> The suffering, the heat, the isolation, the wind, the loss of
>   everything,
> the cold, the deaths.
> Why do we remember?
> Lest we forget, so not to repeat the incarceration.
> Why do we remember?
> So future generations will remember the injustices by the
>   government

and the sufferings by the people.

How do we remember?

By continuing this pilgrimage and other observances.

—From the April 24, 1993, "Day of Remembrance"
interfaith service at Manzanar National Historic Site,
Inyo County, California

If you arrive early at the annual pilgrimage, on the last Saturday of every April, you can join the walking tour led by park rangers and former internees, who fifty years later can still find their way around the unmarked paths, pointing out where their family and friends used to live, while sharing stories about the residents who are now long gone.

Each year, a memorial service and picnic are held in the far northwest corner of the camp in front of the old cemetery that is marked by an eight-foot "Soul Consoling Tower," a white granite obelisk erected by internees in 1943 and now surrounded by half a dozen remaining graves. Only one bears a name on its tombstone: Jerry Ogata, who died in camp when he was just three months old. Of the eighty-six internees who were buried at camp, most were exhumed and reburied after the war. The cemetery is now one of the most visited sites in the camp, and the six remaining graves are covered with coins, flowers, and origami birds left behind by visitors who stop to pay their respects throughout the year.

I am told that in the previous year, over two thousand people turned out for the pilgrimage to commemorate the fifty-year anniversary of the signing of Executive Order 9066. At today's gathering, there are at least five-hundred pilgrims and no less than four generations of Japanese Americans in attendance. The crowd is varied. Most are college-age young men and women, some are former internees. Most of the people here today are Japanese American, the rest are a mix of Anglo, Latino, Jewish, and African American families and friends. There is at least one busload of elders from Little Tokyo in Los Angeles. I am touched by the sight of some who insist on walking or rolling through the desert sand on canes or in wheelchairs.

In the program to today's service, I learn that in the bitter cold month of December 1969, "a group of 150 people, mostly young, mostly Japanese American," drove out to this desert for what they presumed was the first pilgrimage to this site.[25] They were humbled to learn that two issei ministers had already been making their own annual pilgrimage to this place for the previous twenty-five years. The two ministers, Rev. Sentoku Maeda and Rev. Shoichi Wakahiro, had been returning to Manzanar in quiet fashion every year since 1945 to pay their respects to the dead and to remember the camps.

At today's memorial, an interfaith service is led by former internees Art Hiraga, a priest from the Maryknoll Catholic Church, and Paul Nakamura, pastor of the Lutheran Oriental Church and Nikkei Ministerial Association, as well as three Buddhist priests from Japan: Rev. Kuroyanagi, Rev. Okuni, and Rev. Asatani. The crowd is asked to participate in the call and response and to pour cups of water back into the dry desert sand. There is a roll call of all the former camps accompanied by a raising of ten banners, each bearing one of their names: Amache, Gila River, Heart Mountain, Jerome, Manzanar, Minidoka, Poston, Rohwer, Topaz, and Tule Lake. Afterwards, Buddhists in the crowd line up to offer prayer, incense, and flowers at the makeshift shrine on the obelisk, which is covered with signs that record the names of all ten former camps.

I am struck by how the memorial service functions as a kind of collective exercise in bearing witness to history across racial, religious, generational, and cultural lines as we are asked to remember and to forgive. I think to myself that the painful history of silence surrounding the camps is ironically complemented by this collective exercise in remembering. The Manzanar Committee makes sure that the memorial pilgrimage ends each year on a note of hope. Each year the service concludes with a communal potluck, *taiko* drumming, and a joyful *tanko bushi* (coal miner's) dance that everyone is invited to join.

On March 3, 1992, Congress passed a bill establishing Manzanar as a National Historical Site. It is the only one of the former internment camps to receive this designation. The hope today is that the site may someday be fully restored as an educational center and memorial park that will render visible the histories of all ten of the World War II Japanese American internment camps. Today, National Park Service rangers are on hand to pass out sheets to the visitors asking them what they would most like to see at the future site. Some of the responses, especially from former internees, are unanimous in their concern for historical accuracy: "You have to have the barbed wire." Or, "How about showing what the toilets were like? How humiliating they were with no privacy." Others make it clear that they do not want sanitized representations of the past: "Don't flower the site over; do not hide the truth about how Americans were rounded up. . . . [You must] portray the harshness of the site as it really was; show the loss of dignity, lack of privacy, forced separation of families, and loss of property—even pets."[26]

I am reminded of what Robert Kinoshita, the production designer for the television film version of *Farewell to Manzanar* (1976), once said: "It makes no difference which camp former internees spent time in, they all remember the dust, the relentless heat, dry landscapes and sense of exile."[27] Many have been unanimous in their insistence of what constitutes the three most important historical symbols of camp experience: the guard towers, the barbed wire, and the original toilets. The public discussion with internees and others has raised complex questions over the visual politics of historical representation and memory. Many have argued that historical authority belongs only to those who have been there and that "firsthand experiences and on-site memories should be told by the internees on video or tape." Others have insisted that the opportunity to use the camp as a politicized educational space must go still farther beyond Japanese American history and uncover those other narratives of forced removal and relocation that have been buried in Owens Valley history: the dispossession of Native Americans from the area by European farmers, who were themselves dispossessed when their land and water were seized as valuable resources by the city of Los Angeles.

The National Park Service, in cooperation with the Manzanar Advisory Council, is currently working on a long-range plan for protecting and restoring Manzanar as a national historic site representing all ten of the internment camps. The questions on everyone's mind today is whether or not it will become a historically correct national park exhibit, or a kinder, gentler, re-creation of a wartime concentration camp. In short, how will Manzanar be remembered? And according to whose memory? It is clear from the conversations today that exactly how the park will be restored as another kind of bittersweet tourist site is still under debate.

The Continuing Struggle over the Politics of Representation at Manzanar

While Congress granted Manzanar the status of National Historic Site in 1992, it did not allocate any special funds to speed the camp's transformation from desert ruins owned by the Los Angeles Department of Water and Power to a national historic landmark under the jurisdiction of the National Park Service. Although the land was officially turned over to the Park Service on April 24, 1997, plans were stalled to restore and develop the camp into its potential role as one of the most visible educational and recreational sites in Inyo County. But even more significantly, Manzanar has also become a hotly contested national site that has literally "split Owens Valley apart" over the visual politics of representation and the inability of former internees, officials, and local citizens—including those who once worked in the camp—from reaching any type of consensus regarding its restoration.[28] In his former role as National Park Service superintendent, Ross Hopkins has said that "Manzanar has been one of the most controversial places [he has] ever worked."[29]

A forty-year veteran of the National Park Service, Hopkins has been called the "lone guardian of Manzanar" and has worked for many years as the site's only employee. As such, he has taken the brunt of what has been a very heated debate over plans to render the camp's history visible in an area where many would rather forget it ever took place. According to Hopkins, the National Park Service has received threats by people who would like to blow up what remains of the camp auditorium, the proposed site for an interpretive visitor center. He has also reported at least one message on his answering machine "from a veteran who told [him] he had traveled to Manzanar, on a pilgrimage of disgust, to urinate on the small plaque that commemorates the site."[30] Indeed, journalist Paul Rogers has written of the local opposition that "some think it gives the area a black eye" while "a few others contend that the [National Park] service is rewriting history." According to Rogers, these debates have become so emotionally charged that even the local newspaper, the *Inyo Register*, has "stopped printing letters about Manzanar."

One of the most quoted voices of local opposition has been World War II veteran William W. Hastings, who has openly debated the historical accuracy of the National Park Service's rendering of the camp. Hastings, a former Marine who fought the Japanese in World War II, has called plans for the park both "un-American," even "treasonous."[31] He claims to have visited Manzanar in 1943 and argues to this day, along with other opponents of the park, that there were neither eight surrounding guard towers nor a forced imprisonment of internees: "They were never interned . . . A concentration camp? That is the biggest lie that ever was."[32]

In response to such accusations, Superintendent Hopkins has said,

> There is this feeling about this place. It is part anger, with some racism, I guess. But there is this shame, too, this guilt. The Japanese and the locals and the vets. The Japanese, the old-timers who were here, and the people around the valley— they don't want to talk about it.[33]

The local debates surrounding Manzanar's physical restoration to a place on the American map raises larger questions about the difficulties inherent in constructing collective national narratives about disturbing chapters in American history that continue to arouse deep-seated memories of anger, shame, and guilt. That so many who were eyewitnesses to history still do not want to talk about those years complicates our desire to render visible and give voice to wartime narratives that have been buried for over fifty years.

On July 28, 1997, local schoolteacher Richard Stewart made national headlines and history as the first official tour guide at Manzanar.[34] Newspaper accounts were quick to point out that Stewart is also a Paiute Indian who also includes a discussion in his tours of the site's indigenous peoples and their dislocation by white farmers as well as the latter's dislocation by the Los Angeles water wars.[35] Stewart is one of the first public voices to connect the multiple histories of forced removal and dislocation that are layered one upon the other in this part of Owens Valley. Although the Los Angeles Department of Water and Power officially turned over the 800-acre site to the National Park Service, the Manzanar National Historic Site continues to suffer from a shortage of funds. Stewart's tours have been funded with a grant by the nearby Eastern California Museum—a longtime champion of Manzanar National Historic Site as well as the local repository of its camp artifacts, research, and history.

Working under fairly primitive conditions— without electricity, running water, or even a portable restroom—Stewart leads up to five tours a day from his headquarters in one of the small stone sentry posts at the site's entrance. He is articulate about the educational mission behind his interpretive tours, which are tailored to meet the interests and demands of park visitors (some of whom are content with fifteen minutes of basic information, while others participate in two and half hours of site exploration). Stewart is adamant about including what he calls the "three levels of history" in his talk that complicate simple narratives about relocation and internment within a larger—and less known—context of displaced peoples over two centuries on American soil.[36] Indeed, the history of Native American displacement haunts most of the ten internment camp sites yet is rarely acknowledged or written into wartime accounts of uprooting and resettlement.[37]

Without elaborate signposts to mark the terrain, most visitors to Manzanar complain that there is nothing there to see. Stewart's role as a local historian and visual tour guide is to teach visitors a different way of looking, where one must literally "examine the site at the level of vegetation in order to read the signs of past life there."[38] Federal law also dictates what national park tour guides like Stewart can show to the public. Barred by the Protective Act of 1979, he is allowed to discuss the indigenous sites at Manzanar, but he cannot include them on any of his tours.

> When all the occupants of Manzanar have resumed their
> places in the stream of American life, these flimsy buildings
> will vanish, the greens and flowers brought in to make life
> more understandable will whither, the old orchard will grow
> older, remnants of paths, foundations and terracing will grad-
> ually blend with the stable texture of the desert. The stone
> shells of the gateways and the shaft of the cemetery monu-
> ment will assume the dignity of desert ruins; the wind will
> move over the land and the snow fall upon it: the hot summer
> sun will nourish the gray sage and shimmer in the gullies. Yet
> we know that the human challenge of Manzanar will rise
> insistently over all of America—and America cannot deny its
> tremendous implications.
>
> —Ansel Adams, *Born Free and Equal,* 1944

While Ansel Adams understood the power of the elements to physically transform Manzanar into a barely visible desert ruins over
time, he also showed a prophetic insight into the lasting power of
what he termed its "human challenge."[39] A half-century later, Adams
would be pleased to know that Manzanar refuses historic invisibility
and has begun its slow process of restoration to our national memory as one of our commemorative national historic sites.

If one cannot make the long journey to Manzanar, one can now
travel there instead as a virtual tourist. The National Park Service has
recently launched its own Internet Website for Manzanar National
Historic Site where one can now log on and witness the transformation of camp ruins into a commemorative site.[40] According to the
latest on-line edition of the *Manzanar Courier,* an "auto-tour"
through the camp has been completed with over one hundred
marked signs (created by tour guide Richard Stewart). The National
Park Service is also at work restoring the barbed-wire fence that
once surrounded the perimeter of the camp, and plans are underway
to open an actual park headquarters and visitor's center in the old

camp auditorium. Since Stewart's first tour in 1997, Manzanar has seen its annual number of visitors jump from 30,000 to 50,000 in 1999. The National Park Service anticipates that this number will increase to as many as 125,000 per year now that the road tour is completed. What is more, Manzanar's recent visibility on the World Wide Web is quickly producing a new generation of virtual tourists who have begun to include this desert site/sight on their eastern California road tours.[41] It remains to be seen how such a virtual mapping of Japanese American internment memory will shape the visual legacy of the camps in the twenty-first century.

CHAPTER FIVE

Another Lesson in "How to Tell Your Friends Apart from the Japs"

The 1992 Winter Olympics Showdown between
Kristi Yamaguchi of the United States
and Midori Ito of Japan

There have been very few historical moments in American popular culture where the bodies of Japanese American women have been allowed to take center stage; and there have been even fewer moments where the representation of their bodies has been subjected to national critical interrogation and visual scrutiny. The 1992 Winter Olympic Games at Albertville offers us a fascinating opportunity to examine contemporary representations of Japanese Americans in the context of what literary critic David Leiwei Li has elsewhere named the "massive American anxiety about the nature of the nation and the contour of its citizenry."[1] In this chapter we will look at the ambivalent media representation of Japanese American figure skater Kristi Yamaguchi as a national sports icon and new kind of multicultural heroine.

In the winter of 1992, I closely followed the media coverage of Kristi Yamaguchi as she prepared to compete in the women's figure skating event at Albertville. During this time, I was also engaged in research on World War II visual representations of Japanese and Japanese Americans. As I followed the media representation surrounding the first-ever Japanese American Olympic heroine, I was struck by what can only be called a recycled representation of anxiety about the visual politics of citizenship and nationality played out upon Yamaguchi's body—and that of her primary rival, Japanese national skater, Midori Ito. This chapter poses the media representation of Yamaguchi and Ito at the center of its inquiry and asks, How do older wartime anxieties of nationhood, citizenship, and loyalty travel across time? Is such a trans-historical comparison and framework insightful? Illuminating? Or merely arbitrary?

Before I turn to the Olympic representation at Albertville, let me turn briefly to some of the most notorious representations of Japanese in American popular culture in 1941 as a kind of visual preface for discussing Japanese American women in contemporary popular culture on the fifty-year anniversary of Executive Order 9066.

Animals of a Different Breed:
Wartime Images from *Time* and *Life* Magazines

> December the seventh of the year 1941 was the day when the Japanese bombs fell on Pearl Harbor. As of that moment, the Japanese in the United States became, by virtue of their ineradicable brownness and the slant eyes which, upon close inspection, will seldom appear slanty, animals of a different breed. The moment the impact of the words solemnly being transmitted over the several million radios of the nation struck home, everything Japanese and everyone Japanese became despicable.　　　—John Okada, *No No Boy*

In the opening pages of his powerful 1957 novel *No No Boy,* John Okada articulates the significance of December 7, 1941, as a historical marker for Japanese American representation during World War II.[2] Not only does this moment especially mark the Japanese as "animals of a different breed," but it also collapses the existing distinctions between the Japanese nationals and Japanese Americans—a confusion and tension over national difference which one can argue continues to persist in the postwar decades of the late twentieth century.

Immediately after the bombing of Pearl Harbor there was a nationwide outbreak of anti-Japanese violence that took the more generic form of anti-Asian violence. While Japanese and Japanese Americans were the specific targets of such attacks, other Asians were victimized as well. *Time* and *Life* magazines both reported that Chinese-American "correspondent Joseph Chiang made things much easier by pinning on his lapel a large badge reading 'Chinese Reporter—NOT Japanese—please.'"[3] Poet Nellie Wong writes of the Chinese community's fear shortly after Pearl Harbor that all Asians might be lumped together as targets of racial hatred and forced removal:

> When World War II was declared
> on the morning radio,
> we glued our ears, widened our eyes.
> Our bodies shivered . . .
> Shortly after our Japanese neighbors vanished
> and my parents continued to whisper:
> We are Chinese, we are Chinese.
> We wore black arm bands,
> put up a sign
> in bold letters.[4]

Likewise across the country, thousands of Chinese and Koreans took to wearing similar ethnic badges identifying themselves "for security purposes."[5] In response to the violence, both *Time* and *Life* magazines published visual primers on December 22, 1941, on "How to Tell Your Friends Apart from the Japs" complete with diagrams of Japanese and Chinese bodies, close-up faces, and a "few rules of thumb" for those wishing to master the difficult task of telling Asians apart from one another:

> There is no infallible way of telling them apart. . . . Even an anthropologist, with calipers and plenty of time to measure heads, noses, shoulders, hips, is sometimes stumped.[6]

Both magazines invoke in pseudoscientific style the language of physical anthropology, physiognomy, and cultural criticism in their

Reading the Japanese face in "How to Tell Your Friends Apart from the Japs." *(Life, 1941.)*

attempt to teach the American public how to distinguish correctly between "our friends" the Chinese and "our enemies" the Japanese.

The following is a selected excerpt from *Time* magazine's attempt at reading the differences between the Japanese and the Chinese body:

> Some Chinese are tall. . . . Virtually all Japanese are short. . . . Japanese are likely to be stockier and broader-hipped than short Chinese.
>
> Japanese—except for wrestlers—are seldom fat; they often dry up and grow lean as they age. The Chinese often put on weight, particularly if they are prosperous (in China, with its frequent famines, being fat is esteemed as a sign of being a *solid citizen*).
>
> Chinese, not as hairy as Japanese, seldom grow an impressive mustache. Most Chinese avoid horn-rimmed spectacles.

Although both have the typical epicanthic fold of the upper eyelid (which makes them look almond-eyed), Japanese eyes are usually set closer together. Those who know them best often rely on facial expression to tell them apart: the Chinese expression is likely to be more placid, kindly, open; the Japanese more positive, dogmatic, arrogant. Some aristocratic Japanese have thin, aquiline noses, narrow faces and, except for their eyes, look like Caucasians.

Japanese are hesitant, nervous in conversation, laugh loudly at the wrong time. Japanese walk stiffly erect, hard-heeled. Chinese, more relaxed, have an easy gait, sometimes shuffle.[7]

Reading the Japanese body in "How to Tell Your Friends Apart from the Japs." *(Life, 1941.)*

While these instructions are unmistakably aimed at teaching us how to decode a potentially treacherous Japanese body—through signs of arrogance, untimely laughter, and choice of eyewear—both articles offer a public pedagogy for how to scrutinize signs of difference in the "inscrutable" Asian body. There is an acute preoccupation in both magazines with reading the meaning of body types: noses, eyelids, hair, height, weight, manner of carriage, and facial expression. *Life* magazine also attempts to make a class-based differentiation between the "highbred" Japanese and their "squat peasant-bred Mongoloid" counterparts. While *Time* notes that some "aristocratic" Japanese can "even look like Caucasians" (with the notable exception of their eyes), *Life* is careful to point out that the "most numerous Japanese anthropological group" looks distinctly Other with their solid, long torsos, short stocky legs, and distinctly round-faced "flat, blob nose" appearance. Hence, "highbred" Japanese look *like us*, while the "peasant-bred" type most distinctly does not. Of course, neither magazine explains why their Chinese models consist almost entirely of healthy young men—some in civilian clothing—who smile for the camera, while their Japanese counterparts consist of stern-faced, middle-aged men in military uniforms.

It is important to remember that these popular magazine images came out directly on the heels of the bombing of Pearl Harbor. Given the particularly brutal campaign of wartime propaganda and enemy representation, they can now be read as fairly tame and even laughable public lessons in physiognomy and physical anthropology for racists.[8] What is more significant is to see them in the larger context of World War II representations of the Japanese. In his excellent coverage of wartime images of race in the Pacific, historian John Dower demonstrates how popular representations of the Japanese took on a distinctly bestial nature:

> A characteristic feature of this level of anti-Japanese sentiment was the resort to non-human or subhuman representation in which the Japanese were perceived as animals, reptiles, or insects (monkeys, baboons, gorillas, dogs, mice, rats, vipers and rattlesnakes, cockroaches, vermin—or more indirectly, "the Japanese herd" and the like).[9]

Dower argues that the single most dominant wartime caricature of the Japanese by writers and cartoonists in the West was the "monkey or ape." He notes that after the war these bestial images of the Japanese—particularly the simian ones—became "almost immediately transformed into an irritated but already domesticated and even charming pet."[10] Yet as Dower has pointed out, this mode of representation has a history that stretches back much farther than Pearl Harbor in the Western imagination:

> The core imagery of apes, lesser men, primitives, children, madmen, and beings who possessed special powers as well— have a pedigree in Western thought that can be traced back to Aristotle, and were conspicuous in the earliest encounters of Europeans with the black peoples of Africa and the Indians of the Western Hemisphere.[11]

Indeed, the earliest encounters between Euro-Americans and Asians in the nineteenth century were often staged alongside African and Native American cultural "specimens" (as well as other "freaks of nature") in the multiple—and often overlapping—sites of the circus side show, the world's fairs and expositions, and the anthropological museum.[12]

While figures of monstrous Japanese are plentiful in World War II propaganda, the threat of the Yellow Peril is typically depicted in images that are bestial, menacing, subhuman, sexualized, and almost always constructed as masculine. Indeed, the feminine is largely rendered invisible in the masculine construction of such militarized minority representations. The mythological radio figure of "Tokyo Rose" is the most powerful single exception to this general rule of wartime representation. In fact, she is the most potent feminized World War II image of the Japanese enemy alien—a unique hybridized American incarnation of the Dragon Lady stereotype and wartime Japanese monster.[13] While there is no one moment of origin for "Tokyo Rose," by the summer of 1943 her name was in circulation throughout the Pacific, and by 1944 certainly well established.[14] Rather than signifying one specific woman in the Pacific, "Tokyo Rose" clearly operated as a composite naming for the several female radio announcers broadcasting Japanese propaganda and music throughout the Pacific Rim; yet, stories about her broadcasts, her modes of seemingly "omniscient" military surveillance, and speculation over what type of Asian body her voice must inhabit were collectively narrativized, revised, and circulated through a distinctly wartime oral tradition among G.I.s.[15] What remains most fascinating is how her distinctly disembodied nature as a feminized, Orientalized, and sexualized military monster operated out of a unique Foucauldian position of desire, surveillance, and horror over the Pacific Rim. What complicates her history still further is the postwar manner in which Japanese American citizen Iva Toguri D'Aquino was subsequently hunted down and framed as this mythical radio figure and found guilty of treason, stripped of her citizenship, and imprisoned for eight years. D'Aquino's history signifies one of the most extreme case studies in the literal deterritorialization of home, citizenship, language, identity, and body of any Japanese American caught on either side of the Pacific during or after the war.

I mention the case of "Tokyo Rose" here as a transition to a closer examination of how the bodies of Japanese American women continue to operate within the field of contemporary representation as sites of struggle and tension between what critic Leslie Bow has termed "duty, desire, ethnic loyalty, and Americanization."[16]

The International Showdown of Kristi Yamaguchi and Midori Ito

> "My, your English is very good."
> —Journalist's comment to Kristi Yamaguchi

The fascination with reading the signifying markers of racial difference on Japanese and Japanese American bodies is not unique to World War II. On the fifty-year anniversary of Executive Order 9066, the signifying codes for friends and enemies, citizens and foreigners, and model and monstrous minorities have been reinscribed on the bodies of gold and silver medalist figure skaters Kristi Yamaguchi of the United States and Midori Ito of Japan.[17] For the first time in Olympic history, the center stage of "the most glamorous gold medal spectacle" was dominated by the presence of Asian women's bodies. One can also read this staged showdown as another example of the late twentieth century crisis in multicultural representation in the United States.[18] Asians in America are no longer targeted by exclusion acts, nor denied the right to naturalized citizenship or land ownership. Indeed, Asian Americans now have some degree of political representation and are even fashioned as "model minorities." Yet the last two decades have also witnessed a dramatic resurgence in antiforeign, anti-Asian xenophobia that has created a particularly racist climate even for fourth-generation Asian Americans.[19]

While the American media was highly conscious of its first Asian American Olympic superstar and the unique nature of the Japanese versus Japanese American battle for the gold, ultimately the politics of representation embedded in these multimedia narratives were, for the most part, largely ignored. In fact, while the showdown between Yamaguchi and Ito was dubbed that of the "artist" versus the "athlete," it was also embroiled in old narratives of Euro-American superiority and the threat of machinelike Japanese athleticism, technology, even physical beastliness. At stake in this representational war were not only the competing narratives of U.S. and Japanese nationalism, but also sad, and confused attempts to delineate, once again, essentialist notions of racial and cultural differences. The representation of Yamaguchi and Ito "on the ice together, worlds apart," distinctly echoes the racialized rhetoric from wartime representations that once instructed us "how to tell our friends apart from the Japs." Yet, if the post–Pearl Harbor primers showed an acute preoccupation with reading the masculine Asian body, the 1992 media representations centered exclusively on reading their feminine counterparts. Furthermore, the dilemma posed by Yamaguchi's Japanese American heritage further compounded this politics of representation. Michael Omi and Howard Winant have pointed out that in the twentieth-century history of Japanese racial formation in the United States, this group's designated category has shifted from "Oriental" to "Other" to "Asian-Pacific American."[20] As the first Japanese American Olympic heroine, the representation of Kristi Yamaguchi offers an intriguing case study not so much in racial formation, however, as in racial *transformation.* Juxtaposed against the more "authentic"

Japanese national, Ito, Yamaguchi was not only *over*re-presented, but even reinvented as "all-American normal."

That "All-American Girl of 1992"

While the racialized codes for what constitutes a friendly American identity no longer require crude signifying buttons pinned to one's lapel, the cultural signifiers for friendly "real" Americans *like us* became re-encoded at Albertville in the body of Yamaguchi the cheerleader, prom goer, sister of the all-star basketball player, and exclusive dater of white men. One must ask in how many ways was Yamaguchi representationally marked not as Oriental, or Other, or even as Asian-Pacific, but as a new type of harmlessly hyphenated American heroine?[21]

Virtually all of the media attention surrounding Yamaguchi straddled the tensions around race, culture, and national identity. Journalist Frank Deford of *Newsweek* certainly pinpointed the sense of media discomfort produced by America's first Japanese American superstar:

> And now: what's a good ole boy to do if there's not only a Toyota in the driveway and a Sony in the bedroom and a Mitsubishi in the family room—but on the screen there, as the band plays the "Star-Spangled Banner," is the All-American girl of 1992, and her name is Yamaguchi?[22]

Embedded in his ironic commentary are all the darker hints of a large-scale economic Japanese invasion threatening to upset the American home and way of life so characteristic of the 1980s rhetoric of Japan bashing. And somehow caught in the middle, Yamaguchi—either American or Japanese—remains suspended in limbo in this impossible and contradictory subject position:

> In a sport where no woman but of white, Northern European birth or heritage has ever won the figs, the battle for the gold and all the lucre it earns sets up a duel between two young

women named Yamaguchi and Ito, whose *bloodlines* both stretch back, pure and simple, to the same *soft, cherry-blossom* days on the one bold *little* island of Honshu. The twist is, though, that if the *powerful* Ito is Midori, of Nagoya, the *delicate* Yamaguchi is Kristi, from the Bay Area, *fourth-generation American.* It's the *chrysanthemum* and the *sword*—on the ice together, *worlds apart.*[23]

In spite of the patronizing representation of the two women, Yamaguchi is ultimately reclaimed as authentically American. In fact, if Ito represents the "powerful" Olympic threat from Japan, Yamaguchi is merely a "delicate" home-grown "chrysanthemum" whom journalists can comfortably call a "fourth-generation" American "raised in Fremont" where her dad is a dentist. Deford assures us that while Yamaguchi "is still a Buddhist," she is also "very much a hyphenated American," albeit in this trivializing order: "Middle-American, California-American," and "beauty-American."[24] He also points out, one supposes as further proof of her American identity, that "her mother, Carole, chuckles that she can't recall any of her three children ever dating anyone but a Caucasian." In fact, Deford argues, ice skating is "practically subversive compared with the hopelessly American activities that Yamaguchi's's siblings have preferred—Lori, her older sister, was on a championship baton-twirling team, and Brett, is at 5 feet 10, a starting guard on his high-school basketball [team]."

In some sense, one could argue that the need to both assert and prove Yamaguchi's hyperassimilation into clichéd American culture is the particular dilemma of the fourth-generation Japanese American *yonsei.* During World War II and the postwar years, the dilemma of the nisei focused on what historian Ron Takaki calls their "sense of twoness" as Japanese Americans caught between the cultures, histories, and languages of two different worlds: their own and that of their issei parents.[25] In her 1953 autobiography, *Nisei Daughter,* Monica Sone explains such a dilemma in this way: "I didn't see how I could be a Yankee and Japanese at the same time. It was like being born with two heads. It sounded freakish and a lot of trouble."[26] On the eve of the Sone family's relocation to the camps, claiming an identity that is both Yankee *and* Japanese seems to her an impossible if not contradictory position bordering on the "freakish."

The nisei were the first generation of Japanese Americans to be subjected to intense pressure to assimilate fully into American culture in order to prove their loyalty and patriotism, thus dispelling the long-standing Orientalist myth of the "unassimilable" alien—a myth which served as the backbone for justifying the roundup and internment of some 120,000 Americans of Japanese descent under Executive Order 9066. As Lt. General John L. Dewitt (then commanding officer of the Fourth Army and Western Defense Command) reasoned in 1943, "There isn't such a thing as a loyal Japanese, and it's just impossible to determine their loyalty by investigation—it just can't be done." For General DeWitt, "the mere fact of having Japanese blood and skin was enough basis for suspicion."[27] If there is a nisei legacy for the sansei and yonsei generations, it is the assumption that assimilation into American culture is now complete. Indeed, the out-marriage rate for Japanese Americans in this generation is the highest of all Asian American groups.

The journalists covering Albertville took great care in reminding us that Yamaguchi and Ito were not only "worlds apart," but went to great lengths to make the former over in unmistakable American fashion. Note *Los Angeles Times* reporter Mike Downy's overt participation in this careful overrepresentation of Yamaguchi as a "normal All-American girl":

> Sixty inches and 93lbs of athleticism on ice. Kristi Yamaguchi is a giggly, not particularly gabby, California girl whose favorite things in the world are going shopping, going rollerblading, and going to San Francisco's 49er football games.
>
> She's not much bigger than a Barbie Doll. She's your everyday, normal All-American girl. . . . Hers is the portrait of an All-American family. Grandfather George was a U.S. Army infantry officer during World War II. Dad Jim is a dentist. Mom Carole is a medical secretary. Brother Brett plays varsity basketball. Sister Lori's a world champion baton twirler. And

itsy-bitsy, ponytailed Kristi is a world champion figure skater, favored . . . to become Olympic champion as well.[28]

In this disturbingly blithe narrative, race is downplayed, internment history is erased, and cultural identity is reencoded into a more recognizable, more palatable, essentialized "all-American" form. If the signifiers for what constitutes Yamaguchi's authentic American-ness (i.e., shopping, rollerblading, frequenting football games, and a marked preference for white boyfriends) were ascribed to one of the Euro-American figure skaters like bronze medal winner Nancy Kerrigan of Stoneham, Massachusetts, or Tonya Harding from Portland, Oregon, they would seem absurd. Applied to Yamaguchi they are meant to convince us beyond the surface of her Japanese blood and skin that she is indeed *like us.* In fact, if we include her dad the dentist, her mother the secretary, her tall brother the basketball player, and her baton-twirling sister, the entire Yamaguchi clan is represented as thoroughly and hopelessly American.

If one looks at Yamaguchi's appearance on the covers of *Sports Illustrated* (March 2, 1992) and *Newsweek* (February 10, 1992) magazines, they further reinforce her all-American iconography within the framework of sports nationalism and red, white, and blue representations of loyalty. On the *Sports Illustrated* cover, Yamaguchi appears with the accompanying caption, "American Dream." Holding up her gold medal, she looks triumphant in the close-up shot. What strikes one immediately is the combination of her smile, girlish ponytail, the glittering gold of her costume and medal, and her long red nails. Given the fact that the feature article says nothing at all about race, or even American dreams, what other covert message does the cover photograph convey? What connections are we meant to draw between the fulfillment of the American Dream and the model minority success story? And what transitional space does Yamaguchi's body here occupy somewhere between the innocent girlhood of ponytails and the much more adult sexuality signified by the long red nails? *Newsweek's* "Olympic Preview" cover poses more unmediated questions. Yamaguchi leaps across the cover, ponytail flying and arms outstretched, in full midair pose under the caption,

A Japanese American sports heroine: Kristi Yamaguchi on the cover of *Sports Illustrated,* 1992.

"America's Kristi Yamaguchi" on the cover of *Newsweek,* 1992.

"Jewel on Ice." One is struck by the dominant red of her costume against the patriotic white and blue of the magazine background. A smaller caption to her left reads, "America's Kristi Yamaguchi." One is left asking, Does she belong to America? And is it important for America to claim her as its own?

If there is any ambivalence in the racial representation of Kristi Yamaguchi as a *different* type of "all-American" hero, this ambivalence all but disappears when she is placed in comparison with Midori Ito. Furthermore, in the time-honored tradition of *Time* and *Life* magazines, there is also a noticeable media preoccupation with measuring the bodies of both Asian women: A great deal of attention is focused on documenting Yamaguchi's and Ito's comparative heights, weights, shoe and dress sizes, and body types. This attention to bodily measurement is conspicuously absent with regard to any of the other women in the Olympics. Although Yamaguchi is twenty-one years old, she is never referred to as a fully developed woman. Instead, she is a "giggly," "itsy-bitsy," 93-pound ponytailed "California girl" who stands all of sixty inches—as opposed to five feet—high. Because she is "not much bigger than a Barbie Doll," we are told she wears incredibly small size three shoes and size one clothes. I will return later in my discussion to the implications of Yamaguchi's adolescent representation.

The Media Fascination with the Body of Midori Ito: "She Is 4 Ft 9 Inches and Built Like a Fireplug"

As Yamaguchi is re-encoded by the journalists at Albertville from Japanese American into "All-American," racial difference and anxiety becomes displaced onto the figure of Midori Ito, who must bear the representational burden as the *real* Japanese *Other* at Albertville. Given the strong Americanization of the former, it is hardly surprising to note that when paired with Ito, Yamaguchi seems to transcend Japanese racial representation altogether and even comes to embody a white "stylish Western ideal" against which her "stout little" rival cannot possibly hope to compete:

Comparative body types: Midori Ito and Kristi Yamaguchi *(Newsweek, 1992.)*

[While] Yamaguchi is almost five inches taller than the 4-foot-
7 Ito and totally of Japanese descent, she perfectly represents
the stylish Western ideal that the stout little Midori is so
envious of. Although absolutely petite, a size 1, 93 pounds,
Yamaguchi is cut high, with a Betty Boop mouth and two
beauty marks wonderfully positioned under the left eye and
the lips. Ito, though, is simply short, her powerful legs bowed
in an old-fashioned way, what the Japanese once called,
unkindly of their women, daikon legs, after the archipelago's
big, squat radishes. In matters of appearance, it doesn't seem
that Yamaguchi and Ito grew up in different lands so much as
if they came from different centuries.[29]

In this juxtaposition, the 1941 *Time* and *Life* distinctions between "high-bred" Japanese who can "even look like Caucasians" is translated into contemporary 1992 terms. Yamaguchi thus represents a new type of Japanese—one where Americanization and assimilation have visibly transformed her into a type of beautiful model minority of modernity: where racial difference becomes muted in favor of Western style. As one who "perfectly represents the stylish Western ideal," she becomes an honorary Caucasian complete with beauty marks and a "Betty Boop mouth," and is *cut high* even though she is only five feet tall.[30] In contrast, Ito is representative of an old world, old-fashioned, even primitive Japan—where marked racial difference remains painfully apparent. Read: *stout little* Midori cursed with what the Japanese still call *daikon aishi* (radish legs). Compared to her modernized and Americanized counterpart, she remains, behind the times, a "squat" peasant-bred Mongoloid on skates. The *Newsweek* journalist confirms this perspective: "In matters of appearance, it doesn't seem that Yamaguchi and Ito grew up in different lands so much as if they came from different centuries." Indeed, they may be "on the ice together," but racially they remain "worlds apart."

Like Yamaguchi, the Olympic representation of Midori Ito is also marked by a curious set of ambivalences. While great media effort has gone into the Americanization of Kristi Yamaguchi, it is most ironic that it is Ito who in some sense best embodies the mythos of the American Dream itself: according to the widely circulated narrative of her life history, Ito grew up as a working-class girl from Nagoya, Japan, who then rose from obscurity and relative poverty on the basis of her personal industry and great talent. In a move that invokes heroic overtones reminiscent of Sylvester Stallone in the endless series of *Rocky* movies, Ito lost the gold medal, but still hit her triple axel in the final moment of competition, thus securing a silver medal and her place in Olympic history.[31] Until 1992, she was also viewed as one of the "fiercest challengers" in the history of international women's figure skating who single-handedly influenced the future direction of the sport.[32] At the same time, she was also viewed as a hopeless contender in the unspoken Western-style beauty pageant that marks the same event. The double media obsession with her threatening athletic superiority as well as her physical inferiority reinvokes old wartime paradigms of the dwarfish, childlike, and primitive Japanese. Yet, in modern fashion, the Japanese female body is here reinscribed as a new embodiment of Japanese super technology. Thus Ito is presented as a kind of relentless and nearly perfect "Japanese jumping bean" machine who is even able to outperform most men.[33] Canadian choreographer Sandra Bezic says of her athletic ability, "She blows away most guys in the field." And according to Olympic coach Evy Scotvold, the only man she has ever seen outjump Ito is former gold medalist Brian Boitano.[34]

Ito's extraordinary physical ability to jump was unprecedented in women's figure skating. Unlike any of her competitors, she could execute "all the categories in figure-skating at age 11, and had perfected them at 12."[35] With a body trained, disciplined, and built to perform feats far beyond the physical ability of virtually every other female Olympic competitor, Ito's technical skills were matchless. Indeed, her arrival at Albertville together with her powerful athletic displays intimidated everyone in the women's figure-skating community:

> When Ito arrived in Albertville, . . . she looked unbeatable. At her first practice she landed three different triple-triple combinations with such ease, such power, that coaches in the stand were burying their eyes in their hands.[36]

Yet, for an athlete who rarely makes a mistake, her Olympic performance literally collapsed under the tremendous pressure of competition. Her repeated failure to execute her jumps cost her the gold medal even though she salvaged second place on the basis of her brave last-minute execution of the first triple axel jump in Olympic women's history.[37]

In spite of her tremendous physical talents, Ito herself is quoted on her own painful sense of physical inadequacy compared to the (white) women of the West:

> I like jumps because they bring me the greatest pleasure. . . .
> All I can really do is jump. Figure skating is a matter of beauty, and Westerners are so stylish, so slender. I wish I could be beautiful like them. . . . I cannot make a mistake because

people not quite so good as I am can win since they have some higher artistry.[38]

The media fascination with Ito's superior technical abilities also extend to a representational fascination with her body in ways that are similar to the measuring and infantilizing of Kristi Yamaguchi's body. In Ito's case, this extends to reading her facial expressions (*childlike, pixielike,* and *wartlike*) and to her bodily measurements. Virtually every report on Ito contained reference to her height (4 feet 7 inches or 4 feet 9 inches), her weight (97 pounds), and, of course, the peculiar shape of her legs. American journalists felt compelled to note their own sense of her physical inferiority compared to Yamaguchi: "It is unlikely . . . that [Ito] will try to imitate the lithe and pretty Yamaguchi," and "Her powerful legs can never allow her the exquisiteness of the Japanese American rival."[39] Note also *Time* magazine's description of Ito in which her image is "indelibly set" in less than flattering terms:

> She is 4ft 9in. and built like a fireplug. But can she fly! At Munich her image was set indelibly, warts and all, when she took off and whirled, airborne, into the stands. That was the embarrassing part. Then she went back out again, her radiant smile lighting up the arena.[40]

Photographic representation would appear to confirm this contrast between the two skaters. In a dramatic visual showdown between Yamaguchi "the artist" and Ito "the athlete," *Newsweek* depicts the two women with a dramatic caption that reads: "The contest for the ladies' figure-skating gold will come down to one jump." On the right-hand side of the two-page photograph, Yamaguchi fills the page from top to bottom border. Posed in a classic arabesque, her head back, her ever-present ponytail flying, she looks graceful, even tall. Her caption reveals for us her vital bodily statistics: "21 years old, 5 feet, 93 pounds, Hometown: Fremont, California." On the opposite page, Ito appears complete with her own captioned personal information and bodily measurements: "22 years old, 4 feet 7 inches, 98 pounds, Hometown: Nagoya, Japan." She is only a few inches shorter, but on the page, her body takes up one third less space than Yamaguchi. As a result, she looks noticeably short, even stumpy, next to the tall, arched grace of her American rival. In the layout, Ito's gaze appears to be locked onto her taller Japanese American opponent. In another *Newsweek* feature, Yamaguchi is decked out in glittering black and gold and stretches gracefully, her legs spread far apart, across two pages. The centerfold bears the headline "American Beauty" and verges on the erotic.[41] The caption tells us, "She's simply on a different level, so elegantly dressed, gliding so stylishly, seamlessly, weaving her moves naturally into the music." In contrast, Ito's image appears framed in a tiny box in the upper left-hand corner of the opposite page. Her body is hunched over backwards as she falls on her bottom, arms askew. Her extremely awkward posture serves as a visual reminder of her failed ability to mime Yamaguchi's elegance. Her caption reads: "After falling on her first jump, it took courage, daring and a triple axel to win a silver medal."[42] Compared to the looming image of Yamaguchi the "American Beauty," the image of Ito is representationally confined and looks decidedly dwarfish and desexualized.

Anyone following the coverage of the winter Olympics would have to note the competing narratives of sports nationalisms. *Time* magazine noted that "television's appetite for photogenic action is insatiable, and pursuits that were once mere cottage industries of athletics have been streamlined and glamorized for the diversion of millions of viewers."[43] There is no question that the representation of Midori Ito in the winter Olympic games at Albertville invoked Japan as a rising economic superpower threatening to compete in global affairs. In this narrative, the industrious Japanese female athlete with the superior body technology threatens to take over the women's figure skating competition—which, until now, has always been an event dominated by the West. Ever self-conscious of her status as a national icon, Ito felt compelled to apologize on television to all of Japan for her failure to win the gold medal for the nation. In the Albertville narrative, Western style prevails and the threat of Japan is contained: the "tiny Japanese" is cut down as an unsuccessful contender and a reminder that the Japanese may attempt to imitate the West, but they cannot outdo, or outperform, good old-fashioned American ingenuity, creativity, and artistry—not to mention beauty.

The Representation of Olympic Sexuality

> Ultimately, what appeals to the sport's audience is whatsoever is most beautiful, whatsoever is most lovely, whatsoever is most sexy. In Europe . . . by far the most popular photograph of any skater in recent years is not anybody jumping, but of [Katerina] Witt coming completely out of the top of her outfit after a simple spin.[44]

When asked what distinguishes women's figure skating from women's gymnastics, one official stated, "Ninety percent of our girls are attractive, and they all have breasts."[45] Carol Heiss, a former gold medalist and current Olympic coach, has told her skaters, "Think like a man, but act and look like a woman."[46] In addition to the show of athletic skills, there is also, as I have argued earlier, the unmistakable element of a competitive Western-style beauty pageant between the athletes. Given the strong interplay between the stereotypical representation of Asian women and exotic sexuality, it is curious that both Yamaguchi and Ito should, for the most part, have escaped the sexualized framing associated with women's figure skating and instead be subjected to the representational confinement of adolescent girlhood and infantilization.

These distinctions become surprisingly clear when one considers the visual impact of the two Asian women joined on the winner's podium by American bronze medalist, Nancy Kerrigan, who was popularly referred to throughout the 1992 Olympics as a tall "Kate Hepburn–style beauty." One can almost read this unique triad of Japanese, Japanese American, and Euro-American bodies as a type of progression. In this reconfiguration, it is obvious that it is Kerrigan who embodies the *real* Western ideal, while Yamaguchi merely serves to mediate between the two more distinctly' oppositional bodies from the East and West. Furthermore, if Ito operates as the infantilized Other of this twenty-something set, with Yamaguchi standing literally in the middle next to the tall and fully developed body of Kerrigan, then one can also read their podium positioning as a visual narrative that traces not only the genealogy of girlhood into adult female sexuality, but even the simultaneous story of the growth and development of a full American identity. Perhaps most importantly, the image of the three women on the podium serves to deflate the false opposition between Ito and Yamaguchi as distinctly different Japanese and American types. By erasing the possibility of their fully developed adult sexuality, both women are rendered, by the American media, as thoroughly safe and nonthreatening.

While my discussion of the Winter Olympics has focused exclusively on Kristi Yamaguchi and Midori Ito, it is important to note that the problematic representation of race, class, and gender also extends to the other competitors in the 1992 women's figure-skating event. Anyone watching the televised competition must have noted the curious construction of the "good girl" and "bad girl" narratives as journalists scrambled for their inside stories. In this fashion, both Yamaguchi and Ito functioned as the good girls of figure skating, while Tonya Harding of Portland, Oregon, and Surya Bonaly of France emerged as the bad girls at Albertville.[47] More specifically, Harding was portrayed as the uppity working-class bad girl and Bonaly (the only competitor of African descent) as the dark wayward native.[48] While it is beyond the scope of this chapter's discussion, it is significant to note that in light of Tonya Harding's scandalous 1994 involvement in the physical assault on Nancy Kerrigan, the Olympic representation of race, class, and gender two years after Albertville begs further consideration and analysis, particularly for the manner in which class, and in this case, the representation of a white American working-class woman, became conflated with race in truly interesting ways. While the more photogenic Kerrigan was fashioned into nothing less than the media darling, Harding was systematically villified by the press and routinely described as "white trash" and "trailer park trash," and even with the overtly racialized epithet "white nigger."[49]

Toward a Conclusion: The Olympic Representation of Race and Multiculturalism under the New World Order

What I have tried to map throughout this discussion is the insidious way in which racial difference was recognized and simultaneously disavowed and re-encoded in the Winter Olympic games at Albertville. With the end of the Cold War, it was apparent in both the 1992 winter and summer games that the Eastern Bloc countries no longer functioned as the adversarial Other to the heroic Subject of the West.[50] It remains to be seen what new directions the narratives of sports nationalism and competition will take. Yet a popular joke in circulation during the 1990s has been that the Cold War is over and that Japan won. In the wake of late twentieth century Japan bashing, it is not coincidental that the representation of Midori Ito was so heavily laden with ambivalence.

By way of closure, I would like to return to the representation of Kristi Yamaguchi, particularly because her participation in the Olympics also coincided with the fifty-year anniversary of the relocation and internment of Japanese Americans under Executive Order 9066. There is no doubt that the shift in U.S. racial demographics has thrown the multicultural representation of American culture into a crisis. Consequently, one must look at the representation of difference at Albertville as part of the current trend wherein the threat of multiculturalism cannot only be safely contained, domesticated, and emptied of any dangerous racial signification or specificity, but history too can be revised and sanitized in kinder, gentler fashion and good minorities shown to make good citizens. It is in this context that I wish to look at how the narratives of internment and relocation operated as a subtext in Yamaguchi's all-American representation.

To their credit, both Frank Deford of *Newsweek* and Mike Downy of the *Los Angeles Times* acknowledged Yamaguchi's Japanese American heritage.[51] Both journalists noted that a particular brand of silence seems to have played a role in Yamaguchi's ethnic heritage and to the effect of internment on her family. After painting a rather vigorous portrait of Yamaguchi's "all-American family," Downy adds:

> [This] is not the complete picture of the Yamaguchi family of Freemont, California. Kristi's mother was born inside a Japanese-American wartime internment camp in Colorado. And her father was four when his family was coerced into selling off its Gilroy farm and most of its belongings before being relocated to a similar camp in Poston, Arizona where they remained for the next three years. "They don't talk about it much," Kristi says.

Similary, Deford briefly alludes to the wartime history and its effect on the Yamaguchis (and on the Itos as well):

> Carole Doi's father was ripped out of the University of Southern California, and, with the rest of his family, sent off to a camp in Colorado. That is where Carole was born. The Dois lost their flower farm in Gardena, just as up north, in Gilroy, the Yamaguchis lost a ranch and all that was theirs, too. But Mrs. Yamaguchi is reluctant to talk about any of that, because, it seems, it was a long time ago and none of them want to dwell on it anymore. Or, if they do, they won't let us know. . . . Probably Midori Ito's mother doesn't want to talk about what happened to her when she was a little girl in the 40's either. It's all very far away by now.

There is nothing new about the wall of silence these journalists here indicate they have come up against. After all, silence has largely dominated Japanese American internment history for the last fifty years. What is new, however, are the current ways in which mainstream American culture has just recently chosen to break its own silence in remembering, even re-visioning, internment history itself as the truest test of Japanese American loyalty in a move that actually recoups minority history into an American success story. The internment narrative in this version details how the Japanese Americans may have suffered as a group (a long time ago), but have since managed to pull themselves up by the bootstraps and become successful model minority citizen subjects. Seen in this light, it makes sense that the representation of Kristi Yamaguchi should transcend the specificity of racial difference as she becomes a new type of all-American hero. Indeed, as a kind of postscript for the final heroic recouping of Yamaguchi's body, it is fitting that an audio-animatronic representation of her body currently performs in another public space of spectacle: on stage at the Epcot Center in Disneyworld, Yamaguchi holds a special place of honor as the only Japanese American in the "Golden Dream" sequence of the highly patriotic show, "The American Adventure"—whose main theme, appropriately enough, is the "making of America and Americans."[52] One could say that the representation of race at the Winter Olympics at Albertville, or onstage at Epcot, signals the arrival of a particular kind of multicultural representation appropriate for a "New World Order" where reconciliation, assimilation, and celebration have replaced the real tensions inherent in an ethnically diverse culture.[53]

A Postscript for Kristi Yamaguchi's Post-Olympic Representation

One of the disturbing mythologies that immediately followed Yamaguchi's post-Olympic career was that her Japanese American ethnicity impaired her ability to profit from her gold-medal performance. Several post-Olympic articles in *Business Week* and U.S. and Canadian newspapers speculated that to marketers, Yamaguchi "wasn't as good as gold" and that her immediate lack of high-profile endorsements was the result of a "sick sense of Japan bashing."[54] The rumors were so prevalent that both Yamaguchi and her coach went on record to challenge them, denying that "her ethnic heritage had limited her endorsement range."[55] Indeed, immediately after the Olympics, she picked up endorsements with Kellogg, Ray Ban, Evian, Kraft, Campbell's Soup, and Hoechst-Celanese Acetate clothing manufacturer. Yet in 1994, Yamaguchi was featured in a television ad pitted against a doubting Dave Thomas—the founder of Wendy's hamburger restaurant. In the space of just two years, Thomas pretends to suffer from short-term historical amnesia and has forgotten who Yamaguchi is, let alone that she was once a gold medal Olympian and national icon.

In past winter Olympic competitions, gold medalists such as Peggy Fleming, Dorothy Hamill, Katarina Witt, and even silver medalist Nancy Kerrigan have managed to turn the combination of gold and sexuality into highly lucrative businesses for themselves. Indeed, attesting to the fact that sex sells, in one of the few visible endorsements Yamaguchi has had since the Olympics (for Hoechst Celanese), she has representationally made the leap from Olympic girlhood to sultry adult sexuality.[56] In one particular ad, she is literally draped from head to toe in gold fabric and jewelry—a sign that she presumably can turn her gold medal into a commodifiable goldmine. Yet another predominant post-Olympic ad campaign appears to emphasize Yamaguchi's all-Americanization at the expense of her Japanese American heritage. In an ad for DuroSoft Colors contact lenses, the metaphor for racial erasure and blond-haired, blue-eyed reinvention is so transparent it verges on cliché: Yamaguchi is shown with one brown eye and one blue-eye on the verge of a final makeover with the explaining caption, "Because a little change is fun!"[57]

Earlier in this chapter, I have argued that Yamaguchi's arrival on the Olympic scene signaled a continuing anxiety of multicultural representation in popular American culture. Whether she is represented as a type of harmlessly hyphenated American heroine, or is subjected to racial erasure and subsequent reinvention as an honorary Caucasian, the discomfort surrounding her representation was certainly aggravated in the months following the Winter Olympic games at Albertville. In *Life* magazine's pictorial year in review for 1992, Yamaguchi was noticeably absent in their brief segment on the Winter Olympics while Nancy Kerrigan appeared on the special issue cover. *Life's* use of the photogenic Kerrigan works to underscore the visual erasure of Yamaguchi and reminds us of our limited ability to envision the face—and color—of our national heroines.

If there is a twentieth-century conundrum for Asian American representation, it is the fact that even after four generations, Americans of Asian descent continue to be read at the surface level of the body as outsiders and immigrants. As Yamaguchi shifted her career from amateur skater to a professional "Star on Ice," the mantle of Asian American Olympic superstar status was passed on to Chinese American skater, Michelle Kwan. Ironically, but perhaps not surprisingly, when Kwan lost the gold medal to Tara Lipinski at the 1998 Winter Olympic Games at Nagano, the MSNBC Website ran the now notorious headline: "American beats out Kwan."[58] Such visual slippage out of citizenship only reinforces what poet Kimiko Hahn has observed about Asians in America, "We are the 'model minority' on the one hand and 'dogeater' on the other: exotic and second class. We are 'forever foreign.'"[59] This book has argued that Japanese American bodies have long been subjected to multiple (mis)readings in American popular culture. The following Epilogue closes this book with a series of multiracial Japanese American and Asian American bodies that offer us complex and even pleasurable trajectories for imaging—and imagining—multicultural, multiracial, and multilingual American representation at the beginning of the twenty-first century.

Epilogue

Imag(in)ing the Multiracial Japanese American Body at the Turn of the Millennium

> I come from a mixed marriage: I'm half-Japanese and half-Yugosla-vian. Folks, you can't make up shit this weird. I'm a Japoslavian.
>
> —Mike Moto, standup comic

> People see me walking down the sidewalk with my European friend and her daughter and assume I'm the nanny or the housekeeper. I don't know where people think I'm from but it sure ain't here! . . . People speak to me in Spanish all the time. I remember this woman who came up to me and started speaking Spanish. I said, "I'm sorry I don't speak Spanish." She thought I was lying—she said, "You're ashamed you're Latina, be proud." . . . It would be great if people could tell that I was Japanese and Finnish right off the bat. But then I'd be pulling a reindeer and . . . a Dachshund dog.
>
> —Amy Hill, from *Beside Myself*

Standup comic Mike Moto and actress Amy Hill not only under-stand what it means to live inside bodies that confound public scrutiny, but have created entire performance pieces out of their visibility as multiracial Japanese Americans whose bodies have ren-dered them racially unreadable at the surface of their skin.¹ If per-formance theorist Peggy Phelan is correct that the politics of repre-sentation is "almost always on the side of the one who looks and al-most never on the side of the one who is seen," then this epilogue brings this book to a close by opening with the outlaw body of multiracial Japanese American performers, writers, and artists who have historically been defined by the gaze of the Other and only more recently by their own acts of self-definition.[2] Moto and Hill are well aware of the signifying power of their multiracial bodies. They each articulate their frustration and pleasure in having bodies that visually refuse to fit into prescribed categories of racial representation. Moto's delight in his strange hybridity as a "Japoslavian" is matched by Hill's witty understanding of the sign system of meaning attached to her body as a Japanese Finn who continually passes as Latina.[3] Their performances remind us of the dramatic lack of national imagination to envision not just a non-white, but a complex multiethnic and multicultural reconfiguration of America.

As this epilogue moves through its concluding litany of real and imaginary Japanese American subjects, I wish to extend the boundaries of visual representation to include literary bodies that can also teach us something about imagining multicultural America at the close of the twentieth century. Critics like Traise Yamamoto have, after all, argued persuasively that literary representations of the Japanese American body are almost always shaped by a visual politics of representation.[4]

While performers like Moto and Hill represent powerful voices articulating the history and experiences of mixed-race Japanese Americans, perhaps no other multiracial writer understands what is at stake in the personal constructing, ordering, and strategizing of one's own self-representation than playwright and poet Velina Hasu Houston.

In the wake of post–September 11, 2001, anti-Asian violence, I am reluctant to claim that the rights of citizenship once challenged under Executive Order 9066 are now fairly locked into place.[5] Indeed, I turn to the work of writers like Houston to remind us that some Japanese Americans continue to engage in visual battle over their claim to American identity. Moreover, the Japanese American body still functions as the site of the battleground. Houston's writings continue a dialogue across time with other Japanese Americans who earlier in this century were also threatened by a visual politics of representation intent on casting them out of the protective membership of the nation and into desert exile.

As the daughter of a World War II Japanese war bride mother and an Afro-Native American G.I. father, Houston has devoted several plays and countless poems and essays to mapping out the complex narrative of her multiracial history.[6] Through her aesthetics, Houston documents the twin dynamic of having a body that is perpetually subjected to visual scrutiny even as she struggles to locate herself in a place called "home" on the American map. Unlike Moto and Hill, Houston expresses little pleasure and a great deal of pain in her recounting of what it is like to have a body that emits racial significations beyond her control.

In one of her early essays, Houston narrates a particularly telling scene of encounter with a white anthropologist who "discovers" the playwright's body in the unveiled space of a Santa Monica steam room:

> Los Angeles . . . A Caucasian woman about fifty years old observes me. Her face is intelligent, analytical and scrutinizing. I am its current object of scrutiny. As she follows me into the showers and maintains a close watch, I wonder if she is a lesbian. After the shower, she brings her clothing to my section to dress. She attempts being inconspicuous, but I am painfully aware of it. She allows me the decency of putting on my lingerie before she moves in for the attack. "Excuse me, miss," she says. "Do you speak English?" I think about it, decide I speak fairly well considering my childhood existence among Japanese immigrants, and nod. She is delighted. Thinking English is my second language, she speaks slowly, with exaggerated enunciation. "I . . . am . . . an . . . anthropologist," she says. I nod readily to speed up her explanation. "I don't see many Micronesians in Los Angeles. You must be a recent transplant," she states. She zealously continues relating her experiences in Micronesia and how her village friend looked just like me. Or vice versa. As she speaks. I wonder silently if Micronesia, tucked away in the South Seas, was a place where African adventurers and Japanese refugees were shipwrecked together centuries ago.[7]

Under visual "attack," as the object of an anthropological gaze, Houston speaks to the discomfort of such encounters that are chronically produced—in ways that are almost always out of her own control—by her multiracial body. In this encounter, Houston reveals a heightened sensitivity to how the visual politics of representation operate as a politics of domination where she is passively reduced to an "object of scrutiny." Her body is literally revealed in the naked space of the steam room and rendered speechless in its vulnerability to the invasive, relentless onslaught of questions of the anthropologist who is visually studying her.

In her writings, Houston narrates many similar scenes where she repeatedly functions as an object of visual scrutiny in public spaces, including taxi cabs, city streets, and shopping malls. Her poem "Amerasian Girl" articulately speaks to the discomfort of the multiracial Japanese American body which must continuously assert its racial and national identity under a barrage of annoying and exhausting misreadings:

> No.
> I'm not schizoid.
> I'm not feeling American today.
> And, no, I am not
> PilipinaThaiSamoanHawaiian
> MexicanBrazilianBurmeseSiamese
> PolynesianTahitianMalaysianMoroccan
> EgyptianIndo-ChineseIndonesianMicronesian
> I have no race,
> no country.
> Only a soul composed of wars
> mixed pride
> and
> agony.[8]

"Not feeling American today," Houston is reconfigured as an alien in the nation and dispossessed of racial identity and citizenship ("I have no race, no country"). Counter to a contemporary discourse celebrating multiculturalism, the effect here of Houston's multiethnic, multiracial, and multicultural heritage is not utopian, but a potpourri of "mixed pride and agony." This poem works to undo the kind of visual rhetoric of Americanism that photographers like Ansel Adams worked so hard to produce a half-century earlier. If anything, "Amerasian Girl" reinforces how such a multiply-marked body problematically exists outside of simple visual categories of racial and national representation, while speaking to the problematic conception of where and how one can safely retreat to a place called "home." Here, Houston must assert her sense of self through a continuous series of negations that have been read onto the surface of her body: "not schizoid/not American/not Pilipina, etc."

The work of multiracial writers like Houston reminds us that in spite of the current tendency to celebrate and even romanticize multiculturalism, there is a genuine dilemma of where one may place a hybrid body that does not fit into any one simple place on a white American map:

> Green tea girl in a land of milk and honey,
> tea in bags without fine leaves to read.
> She learns to drink the blacker brew
> with nothing to sweeten the bitter truth.
> She learns a different *gaman* to survive
> in a land where the soul is in the fist.
> But is it her land; they call it their land.
> One moment she is a *Jap* without a home,
> Another moment a *nigger*, homeless yet.[9]

Suspended between racist configurations of identity, Houston feels stripped of any possibility of belonging to the nation. Cast out of home, identity, and homeland, her hybrid body does not allow her the possibility of visual assimilation into American culture like so many of the nisei who came before her. The metaphoric "homelessness" of Houston's "Green tea girl in a land of milk and honey" is rendered particularly "bitter" given the special brand of racism she encounters as an Afro-Asian American woman who must face the violence of rejection from both sides of her genealogy.

The multiracial Japanese American poet Ai similarly forces us to question the enforced exile that accompanies the personal and painful politics of location for the Afro-Asian Japanese American woman. While Ai has been a prolific contemporary poet, it is interesting that her creative writing does not directly engage her complex multiracial heritage as a woman who is self-defined and fractured into a "½ Japanese, ⅛ Choctaw, ¼ Black, 1/16 Irish" Catholic girl [who grew up] in the unlikely home-lands of Texas, Las Vegas, and San Francisco in the 1950s."[10] While her creative writing is autobiographically unmarked, Ai discloses in one rare 1978 personal interview how her mother once advised her "to tell people she is 'Indian' if anyone asks . . . in order to avoid being treated like a freak."[11] Unable to find a home in the Japanese or the African American communities, Ai explains how she found solace instead as an undergraduate majoring in "Oriental Studies"—an academic home she says where she was surrounded by white and Chinese students.

In one of the most poignant articulations that pedagogically enables a politics of representation for the multiracial woman of color, she writes, "I have learned well the lesson most multiracial people must learn in order to live with the fact of not belonging: there is no identity for me 'out there.'"[12] Although Ai once positioned herself as "aesthetically Japanese," her open acknowledgment of "not belonging" anywhere "out there" should caution us to the fact that not all multiracial women of color find the radical possibility for openness, interrogation, and double-vision that is celebrated in the paradigm of border crossings and multiculturalism. Instead, such crossings are also fraught with difficulties and personal pain.

Poet Thelma Seto offers us another such literary representation of the perils of cross-racial Japanese American mixing in her remarkable poem, "The Archipelago of My Bones":

> I am a mixed-blood animal that talks,
> The progeny of a world war
> displacing more than people.
> One small human conceived by a man too smart to fight
> barbed wire

of either concentration camp
or Japanese ghetto,
and a woman with the vision and courage to fall in love
with the yellow peril it was illegal
for her to marry.
I am the synchronicity of their mutiny.[13]

"The Archipelago of My Bones" maps the geography of the multiracial outlaw body produced through the "illegal" pairing of a white mother and a Japanese American father. As the product of their postwar interracial union, Seto's narrator reclaims the power of her own voice to talk back to a world unable to accept the terms of her illicit creation. She is a "mutinous" body—a "mixed blood animal" who bears the memory of her parents' transgressive union, her father's punishment in the wartime internment camps, and the family's complicated history of continental crossings.

At the turn of the millennium, Seto's narrator sadly observes that America is "still too young for [its] mixed-race kind" even though "we hide in the branches of every family tree." Standing on the edge of white and Japanese America, the narrator calls out the racism and self-hating schizophrenia of both and admits she feels most at "home," self-exiled in that geographic "Oriental" third space "between East and West"—in "the purple hills of Natanz, Persia" where she was born and raised, and where her expatriate "bones" are rooted.

I post the poetic articulations of Houston, Ai, and Seto here as a cautionary segue to the representation of multiracial Japanese Americans who find pleasure in the deliberate confusing and mixing of boundaries in their often complex, mixed-race genealogies.

From Pleasure to Danger—Envisioning "Safe Sex" Miscegenation

In my attempts to understand race and mixing I began to search for faces like mine in the immediate world. I had no idea how dangerous that could be.

—Carol Camper's *Miscegenation Blues*

One of the most fascinating visual exercises in miscegenation at the end of the twentieth century appeared in the fall of 1993, when *Time* magazine devoted an entire special issue to a discussion of "How Immigrants Are Shaping the World's First Multicultural Society" in the United States. The cover of this special issue was particularly striking for its close-up portrait of the face of a light-skinned mixed-blood woman of color whose arresting symmetrical features, dark green eyes, lipstick smile, and actual pores appeared very lifelike.[14] Her face was pasted against a muted backdrop of hundreds of tiny head shots of equally light-skinned men and women from across a rainbow coalition of color. The copy on the cover cautioned the reader and holder of the magazine's cover gaze to "take a good look at this woman" who was "created by a computer from a mix of several races" giving us a "remarkable preview of 'The New Face of America.'" *Time*'s Asian American computer imaging specialist, Kin Wah Lam, crossed fourteen different photographic racial types (hand picked by the magazine's assistant picture editor) to morph this *hapa mestiza* cover girl.

> The woman on the cover of this special issue of *Time* does not exist—except metaphysically. Her beguiling if mysterious visage is the product of a computer process called morphing—as in metamorphosis. . . . The highlight of this exercise in cyber-genesis was the creation of the woman on our cover, selected as a symbol of the future, multiethnic face of America. . . . She is: 15% Anglo-Saxon, 17.5% Middle Eastern, 17.5% African, 7.5% Asian, 35% Southern European and 7.5% Hispanic. Little did we know what we had wrought. As onlookers watched the image of our new Eve begin to appear on the computer screen, several staff members promptly fell in love. Said one: "It really breaks my heart that she doesn't exist." We sympathize with our lovelorn colleagues, but even technology has its limits. This is a love that must forever remain unrequited.[15]

Managing editor James Gaines professes the magazine's innocence in this computerized racial experiment emphasizing that they "make

Time's multicultural cover girl. *(Time, 1993.)*

no claim to scientific accuracy" and instead present Lam's "chimerical results in the spirit of fun and excitement." Yet, what *Time* refers to as an experiment in "cyber-genesis" can also be read as an allegory of postmodern "safe-sex" miscegenation where illicit interethnic couplings occur in sanitized virtual space under the watchful eyes of the magazine's all-male pro-creative editorial team.

Time's special issue attempts an objective representation for imagining what multicultural America will look like by the middle of the twenty-first century, by when it is estimated the national population will swell to some 392 million people. One of the undercurrents running throughout this special issue is the unmistakable anxiety over what embodied form this new population will take and how new immigrants and an increasing ethnic minority population will impact crime, disease, an overburdened school system, and welfare rolls. It is both significant and ironic that while *Time* identifies Hispanics and Asians as two of the most rapidly growing ethnic groups in the United States, their multiracial cover girl fails to mirror such a corresponding racial composition. Indeed, her "Hispanic" and Asian heritage are not only muted at a combined 15 percent but have melted into her hybrid body's overall racial configuration. The magazine editors tells us that she is 15 percent Anglo-Saxon, 35 percent Southern European, and 17.5 percent Middle Eastern. Because she is safely constructed as well over 50 percent white, she can certainly "pass" as such on the basis of her light skin and Euro-features. As such, she operates in *Time's* special issue as the safest kind of multiracial body: she is carefully crafted as an honorary white woman of color, with just enough Asian and Hispanic blood to give her a hint of "beguiling and mysterious" erotic promise. One could say that she is not so much an experiment in "cyber-genesis" as in "cipher-genesis" in that the mask of her smiling visage conveys blankness rather than an interior subjectivity.

In *Time's* editorial notes, this "new Eve" visually functions as the object of both racial difference and desire. Whether she is first seen on *Time's* computer graphics screen or later on the cover of the nationally circulating magazine, she becomes everyone's cyber-cipher—a screen onto which we can all project our fantasies. I pose her here as a "beguiling" screen onto which I impose our racialized and gendered fantasies of the nation, metonymically encoded as the "new face of America."

This "new Eve" undoes national anxieties over monstrous forms of multiculturalism that may threaten to inhabit, breed, or dominate the twenty-first century. If anything, she is a safe, sanitized, fair-skinned creation who has been fashioned along the pleasing lines of *Time*'s Euro-American imaginary—which has taken great care to regulate and re-vision the darker threat of multicultural bodies multiplying in the twenty-first century.

Toward a Conclusion: Imag(in)ing Other Possibilities for a Late Twentieth-Century Japanese American Body

In closing this book, I wish to invoke four final bodies that help us to envision the politics of race, class, and gender representation. The first body works to disrupt simple notions of multiculturalism with its violent, wistful vision for a borderless future, the second comes from a painting where the Asian woman is configured as a cyborg, the third operates as another cyborg figure conjured from the comic imaginary world of the Japanese *manga,* and the fourth is a Japanese American adult entertainer and performer in charge of the business of her own visual representation. All four figures invoke in their own way narratives of illicit creation, miscegenation, and a desire for imagining and envisioning new possibilities for multicultural visual representation at the turn of the millennium.

In one of her most provocative essays, feminist critic Donna Haraway invokes the literary figure of mixed-blood Japanese computer hacker Lisa Foo from science-fiction writer John Varley's famous short story, "Press Enter."[16] Haraway is fascinated with how Foo operates as a kind of hopeful metaphor for navigating and "hacking" our way through complex systems of knowledges and technologies in her role as an expert penetrator of high-security information systems in cyberspace. While Varley's narrative description is not exactly flattering, he nevertheless paints a vivid portrait of the textual surface of her hybrid Japanese American body:

> Where does one start in describing Lisa Foo? Remember when newspapers used to run editorial cartoons of Hirohito and Tojo, when the *Times* used the word "Jap" without embarrassment? Little guys with faces wide as footballs, ears like jug handles, thick glasses, two big rabbity buck teeth, and pencil-thin mustaches. . . . Leaving out only the mustache, she was a dead ringer for a cartoon Tojo. She had the glasses, and the ears, and the teeth. But her teeth had braces, like piano keys wrapped in barbed wire. And she was five-eight or five-nine and couldn't have weighed more than a hundred and ten.[17]

Varley's mixed-blood character is not only constructed as a postmodern computer geek/genius but as a mixed-blood Japanese woman in America who has begun the arduous process of transforming her body with orthodontic and cosmetic surgery. She also embodies the Asian immigrant model minority success story through a trajectory that has taken her from a life as a former street hustler, to child prostitute, to postwar refugee, to an American graduate of Caltech. Foo intrigues Haraway and others for her complex multicultural, multilingual, and multiracial history which charts the horrors of violent warfare, miscegenation, uprooting, and exile.

In a passage that speaks to the violent complexity of Foo's origin story, Varley describes how this hybrid Japanese character literally carries the burden of historical representation on her body:

> It's no accident I look Japanese. My grandmother was raped in '42 by a Jap soldier of the occupation. She was Chinese, living in Hanoi. My mother was born there. They went south after Dien Bien Phu. My grandmother died. My mother had it hard. Being Chinese was tough enough, but being half Chinese and half Japanese was worse. My father was half French and half Annamese. Another bad combination. I never knew him. But I'm sort of a capsule history of Vietnam. . . . I've got one grandfather's face and the other grandfather's height [and silicone] tits by Goodyear.[18]

Through this recitation, Foo boasts a genealogy that literally encapsulates the violent history of Vietnam. Lisa Foo is a unique and disturbing figure in the field of Asian American representation and most readers are resistant to and dissatisfied with the horrific, even pornographic, terms of her final undoing at the end of the narrative.[19] As a racially transgressive body who penetrates too many high-security Internet borders, Foo becomes both a dangerous and a deadly repository of too much knowledge. Destroyed in a microwave oven, the final violence of her execution mimes the horrific violence inflicted upon her grandmother. Disturbed by Varley's violent termination of Lisa Foo, critics like Haraway have insisted upon exercising the creative license of feminist guerrilla reading practices to rewrite the ending of the story and recuperate this fascinating figure for her metaphorical and mythological potential as a Beatrice-like guide through the postmodern matrices of power, knowledge, and pleasure. Lisa Foo anticipates the feminist revisioning of the figure of the cyborg.

The figure of the cyborg is, in its most literal sense, a cybernetic organism, a "hybrid of machine and organism, a creature of social reality as well as a creature of fiction"—a boundary that critics like Haraway reminds us is "an optical illusion."[20] In Haraway's famous "Cyborg Manifesto," the latter is a creature that also embodies enormous possibilities for creative resistance and provides us with a way to think about "transgressed boundaries, potent fusions, and dangerous possibilities which progressive people might explore as one part of needed political work."[21]

In a creative stretch of argument and imagination, Haraway positions women of color as a type of cyborg identity—one that is "synthesized from fusions of outsider identities."[22] One can imagine this woman of color cyborg as part trickster and woman warrior who moves among and between the lines of different cultural spaces, landscapes, and languages. She is a fusion of Audre Lorde's "sister/outsider," Patricia Hill Collins's "outsider within," Trinh T. Minh-ha's "inappropriate/d Other," Gayatri Spivak's well-heeled shuttler between margins and center, and Gloria Anzaldúa's "new mestiza," possessed with the learned powers of reading, deciphering, deconstructing, maneuvering, and, above all, surviving in what Haraway calls the "webs of power" that surround her.[23]

Asian American actress, musician, poet, novelist, and playwright Jessica Hagedorn reads these "webs of power" very well. The place of contradictions, multiple languages, and monstrous, alien, and other outsider identities signify a kind of home base for her from within which she positions herself both as a writer and a performance artist:

> As a young actress, it was already very clear that I would be relegated to extremely limited roles in theater and film; because I was female and a person of color, these were two strikes against me. Fortunately, I was also a writer. Writing took precedence in my life because I knew writing was my salvation. It was a medium in which I had power and control; I could create my own world as I envisioned it, filled with so-called aliens, "others," exiles, mulattos, mestizos, outlaws, saints and criminals . . . whatever. It would be a world many others would recognize—rich in contradictions, complicated rhythms, and often infused with sensibilities, languages, and dialects other than English.[24]

Haraway reminds us that "releasing the play of writing is deadly serious," noting that "the poetry and stories of U.S. women of color are repeatedly about writing" and the "power to signify."[25]

One of the most critical sightings/sitings of the Asian woman as a cyborg occurs on the cover of Haraway's *Simians, Cyborgs, and Women: The Reinvention of Nature.*[26] The cover portrait, by artist Lynn Randolph, was created in 1989 in conversation with Haraway's landmark cyborg essay. The human model for Randolph's "Cyborg" is Grace Lee, who was a visiting student from China.[27] In this painting, the Asian woman hovers over a computer keyboard, her arms and hands merging with machine (fig. 29). Behind her, a living white tiger drapes its body around her in an intimate gesture that merges the human with the animal in its embrace. Their forearms are skeletal, and the borders of skin and bone are fully revealed and are virtually indistinguishable. Randolph's cyborg sits before a desert

Lynn Randolph's "Cyborg" sitting at her workstation.
(Used by permission of Lynn Randolph.)

landscape of pyramids bordered by a range of blue mountains, behind her is a map of galaxies, or possible worlds. She is a creature conjured from the artist's imaginary—her body literally plugged into a global, universal circuit board.

Haraway's sighting/siting of the Asian woman of color as cyborg is both problematic in its gesture toward what she calls "real life cyborgs"—the Asian women whose bodies are centrally positioned in the microelectronic global assembly line—as well as highly suggestive for its daring glimpse into the imagined promise of a subjectivity that is both utopian, multiple, and hybridized. To Haraway's credit, in a 1991 interview she reconsiders the manner in which she had formerly, and all too easily, positioned the Asian female factory worker as a type of cyborg embodiment; in addition, Haraway notes that if she were to actually rewrite the "Cyborg Manifesto" she would, in fact, "be much more careful about describing who counts as a 'we,'" in the rhetorical statement, "We are all cyborgs."[28] I would like to caution, too, that any gesture positing the body of the Asian woman as a type of cyborg embodiment must also interrogate her material and representational location and integration in the historical and politically specific context of what Laura Hyun Yi Kang identifies as the machinery of global capital accumulation and assembly-line production.[29] For the purposes of my discussion, I posit the figure of the Asian female cyborg in order to challenge an oppressive history of visual representation of Asian Americans.

In the search for imaginary incarnations of powerful Asian female bodies in contemporary American cultural representations, I move from Lynn Randolph's cyborg to the figure of Japanese supercop Kiddy Phenil, conjured from the creative imaginary of Kia Asamiya's science fiction comic, *Silent Mobius*.[30] In this Japanese *manga* series—set in futurist Tokyo A.D. 2026—the all-female "Astral Military Police" squad patrols the borders of the visible as well as the invisible in their hunt for supernatural entities that threaten the well-being of the city. They are among the elite few who possess the technological surveillance tools and the psychic abilities to access both the seen and unseen worlds. Kiddy Phenil is a "megadyne combat model" *hapa* cyborg woman warrior who tests the limits of her newly

Kiddy Phenil–*hapa* cyborg patroller of visible and invisible worlds. *(Used by permission of Kia Asamiya/Studio Tron.)*

refashioned body in this series. She is made monstrous through a fusion of machine technology and Anglo-Japanese anatomy.

> This is my body . . . seventy percent of my body is bionic, covered with synthetic flesh. Three years ago, after being cut to

pieces, I was barely saved by a cyber-graft operation. . . . [The] parts for my combat graft were developed from megadyne technology. In order to kill a megadyne, I became one. Eventually, I started to hate this body. I wasn't feminine anymore. I was a superhuman—thing. I hated this body even though I wanted it.[31]

Her body fascinates in its physical hybridity and catches the reader's eye. In addition to her green hair, dark brown skin, and eyes that appear to shift from blue to brown in every other cartoon frame, she has the typical fine-boned, highly angled European face of so many Japanese cartoon creations. The narrative of the series tracks her ambivalent relationship to her own body's technology and superhuman abilities as she learns to understand its limits, its gendered feel and look, its tools, and its special power to intuit and survey unseen forces.

As cultural critic Jennifer Gonzales has observed, Kiddy is "typical of contemporary (mostly male-produced) cyborg fantasies: a powerful, yet vulnerable, combination of sex toy and techno-sophisticate," who is also an "'exotic' vindictive cyborg who passes—as simply human."[32] As she peels her "chocolate" brown skin back to reveal her mechanical body parts, Kiddy is "all about the seduction of the strip tease, the revelation of the truth, of her internal coherence; which, ultimately, is produced by the super-technicians of her time."[33] Gonzales reminds us that "her real identity lies beneath the camouflage of her dark skin—rather than on the surface."[34]

If Lisa Foo is destroyed by the violence of technological intervention, then Kiddy Phenil's cyborg body is born out of the violence of the same. Unlike Foo, who is no match for the unseen forces she must encounter in "Press Enter," Kiddy is customized for both battle and survival. She is also masterfully proficient in the reading and deciphering of systems of knowledge even while continuously threatened with destruction in the comic narrative. If Kiddy Phenil has a fictive kinship with any other powerful female figure in Japanese American representation, it is with that other, older fictional creation from the American wartime imaginary, Tokyo Rose—who, as I have argued earlier in this book, has been represented as monstrous, oppositional, and even panoptical in her uncanny ability to survey the entire Pacific Rim at a glance. Like Kiddy Phenil, Tokyo Rose also functions as an imaginary patroller of the visible world—even as she inhabits a body that exists outside the confinement and rules of a fixed system of visual representation.

The Business of Japanese American Self-Representation in the Twenty-First Century

> Hi! I'm Asia Carrera—often referred to as "that Eurasian XXX pornstar who's always on Playboy and Spice" by pornofans, or the "World's Cutest Dictator" by cyberfans! I don't feature dance, and I avoid public appearances whenever possible, so the best way to get to know me is through my web site. I'm a 100% self-taught computer geek, and I take pride in running my whole site myself, from start to finish—because that's the way dictators do things!
>
> —Asia Carrera, www.asiacarrera.com

> The visual is inherently pornographic.
> —Frederic Jameson, *Signatures of the Visible*

In closing this book, I wish to return to the image of the Japanese American female body—her hands plugged into a computer keyboard in command of information technology and the tools of representation. In counterpoint to Lynn Randolph's painting of the Asian "Cyborg" and John Varley's computer geek/genius Lisa Foo, let me conclude with another Asian female figure sitting at the controls of her computer workstation—that of a Japanese American pornstar and self-trained "computer geek" who masquerades in the field of visual representation under the first-person pseudonym of "Asia."

Asia Carrera offers those of us who study Japanese American visual representation an intriguing case study for the postmodern practice of what Pratibha Parmar has called the "heterogeneous realities in constructing ourselves through the hybridity of cultural practices."[35] As the daughter of a German mother and a postwar

Asia Carrera—Japanese American *hapa*cyborg or "real life nerd of porn" at her computer workstation.
(Asia Carrera. Used by permission.)

immigrant Japanese father, Carrera is highly aware of the signifying power of her "exotic" Japanese American body and has firmly staked out her place in the specialized adult-entertainment genre of "Asian representation," where she has made an art form—and a profitable business—out of performing in video and on the World Wide Web.[36]

When asked about the ethnic origins of her stage name, she responds with a self-conscious narrative about race, hybridity, and practicality, "I picked Asia because I'm Asian, and I think it's a pretty name, and Carrera from actress Tia Carrere, but I spelled it differently to prevent lawsuits."[37] Well aware of how the surface politics of representation operate as illusion, Carrera is glib about the effects of her bodily transformation through extensive cosmetic surgery and the application of make-up tricks.[38] Her Website offers us a virtual behind-the-scenes tour as she transforms herself from a casual Californian in "baggy jeans" and "combat boots" to a glamorous "Asian" porn star:

> The truth is the porn star act I play in the movies is just that—an act. You'll never catch me wearing any of that pornoland wardrobe in real life—I don't even bother with makeup on my own time. I stick to baggy jeans, t-shirts, flannels, and my trusty combat boots, 'cause I'm sure as heck not going through 2–½ hours of curling, teasing and primping just to sit at my computer![39]

What is clear from touring her Website is that she is an expert in the art of her own self-construction, having logged hundreds of hours composing the parts (hair, make-up, costume, etc.) that comprise the whole of her screen persona; after all, "Asia Carrera" is a phantasmatic invention designed for visual pleasure, separate from who the actress/Webmaster is in "real life." Literary critic Traise Yamamoto has argued that "masking" is a resistant strategy enacted upon the Japanese American body through which subjectivity may be claimed.[40] "Asia Carrera" is an expert in such a strategy and, as a result, the businesswoman behind the porn star is ironically hidden from full view—her real name (and email) are never divulged. As one who makes her living by the full global display of her body, the woman behind the "Asia Carrera" mask is unreadable and slips tricksterlike outside of representation.

The literal master of her own domain, she calls herself the "little dictator" and invites us to look at her stunning creation. With over 20 million "hits" to her website, it is apparent that the public cannot resist her invitation. If critic Peggy Phelan is right that the politics of representation "is almost always on the side of the one who looks and almost never on the side of the one who is seen," then Asia

Carrera functions as an intriguing Japanese American exception to the rule.[41]

This book has been concerned with questions of how Japanese America has been imaged and imagined in twentieth-century American visual culture as well as how the Japanese American body has functioned as a racialized and gendered sight/site of representation. In an articulate summary of the trouble with the visual, Phelan cautions,

> As a representation of the real the image is always, partially, phantasmatic. In doubting the authenticity of the image, one questions as well the veracity of she who makes and describes it. To doubt the subject seized by the eye is to doubt the subjectivity of the seeing "I."[42]

She reminds us that in studying the visual "representation of the real," one needs to question the stability of both sides of the gaze. In my visual interrogation of the public spaces of the internment camps, the national museum exhibition hall, the culture of ruins at Manzanar, the Olympic ice-skating ring, and the open windows of the World Wide Web, I have tried to map such instability in the ideological field of Japanese American representation. In *Imaging Japanese America,* I have tried to engage the visual politics of the gaze both from the side of those who look and from the side of those who are seen. It is my hope that this book has opened up a space for conversation between both sides.

NOTES

NOTES TO THE INTRODUCTION

1 Renee Tajima-Pena, "No Mo Po Mo and Other Tales of the Road," in Darrell Y. Hamamoto and Sandra Liu, eds., *Countervisions: Asian American Film Criticism* (Philadelphia: Temple University Press, 2001), 253.

2 Peggy Phelan, *Unmarked: The Politics of Performance* (New York and London: Routledge, 1993), 26.

3 Tajima-Pena's guide through *My America* offers one of the most astute observations in the film for the politics of reading the Asian American body. In a close-up monologue, Chinese American actor Victor Wong waxes theoretical about how the racial politics of a white American gaze frames not only his own, but all Asian faces: "This face, even though it's Chinese American . . . you can say that he's a Korean, or he's a Vietnamese, or he looks Japanese. They couldn't tell the difference. But in this last century, there were three wars fought in the far east: the war in Japan, the war with Korea, and the war in Vietnam. I think most Americans think of it as one huge war with Asia and so they're used to thinking of this face even subconsciously as their enemy." At the end of his monologue, the camera fades to an extreme close-up of Asian names on the Vietnam Memorial wall—a gesture underscoring Tajima-Pena's insistence on laying claim to the rights of citizenship paid for by Asian Americans through a history of service and sacrifice to the nation.

4 See Lisa Lowe's famous essay, "Heterogeneity, Hybridity, Multiplicity: Asian American Differences" in *Immigrant Acts: On Asian American Cultural Politics* (Durham, NC: Duke University Press, 1996).

5 Dorinne Kondo, *About Face: Performing Race in Fashion and Theater* (New York: Routledge, 1997), 10.

6 Mitsuye Yamada, "Looking Out," in *Camp Notes and Other Poems* (Latham, NY: Kitchen Table Press, 1976), 39.

7 Yamada, "Mirror Mirror," in *Camp Notes and Other Poems*, 56.

8 This will form part of my discussion in the Epilogue, where I engage the September 1993 special "multicultural" issue of *Time* magazine on "The Changing Face of America."

9 The field of Asian American visual culture has recently begun to grow. Some of the most exciting work has been done by the following scholars: Gina Marchetti, *Romance and the Yellow Peril* (Berkeley and Los Angeles:

University of California Press, 1993); Darrell Y. Hamamoto, *Monitored Peril: Asian Americans and the Politics of TV Representation* (Minneapolis: University of Minnesota Press, 1994); Jun Xing, *Asian America through the Lens: History, Representations, and Identity* (Walnut Creek, CA: AltaMira Press, 1998); Peter Feng, *Identities in Motion: Asian American Film and Video* (Durham, NC: Duke University Press, 2002); Laura Hyun-Yi Kang, *Compositional Subjects: Enfiguring Asian/American Women* (Durham, NC: Duke University Press, 2002).

10 David Palumbo-Liu, *Asian/American: Historical Crossings of a Racial Frontier* (Stanford, CA: Stanford University Press, 1999), 6.

11 David Leiwei Li, *Imagining the Nation: Asian American Literature and Cultural Consent* (Stanford, CA: Stanford University Press, 1998), 1.

12 Ibid., 3.

13 Ibid., 3–4.

14 Roger Daniels, *Asian America: Chinese and Japanese in the United States since 1850* (Seattle: University of Washington Press, 1988), 210.

15 *The View from Within: Japanese American Art from the Internment Camps, 1942–1945* (Los Angeles: Japanese American National Museum, 1992).

16 In the immediate aftermath of September 11, 2001, there was a substantial body of visual renderings of the Statue of Liberty as an animated icon that was roused into a state of fury and maternal anger. In some of these Internet and print-media cartoons, she was seen carrying a baby and wielding an assault rifle as she prepared to step down from her pedestal, roll up her sleeves, and do the dirty work of defending her nation.

NOTES TO CHAPTER ONE

1 Ferris Takahashi, "Nisei! Nisei!" in *Speaking for Ourselves,* Lillian Faderman and Barbara Bradshaw, eds. (Atlanta: Scott Foresman, 1969). Cited in Elaine Kim's *Asian American Literature: An Introduction to the Writings and Their Social Context* (Philadelphia: Temple University Press, 1982), 72. Ferris Takahashi is a Caucasian writer married to a Japanese American. She has also published under the psuedonyms M. H. Constable and Mary Takahashi.

2 Daniel Okimoto, *American in Disguise* (New York: Walker/Weatherhill, 1971), 5.

3 Ibid., 5.

4 Kim, *Asian American Literature,* 81.

5 Monica Sone, *Nisei Daughter* (Seattle: University of Washington Press, 1979), 158–159. President Franklin Roosevelt's signing of Executive Order

9066 set in motion the process for the relocation and internment of some 120,000 Japanese Americans on the West Coast.

6 See my discussion in chapter 5 of the articles published by *Time* and *Life* magazines two weeks after the bombing of Pearl Harbor that explicitly attempt to map the differences in Chinese and Japanese faces for a white American audience.

7 Mary Oyama, "My Only Crime Is My Face," *Liberty,* August 14, 1943, 58. Also see "An American with a Japanese Face," *Christian Science Monitor,* May 22, 1943.

8 This response to American wartime images of the Japanese outside the relocation camps comes from Emily Medvec's introduction to *Adams's Born Free and Equal: An Exhibition of Ansel Adams Photographs: Fresno Metropolitan Museum of Art, History, and Science* (Washington, DC: Echolight, 1984), 8.

9 John L. DeWitt, "Final Recommendation of the Commanding General, Western Defense Command and Fourth Army, Submitted to the Secretary of War, February 14, 1942," in *Final Report: Japanese Evacuation from the West Coast, 1942* (Washington, DC: Government Printing Office, 1943): 34, 9. Emphasis mine.

10 Jan Zita Grover, "The Winner Names the Age," *AfterImage,* April 1988, 14.

11 John Armour and Peter Wright, eds., *Manzanar* (New York: Times Books, 1988), 38. It is now a matter of historic record that even those with as little as one-sixteenth Japanese blood were subjected to relocation and internment.

12 John W. Dower has produced what is perhaps the most compelling work thus far on U.S. wartime racism directed at the Japanese. See *War without Mercy: Race and Power in the Pacific* (New York: Pantheon Books, 1986). Dower's discussion of the subhuman representation of the Japanese as animals, reptiles, and insects in the wartime imaginary of the U.S. speaks powerfully to the relevance of treatment of the Japanese Americans.

13 John C. Welchman, "Turning Japanese (In)," *Artforum* 27 (April 1989): 152.

14 Marita Sturken, "Absent Images of Memory: Remembering and Reenacting the Japanese Internment," *Positions* 5:3 (1997): 691.

15 According to Welchman, there are some 13,000 War Relocation Authority photographs in addition to those taken by Farm Security Administration, Fourth U.S. Army, and Western Defense Command. These photographs form a visual public record, but until their recent digitizing on the University of California, Berkeley, Internet library, they have been out of public sight.

16 For a fascinating compilation of internee home movies shot in the camps,

see Karen L. Ishizuka and Robert Nakamura's video, *Something Strong Within* (1995).

17 Ansel Adams, *Born Free and Equal: Photographs of the Loyal Japanese-Americans at Manzanar Relocation Center, Inyo County, California* (New York: U.S. Camera, 1944).

18 Ralph Palmer Merritt was the second director of Manzanar War Relocation Center. Merritt, who grew up in Inyo County, was generally acknowledged to be a fair and liberal-minded administrator. Adams dedicates the book to him.

19 Armor and Wright, from introductory essay, "The Photographers of Manzanar," in *Manzaanr*.

20 It should be noted that both the text and photos of *Born Free and Equal* were also approved by Manzanar camp director Ralph P. Merritt.

21 See Dorinne K. Kondo's excellent work on Asian American representation, *About Face: Performing Race in Fashion and Theatre* (New York: Routledge, 1997).

22 Grover, "Winner Names the Age," 15.

23 The "No No Boys" were those young Japanese American men who answered "no" to questions 27 and 28 on the "loyalty oaths" which internees over the age of seventeen were forced to sign. These questions asked internees to forswear allegiance to Japan and to agree to defend the United States against its enemies.

24 See Carl Mydan's compelling photo-essay, "Tule Lake," *Life*, March 20, 1944, 25–35.

25 Adams, *Born Free and Equal*, 102.

26 The only image of Japanese American schoolboys Adams includes in *Born Free and Equal* features two high school students who are singing in the front row of the camp choir. With their hands folded quietly in their laps, the two teenagers present a visual study in obedient body language and offer a dramatic contrast to the disobedient bodies of young men in Carl Mydans's *Life* magazine photographs at Tule Lake. Adams also includes one photograph of the Japanese American combat team in action. It is the only photograph of Japanese Americans taken outside of Manzanar. Included in *Born Free and Equal*, the photograph visually reinforces the patriotic wartime discourse of the loyal Japanese American body.

27 Karin Becker Ohrn, *Dorothea Lange and the Documentary Tradition* (Baton Rouge: Louisiana State University Press, 1980), 140.

28 Kim, *Asian American Literature*, 87.

29 Ibid., 81.

30 Ibid., 129.

31 Ibid.

32 The term "American in Disguise" comes from Daniel Okimoto's autobiography, *American in Disguise* (New York: Walker/Weatherhill, 1971), 24.

33 Gloria Anzaldúa, *Borderlands/La Frontera: The New Mestiza* (San Francisco: Aunt Lute Book, 1991), 63.

34 Kim, *Asian American Literature*, 134.

35 Adams, *Born Free and Equal*, 23.

36 Grover, "Winner Names the Age," 15.

37 Adams, *Born Free and Equal*, 145.

38 This photograph is not included in the original pages of *Born Free and Equal*, rather it is included in Armor and Wright's *Manzanar*. I include it in my discussion because it is one of the most compelling domestic portraits of the internees' living quarters in Adams's collection.

39 Many Japanese American couples hastily married before relocation in order to avoid being separated in the camps. I am assuming that Mr. and Mrs. Dennis Shimuzu are one such newlywed couple.

40 Jeanne Wakatsuki Houston, *Farewell to Manzanar* (Boston: Houghton Mifflin, 1973), 73–74.

41 Adams, *Born Free and Equal*, 24.

42 Ibid., 36, 33.

43 This idea that the majesty of the Sierra Nevadas was good for the internees echoes a sad logic heard elsewhere where the camp experience has been read as positive and character building and not as a shameful or oppressive incident in U.S. history. According to Elaine Kim, many of the autobiographical works dealing with the internment have been praised by critics for what they note is an apparent lack of bitterness on the part of the internees.

44 Questions number 27 and 28 on the Loyalty Oath administered in the camps were the crucial ones in determining whether or not internees would be granted clearance for leave from the camps or else be grouped as "disloyal" subjects. For the issei (who were barred from obtaining U.S. citizenship) answering *yes* to question 28 proved problematic in that it theoretically would leave them in a precarious position as stateless subjects.

45 In Canada, the Japanese and Japanese Canadians were not only subject to internment during the war, but afterwards were officially barred from moving back to the west coast of British Columbia. Removal policies in Canada were in general much harsher than in the United States. Joy Kogawa's novel *Obasan* is one of the few works to document the Japanese Canadian internment experience in detail.

46 Abdul R. JanMohamed and David Lloyd, "Introduction: Minority

Discourse—What Is to Be Done?" *Cultural Critique* 7 (Fall 1987): 10. This volume has been reprinted in book form as *The Nature and Context of Minority Discourse* (New York: Oxford University Press, 1990).

47 Adams, *Born Free and Equal*, 35.

48 Grover, "Winner Names the Age," 16.

49 Armor and Wright's *Manzanar* appears to have been published to coincide with the successful 1988 Civil Liberties Act that supported reparations and a national apology to surviving internees.

50 I was unaware that so many portraits of Japanese American schoolgirls were included in *Born Free and Equal* until I looked at the original publication. In Adams's publication, the photographs are blown up to full-page size, giving them equal status to his narrative text.

51 Adams, *Born Free and Equal*, 9.

52 Ibid., 9.

53 Ibid.

54 In some sense, the camps are like the American Indian boarding schools of the early twentieth century where young native boys and girls were disciplined and trained as industrious citizens of the nation.

55 Adams, *Born Free and Equal*, 25.

56 Ibid., 13.

57 Ibid., 80, 84.

58 See Graham Howe, Patrick Nagatani, and Scott Rankin, eds., *Two Views of Manzanar: An Exhibition of Photographs by Ansel Adams/Toyo Miyatake* (Los Angeles: Frederick S. Wight Art Gallery, University of California, Los Angeles, 1978). Commentators such as Howe et al. have noted with irony the stylistic similarity and clarity in Adams's close-up photographs of the surface of the human face and the surface face of the land.

59 The photograph of Benji Iguchi is reprinted in the pages of Armor and Wright's *Manzanar* and does not appear in the original pages of *Born Free and Equal*.

60 Howe et al., *Two Views*, 11.

61 Ohrn, *Dorothea Lange and the Documentary Tradition*, 122.

62 Ibid., 148.

63 The epigram by Dorothea Lange is cited by Roger Daniels in "Dorothea Lange and the War Relocation Authority: Photographing the Japanese Americans," in *Dorothea Lange: A Visual Life*, Elizabeth Partridge, ed. (Washington, DC, and London: Smithsonian Institution Press, 1994), 46. According to Daniels, Lange remained on the War Relocation Authority staff until September 1943, but most of her photographs of the Japanese American internees were taken between March and September 1942.

64 See Maisie and Richard Conrat's foreword in *Executive Order 9066* (Los Angeles: University of California, Los Angeles, Asian American Studies Center, 1972).

65 Maisie and Richard Conrat write that their involvement with *Executive Order 9066* began as early as 1965 when the latter worked as an assistant to Dorothea Lange. With Lange's support, the California Historical Society officially sponsored the exhibit in 1972—a decade ahead of the visibility that the redress and reparation movement would bring to the internment experience. In 1992, the University of California's Asian American Studies Center republished the original catalog for *Executive Order 9066* to coincide with a year-long series of conferences, exhibits, and special performances commemorating the fifty-year anniversary of the signing of Executive Order 9066.

66 Ohrn, *Dorothea Lange*, 22. I believe that the fascination with Lange's photographs during the 1970s and early 1980s had much to do with her moving depictions of the evacuation process just when the Japanese American redress and reparation movement was gaining momentum. Given the movement's political agenda of casting the internment as an unnecessary historical tragedy, Ansel Adams's aestheticized portraits of internees at Manzanar were visually inappropriate as historical evidence.

67 Karen Tsujimoto, *Dorothea Lange: Archive of an Artist* (Oakland: Oakland Museum of California, 1995).

68 Linda A. Morris, "A Woman of Our Generation," in Partridge, *Dorothea Lange*, 26.

69 Ohrn, "What You See Is What You Get," *Journalism History* 4:1 (Spring 1977): 21.

70 Milton Meltzer, *Dorothea Lange: A Photographer's Life* (New York: Farrar, Straus and Giroux, 1978), 241.

71 Ohrn, "What You See is What You Get," 22.

72 Ibid., 21.

73 Grover, "Winner Names the Age," 17.

74 Roger Daniels also notes that Clem Albers and Russell Lee were also sensitive WRA photographers.

75 Ohrn, *Dorothea Lange*, 124.

76 See Dorothea Lange and Paul Taylor's *An American Exodus: A Record of Human Erosion* (New York: Reynal and Hitchcock, 1939), and Erskine Caldwell and Margaret Bourke-White's *You Have Seen Their Faces* (New York: Modern Age Books, 1937).

77 I have yet to look at Lange's complete 1930s Farm Security Administration archive of photographs in order to validate my claim. However, from what

work I have seen both by her and other FSA photographers there does indeed seem to be an absence or an invisibility of Japanese and Japanese American farmers who lived and worked up and down the West Coast from the turn of the century up until their internment.

78 I borrow this expression from Erskine Caldwell, who in a preface to a later edition of *You Have Seen Their Faces* reflects: "The tortured face of poverty was not an appealing sight in the Deep South in the 1930s when [the book] was first published . . . [and now] forty years later in the 1970s, whether in full view or in profile, the shriveled visage has not been improved by the passing of time."

79 In the rush to evacuate, many farmers left fields unharvested, others in their frustration mowed under perfectly good fields abundant with crops ready for harvest. Many of Lange's photographs of farmers in the fields bear a resemblance to Ansel Adams's portraits at Manzanar depicting the close relationship of the Japanese American to the land.

80 This photograph appears cropped as a portrait of the unsmiling schoolgirl in Partridge's *Dorothea Lange: A Visual Life*; Dorothea Lange's *Dorothea Lange* (New York: Museum of Modern Art, 1966); Keith F. Davis's *The Photographs of Dorothea Lange* (Kansas City, MO: Hallmark Cards in Association with H. N. Abrams, New York, 1995); and Dorothea Lange's *Dorothea Lange: Photographs of a Lifetime* (Millerton, NY: Aperture, 1982). The cropped photograph has also been blown up to larger than life dimensions and is installed in the Smithsonian Institution's American History Museum's permanent exhibition on the internment, "A More Perfect Union." One wonders if the close-up cropping is meant to invoke a visual resemblance to Ansel Adams's close-up portraits of Japanese American schoolgirls.

81 Mark Constantine and Annie Nakai, "Executive Order 9066," *San Francisco Examiner,* February 16, 1992.

82 Mitsuye Yamada, "The Evacuation," in *Camp Notes* (New Brunswick, NJ: Rutgers University Press, 1992), 13.

83 My students routinely note when looking through the visual archives of these photographs that there is a preponderance of images of happy Japanese American travelers boarding trains and buses on their way to the assembly centers.

84 Carl Mydans's 1942 photo-essay for *Life* magazine certainly exemplifies this mode of benevolent Japanese American representation, where smiling volunteers travel—under armed military escort—to prepare what looks more like a mountain summer camp rather than a concentration camp for

fellow internees. See Mydans's "Coast Japs Are Interned in Mountain Camp," *Life*, April 6, 1942, 15–19.

85 The War Relocation Authority films on the internment experience are benevolent visual exercises in rendering how harmless the camps were and argue for their existence out of military necessity. They are narrated by the WRA's first director, Milton S. Eisenhower.

86 Paul S. Taylor, *An American Exodus: A Record of Human Erosion* (New York: Reynal and Hitchcock, 1939).

87 Lange's images of the internees at the converted racetrack known as Tanforan Assembly Center were marked "impounded" by WRA officials presumably for their clear depiction of the crude conditions of the camp's early days.

88 One of the few landscape portraits Lange took of Manzanar depicts the Sierra Nevadas in a majestic form reminiscent of Adams, but what steals one's attention is the presence, beneath a flapping American flag, of two running bodies ducking for cover from what is a very strong and routine dust storm.

89 Sally Stein, "Peculiar Grace: Dorothea Lange and the Testimony of the Body," in Partridge, *Dorothea Lange*, 81.

90 Ibid., 81.

91 Armour and Wright, *Manzanar*, 4.

92 In many ways, I believe that the photographs of children, both those tagged for evacuation as well as those in the camps, remain the most moving images of the internment experience.

93 Sylvia E. Danovitch, "The Past Recaptured? The Photographic Record of the Internment of Japanese-Americans," *Prologue: The Journal of the National Archives* 12, no. 2 (Summer 1980): 98–99. She has an excellent discussion of the small, visual gestures of resistance in the WRA evacuation photographs and is the first to identify the World War I veteran who is wearing his uniform for evacuation. Danovitch also points out a photograph of an issei woman who appears to have tucked her numbered identity tag inside of her coat as another possible gesture of resistance to the physical humiliation surrounding the evacuation process.

94 Stein, "Peculiar Grace," 84.

95 Ohrn, *Dorothea Lange*, 2.

96 Ibid., 2–3.

97 Ibid., 3.

98 This quote was originally taken from Dorothea Lange's "The Making of a Documentary Photographer," an oral history conducted in 1960–61 by

Suzanne Riess for the Regional Oral History Office, University of California, Berkeley, 1968, 27. It is cited in Karen Tsujimoto, *Dorothea Lange: Archive of an Artist* (Oakland: Oakland Museum of California, 1995), 5.

99 Apparently Chiura Obata, one of the most brilliant interned artists, has also noted in his diary a similar sense of irritation with Lange's intrusive photography during the evacuation. He recalls her ordering vehicles to be moved in order to accommodate her shots. His diary is now in the special collections archive at the Smithsonian Institution's American History Museum.

100 John Okada is perhaps the first Japanese American writer to explore the effects of internment on nisei masculinity in *No No Boy, a Novel* (Tokyo and Rutland, VT: C. E. Tuttle, 1957).

101 David Mura, *Where the Body Meets Memory: An Odyssey of Race, Sexuality, and Identity* (New York: Doubleday, 1996), 19.

102 Ibid., 246.

103 Constantine and Nakai, "Executive Order 9066."

104 See Estelle Peck Ishigo's autobiography, *Lone Heart Mountain* (Los Angeles: Communicart, 1972, 1989), as well as Karl Yoneda's autobiography recounting his and his wife Elaine's experiences as an interracial couple under internment and his postinternment years as a radical left-wing activist in the United States, *Ganbatte: Sixty Years of Struggle as a Kibei Worker* (Los Angeles: Resource Development and Publication, Asian American Studies Center, University of California, Los Angeles, 1983).

105 Cynthia Takano, "Manzanar: Life in an Internment Camp through a Photographer's Eyes," *Rice,* August 1987, 61.

106 I take this information from Howe et al., *Two Views.*

107 Ibid., 10.

108 Ibid.

109 Ibid., 11. Emphasis is mine.

110 One of the difficulties of writing about Miyatake's photo-documentary of life in the camps is the scarcity of published materials in English dealing with his work.

111 This quote is taken from the press release for the exhibit, "Picturing History: Manzanar" at the Ansel Adams Center for Photography, San Francisco, California, April 28–October 18, 1998. Fidel Daniell also discusses Toyo Miyatake as an "'illegal' [photographer] of daily life and ceremonial occasions" in "A Rewriting of History," *Artweek* 17 (May 1986): 10.

112 These photographs are cataloged in Howe et al., *Two Views,* as well as in Atsufumi Miyatake, Taisuke Fujishima, and Eiko Hosoe, *Toyo Miyatake: Behind the Camera* (Tokyo: Bungei Shunju, 1984).

113 The one exception to this rule is Richard Chalfen's excellent study of Japanese American family photo albums, *Turning Leaves: The Photograph Collections of Two Japanese American Families* (Albuquerque: University of New Mexico Press, 1991).

114 John C. Welchman, "Turning Japanese (In)," *Artforum* 27 (April 1989): 155.

115 Ibid., 155.

116 Michael Several, "Photographic Memories," *Public Art Review,* Spring/Summer 1996, 24.

117 This is the only photograph by Adams that is included in Maisie and Richard Conrat's 1972 collection, *Executive Order 9066*.

118 My students have noted the irony in the upper right side of the photograph of the name, "White & Co." Director Alan Parker has also re-created this photograph as a stage set in his feature film, *Come See the Paradise* (1990).

119 I will discuss this exhibit more fully in chapter 4.

120 See Danovitch, "The Past Reaptured?"

121 Ibid., 98, 92.

122 Takano, "Manzanar," 61.

123 Several, "Photographic Memories," 24.

124 Ibid.

125 Archie Miyatake's comment is quoted in Cynthia Takano's "Manzanar," 61.

126 Ron Tanaka was born in Poston War Relocation Center in 1944. His poem, "Appendix to Executive Order 9066," appears in *Ayumi: A Japanese American Anthology,* Janice Mirikitani, et al., eds. (San Francisco: Japanese American Anthology Committee, 1980).

127 What does it mean, for instance, that in spite of all the literature produced by Japanese American writers, the only time the Japanese American internment history has made it onto the "best seller" book list has been when romance writer Danielle Steele has undertaken internment as a theme in her novel, *Silent Honor* (1996), or when David Guterson includes the experience in his novel, *Snow Falling on Cedars* (1994).

128 Several, "Photographic Memories," 22.

129 Also located on this "street of memory" is the Japanese American National Museum. It was originally housed alongside the Buddhist temple, expanded in 1998 to its new 4,000-square-foot home, and has become a major force as a repository of local and national cultural history. Indeed, the museum has become a cutting-edge model for what multicultural museums in the new millennium can accomplish.

130 See *The View from Within: Japanese American Art from the Internment*

Camps, 1942–1945 (Los Angeles: Japanese American National Museum, 1992).

NOTES TO CHAPTER TWO

1 Both Hisako Hibi and Charles Mikami are quoted from their interviews in Deborah Gesensway and Mindy Roseman, *Beyond Words: Images from America's Concentration Camps* (Ithaca, NY: Cornell University Press, 1987), 21.

2 *The View from Within* was jointly authored by the Japanese American National Museum, the UCLA Wight Art Gallery, and the UCLA Asian American Studies Center. See *The View from Within: Japanese American Art from the Internment Camps, 1942–1945* (Los Angeles: UCLA Office of Instructional Development, 1993). Other notable published collections of Asian American art include Mayumi Tsutakawa's *They Painted from Their Hearts: Pioneer Asian American Artists* (Seattle: Wing Luke Asian Museum, University of Washington Press, 1994). This book serves as an excellent resource for Pacific Northwest artists and includes the work of several Japanese Americans not included elsewhere. Also see Allen H. Eaton's *Beauty behind Barbed Wire: The Arts of the Japanese in Our War Relocation Camps* (New York: Harper and Bros., 1952) for its unique cataloguing of internment camp arts and crafts.

3 Mine Okubo,. *Citizen 13660* (Seattle: University of Washington Press, 1983).

4 Gesensway and Roseman, *Beyond Words*, 9.

5 Ibid.

6 See Yuji Ichioka's *Views from Within: The Japanese American Evacuation and Resettlement Study* (Los Angeles: Resource Development and Publication, Asian American Studies Center, University of California, Los Angeles, 1989) and Peter Suzuki's "Anthropologists in the Wartime Camps for Japanese Americans: A Documentary Study," *Dialectical Anthropology* 6 (1981): 23–60, which was also reprinted in *The Big Aiiieeeee! An Anthology of Chinese American and Japanese American Literature,* Jeffery Paul Chan, Frank Chin, Lawson Fusao Inada, and Shawn Wong, eds. (New York: Meridian, 1991). Also see Violet Kazue Matsuda de Cristoforo's self-published affidavit, "A Victim of the Japanese Evacuation and Resettlement Study (JERS)," as reprinted in *The Big Aiiieee!*

7 Suzuki, from his statement before the Commission on Wartime Relocation and Internment of Civilians in 1981 in *The Big Aiiieeeee!* 369.

8 Chin, *The Big Aiiieeee!* 369–370.

9 See Daniels's editorial note to Asael T. Hansen's "My Two Years at Heart Mountain: The Difficult Role of an Applied Anthropologist," in *Japanese Americans: From Relocation to Redress*, Roger Daniels, Sandra C. Taylor, and Harry H. L. Kitano, eds. (Seattle: University of Washington Press, 1986), 33.

10 Gesensway and Roseman, *Beyond Words*, 12.

11 See bell hooks, "Culture to Culture: Ethnography and Cultural Studies as Critical Intervention," in *Yearning: Race, Gender, and Cultural Politics* (Boston: South End Press, 1990), 125.

12 Toni Morrison, "The Site of Memory," in *Inventing the Truth: The Art and Craft of Memoir*, William Zinsser, ed. (Boston: Houghton Mifflin, 1987), 110–111.

13 bell hooks, "Feminist Scholarship: Ethical Issues," in *Talking Back: Thinking Feminist, Thinking Black* (Boston: South End Press, 1989), 42–43.

14 Mine Okubo, from an interview with Betty La Duke in *The Forbidden Stitch: An Asian American Women's Anthology*, Shirley Geok-lin Lim, Mayumi Tsutakawa, Margarita Donnelly, eds. (Corvallis, OR: Calyx Books, 1989), 190. The quote by Okubo in the epigram is from Gesensway and Roseman, *Beyond Words*, 66.

15 Elaine Kim, *Asian American Literature: An Introduction to the Writings and Their Social Context* (Philadelphia: Temple University Press, 1982).

16 Art Spiegelman's *Maus: A Survivor's Tale* (New York: Pantheon Book, 1986) is of course a much darker work exploring as it does the history and experience of the Jewish death camps in Europe during World War II.

17 Two other striking visual autobiographies of the internment camp experience are Jack Matsuoka's *Camp II, Block 211: Daily Life in an Internment Camp* (San Francisco: Japan Publications, 1974), and Estelle Peck Ishigo's *Mountain Lone Heart Mountain* (Los Angeles: Communicart, 1972). For the best-known camp autobiographies, see Monica Sone, *Nisei Daughter* (Seattle: University of Washington Press, 1979 [1953]), Jeanne Wakatsuki Houston, *Farewell to Manzanar* (New York: Bantam Books, 1973); and Yoshiko Uchida, *Desert Exile: The Uprooting of a Japanese American Family* (Seattle: University of Washington Press, 1982).

18 Kristine C. Kuramitsu, "Internment and Identity in Japanese American Art," *American Quarterly* 47, no. 4 (December 1995): 626.

19 Okubo once told me in conversation that she still receives letters from around the world from fans of the book, particularly from Asia and former Eastern bloc countries.

20 Because it straddles both literary as well as visual representations, I believe that *Citizen 13660* sadly falls between the cracks of most discussions about

Asian American autobiographical writing. Some of the most helpful published discussions of Okubo's work appear in Betty La Duke, *Women Artists: Multi-Cultural Visions* (Trenton, NJ: Red Sea Press, 1992); Shirley Sun, *Mine Okubo: An American Experience* (Oakland, CA: Oakland Museum, 1972); and Kuramitsu, "Internment and Identity in Japanese American Art," 619–658. Also see the videotaped interview with Okubo in Betty La Duke's "Persistent Women Artists: Pablita Velarde, Mine Okubo, Lois Mailou Jones" (Ashland, OR: Southern Oregon State College Productions, Distributed by Reading and O'Reilly, Inc., 1996).

21 Pamela Stennes Wright, "Hitting a Straight Lick with a Crooked Stick": Strategies of Negotiation in Women's Autobiographies from the U.S. 1940s: Zora Neale Hurston, Mine Okubo, and Amelia Grothe," Ph.D. diss., University of California, San Diego, 1993, 139.

22 Ibid.

23 Although it is beyond the scope of this chapter to include discussion of the impact and importance of Mine Okubo's lifework as a major Asian American artist of the twentieth century, it should be noted that she produced an impressive and internationally renowned body of work in the past sixty years. Her work continues to be exhibited around the country and has been honored at such sites as the Smithsonian Institution, the National Women's Gallery, and the Japanese American National Museum. The best published collection of her work remains the Oakland Museum's Shriley Sun's exhibit catalog, *Mine Okubo*. Sun's commentary on Okubo's work in the catalog is outstanding and the most comprehensive to date on the broad range of the artist's work.

24 In addition to the publication of sketches in *Citizen 13660*, Okubo also completed hundreds of charcoal, gouache, and watercolor paintings which make up a larger body of artwork from her days in camp.

25 From the "Preface" to the 1983 edition of *Citizen 13660*.

26 Gesensway and Roseman, *Beyond Words*, 71.

27 bell hooks, *Feminist Theory from Margin to Center* (Boston: South End Press, 1984), 3.

28 Caren Kaplan, "Deterritorializations: The Rewriting of Home and Exile in Western Feminist Discourse," in *Cultural Critique* 6 (Spring 1987): 181.

29 I have had students at Wellesley College comment to me that they initially assumed Mine Okubo was a man, given the great freedom of movement she demonstrates in the camp sketches and her display of independence and resistance.

30 Gloria Anzaldúa, *Borderlands/La Frontera: The New Mestiza* (San Francisco: Aunt Lute Books, 1991), 38.

31 Ibid., 38–39.

32 Okubo, *Citizen 13660*, 12.

33 W. E. B. Du Bois is the first to articulate this trope of "double consciousness" in *The Souls of Black Folk: Essays and Sketches* (Chicago: A. G. McClurg, 1903). Both Elaine Kim and Gloria Anzaldúa rework this trope as the double vision of Asian American writers and the mestiza's borderlands consciousness.

34 Kim, *Asian American Literature*, 88.

35 Okubo, in La Duke, *Women Artists*, 188.

36 Sun, *Mine Okubo*, 22.

37 Ibid., 23. Note: These charcoal drawings are included in *Mine Okubo: An American Experience*.

38 Ibid., 23.

39 Okubo, *Citizen 13660*, 32.

40 Gesensway and Roseman, *Beyond Words*, 71.

41 Ibid., 69.

42 Dorrine Kondo, "Dissolution and Reconstruction of Self: Implications for Anthropological Epistemology," *Cultural Anthropology* 1 (1986): 74–88.

43 Okubo, *Citizen 13660*, 60.

44 Okubo, in Gesensway and Roseman, *Beyond Words*, 69. Yoshiko Uchida also remembers Okubo as an eccentric artist who lived "a few stalls down" from their family at Tanforan and placed a "Quarantined—Do Not Enter" sign on her door, which ironically served to attract rather than repel unwanted attention; in *Desert Exile: The Uprooting of a Japanese-American Family* (Seattle: University of Washington Press, 1982), 96.

45 Okubo, *Citizen 13660*, 108.

46 Many of the artists interviewed in *Beyond Words* attest to this fact.

47 Okubo, *Citizen 13660*, 75.

48 Ibid.

49 Traise Yamamoto, *Masking Selves, Making Subjects: Japanese American Women, Identity, and the Body* (Berkeley and Los Angeles: University of California Press, 1999), 103.

50 Mine Okubo, from the 1983 Preface to *Citizen 13660*.

51 Kamala Visweswaran, "Defining Feminist Ethnography," *Inscriptions* 3 and 4 (1988): 29.

52 Yamamoto, *Masking Selves*, 210.

53 Kuramitsu, "Internment and Identity," 640.

54 For a discussion of the intergenerational fallout of the internment experience in the work of other contemporary Japanese American installation artists, see Karin Higa's and Traise Yamamoto's essays in *Finding Family*

Stories: Heeyeon Chang, Michael Cho, Glenn Kaino, Soo Jin Kim, Karen Kimura, Yong Soon Min, Linda Nishio, Julie Sim-Edwards: September 15, 1995–January 9, 1996 (Los Angeles: Japanese American National Museum, 1995).

NOTES TO CHAPTER THREE

1 See Roger Daniels, *Asian America: Chinese and Japanese in the United States since 1850* (Seattle: University of Washington Press, 1988), 210, and Traise Yamamoto, *Masking Selves, Making Subjects: Japanese American Women, Identity, and the Body* (Berkeley and Los Angeles: University of California Press, 1999), 210.

2 Mine Okubo, from an interview with Betty La Duke in *The Forbidden Stitch: An Asian American Women's Anthology*, Shirley Geok-lin Lim, Mayumi Tsutakawa, Margarita Donnelly, eds. (Corvallis, OR: Calyx Books, 1989), 190.

3 Glen Masato Mimura, "Antidote for Collective Amnesia? Rea Tajiri's Germinal Image," in *Countervisions: Asian American Film Criticism*, Darrell Y. Hamamoto and Sandra Liu, eds. (Philadelphia: Temple University Press, 2000), 150.

4 Kent A. Ono, "Re/membering Spectators: Meditations on Japanese American Cinema," in Darrell Y. Hamamoto and Sandra Liu, eds., *Countervisions: Asian American Film Criticism* (Philadelphia: Temple University Press, 2000), 130.

5 Marita Sturken, "Absent Images of Memory: Remembering and Reenacting the Japanese American Internment," *Positions* 5:3 (1997): 687–707. Filmmaker Rea Tajiri also cleverly reworks Tracy's search for the missing Japanese American man in *Bad Day at Black Rock* as an extended metaphor for her own family's missing history of the camps in her documentary, *History and Memory* (1991).

6 I am indebted to Darrel Hamamoto, who brought this film to my attention.

7 See John W. Dower, *War without Mercy: Race and Power in the Pacific War* (New York: Pantheon Books, 1986).

8 Chester Tanaka's pictorial history of the 442nd is particularly compelling as a rare visual study in Japanese American masculinity. See *Go for Broke: A Pictorial History of the Japanese American 100th Infantry Battalion and the 442nd Regimental Combat Team* (Richmond, CA: Go for Broke, 1982).

9 I find it interesting that in Deborah Gee's *Slaying the Dragon* (1988), John Korty, the director of *Farewell to Manzanar* (1976), mentions that this film

was almost remade from the point of view of a white character who tells the story of what happened to the Japanese Americans during World War II. Korty points out, with irony, how this concept was initially touted by "one of the highest-ranking African American producers" in Hollywood, who was afraid that unless they restructured the narrative no one would be able to relate to the story.

10 Philip Kan Gotanda, "The Wash," in *Between Worlds: Contemporary Asian-American Plays,* Misha Berson, ed. (New York: Theatre Communications Group, 1990), 30.

11 Misuye Yamada, "Thirty Years Under," in *Camp Notes and Other Poems* (Latham, NY: Kitchen Table, Women of Color Press, 1976), 32.

12 Jeanne Wakatsuki Houston, public lecture, University of California, Santa Cruz, January 28, 1993.

13 Darrell Y. Hamamoto, *Monitored Peril: Asian Americans and the Politics of TV: The Politics of Representation* (Minneapolis: University of Minnesota Press, 1994), 66.

14 Ibid., 66.

15 The film version of *Farewell to Manzanar* has periodically shown up on the Disney channel on cable television.

16 Thanks to the collective efforts of California's lieutenant governor, Cruz Bustamante, Universal Studios, the Civil Liberties Public Education Project of the California State Library, and members of the Japanese American community, Universal Studios has produced and released video copies of the film for every public school and library in the state of California. In addition, publisher McDougal-Littell has agreed to provide 8,500 copies of Houston's book and a teaching guide that will be included with the video.

17 Mimura, "Antidote for Collective Amnesia?" 153.

18 Janice Tanaka's outstanding documentary, *Who's Going to Pay for These Donuts, Anyway?* (1992), is certainly the most powerful exception to this rule of representation. The film appeared on the fifty-year anniversary of the signing of Executive Order 9066. Tanaka's moving and poignant film focuses on her own father as a moving case study for the brutalizing effects of relocation, internment, and imprisonment on the male body and psyche. This film tracks Tanaka's search for her long-absent father, who has not been seen by the family since the years just after the internment until he is discovered in 1989 in a Los Angeles halfway house for the mentally ill. As an angry and politically outspoken young man in the camps, her father was roughed up by the FBI, declared mentally ill, and subsequently institutionalized for over a decade. The long years of

electro-shock, drug therapy, and trauma have left her father painfully oscillating on screen between moments of extreme memory loss as well as lucid recollection.

19 Hisaye Yamamato, "The Legend of Miss Sassagarawa," in *Seventeen Syllables and Other Stories* (Latham, NY: Kitchen Table Press, 1988).

20 Gotanda, "The Wash," 30. There are a numer of contemporary Japanese American visual artists who also explore the intergenerational fallout of the internment experience. Artist Roger Shimomura has produced some of the best work on internment camp history in his series, "An American Diary." For an excellent discussion of contemporary artists Glenn Kaino, Karen Kimura, and Linda Nishio, see Karin Higa's essay, "Finding Family Stories," in *Finding Family Stories: An Arts Partnership Porject, 1995–1998* (Los Angeles: Japanese American National Museum, 1998).

21 There is, of course, a fascinating gendered discourse surrounding silence and speech in Asian American literature. For the most in-depth analysis of this topic, see King-Kok Cheung's *Articulate Silences: Hisaye Yamamoto, Maxine Hong Kingston, Joy Kogawa* (Ithaca, NY: Cornell University Press, 1993).

22 Jun Xing, "Imagery, Counter Memory, and the Re-visioning of Asian American History: Rea Tajiri's *History and Memory: For Akiko and Takashige*," in *A Gathering of Voices on the Asian American Experience*, Annette White-Parks, ed. (Ft. Atkinson, WI: Highsmith Press, 1994). For some of the most provocative critical discussions of *History and Memory*, see Marita Sturken's "Absent Images of Memory: Remembering and Reenacting the Japanese American Internment," *Positions* 5:3 (1997): 687–707; Kent A. Ono, "Re/membering Spectators: Meditations on Japanese American Cinema," in *Countervisions: Asian American Film Criticism* (Philadelphia: Temple University Press, 2000); Glen Mimura's "Antidote for Collective Amnesia? Rea Tajiri's Germinal Image," also in *Countervisions*; Abe Mark Nornes's "Our Presence Is Our Absence: 'History and Memory,'" *Asian America: Journal of Culture and the Arts* 2 (Winter 1993): 167–171, and Darrel Y. Hamamoto's discussion of it in *Monitored Peril?*

23 For one of the most fascinating collections of found footage (home movies) of the Japanese American internment camps, see Robert A. Nakamura's edited compilation, "Something Strong Within" (1995).

24 Ono, "Re/Membering Spectators," 151.

25 Gina Marchetti, *Romance and the Yellow Peril: Race, Sex, and Discursive Strategies in Hollywood Fiction* (Berkeley and Los Angeles: University of California Press, 1993), 2.

26 While Ishigo mentions in her autobiography that there were many white

family members in the camp at Heart Mountain, Wyoming, I am not aware of any one study which tabulates the numbers of Caucasians and other non-Japanese Americans held in the camps who refused separation from Japanese and Japanese American family members. Both Karl Yoneda's *Ganbatte: Sixty Years of Struggle as a Kibei Worker* (Los Angeles: Resource Development and Publication, Asian American Studies Center, University of California, Los Angeles, 1983), and Jeanne Wakatsuki Houston's *Farewell to Manzanar* (Boston: Houghton Mifflin, 1973), include some discussion of this topic. The latter refers to an African American woman who covered her hair so she could escape detection and remain undisturbed with her Japanese American spouse.

27 Estelle Peck Ishigo, *Long Heart Mountain* (Los Angeles: Communicart, 1989), 33.

28 I place *Lone Heart Mountain* alongside Mine Okubo's *Citizen 13660* (1946) as an excellent example of visual autobiography of the internment experience.

29 Although she notes that there were a number of "blond, brown, and red-haired" internees in the camps, Ishigo's black and white pencil and charcoal sketches depict only Japanese and Japanese American subjects. Her portraits are stark and lack the detail of individual faces as if to signify instead the personal effects of relocation on a more abstract Japanese American community.

30 Glen Masato Mimura has also suggested that the desert needs to be reterritorialized for its crucial role in Asian American history, where Asian American subjects have tended to fall out of historical representations of the American West.

31 Films like *Mitsuye and Nellie: Asian American Poets* (1981), *History and Memory* (1991), *Farewell to Manzanar* (1976), and *Manzanar* (1971) also use the recurrent image of camp ruins in ways that suggest the unearthing of historical memory and the breaking of silence.

32 While my discussion has focused on the representation of Estelle Ishigo, Okazaki briefly depicts the body of Arthur Ishigo as another figure bearing the trace of historical trauma. In particular, the final scenes of the film record the dramatic physical transformation that occurs as Arthur ages perceptibly in the camps working as a full-time laborer. In Okazaki's narrative, Estelle Ishigo recalls how, when they "were first interned, [Arthur] was strong and alive." Yet, in "three-and-a-half years, he seemed to have aged twenty years. He grew morose and sentimental. In the evening he would sit quietly or play his bamboo flute reminiscing and dreaming of what might have been." It is interesting that the final shot of

Days of Waiting visually reverses the movement of Estelle and Arthur Ishigo's physical decline by returning to close-up images of them as children unmarked by hardship, loss, and trauma.

33 In my own experience with teaching *Days of Waiting* to undergraduates, I have noticed that this film triggers the most reactions of all the films I show about relocation and internment. Occasionally, Asian American students have expressed outrage over what they initially perceive to be unexamined whiteness at the center of this film about Asian American history. Likewise, I have noticed that many white students find themselves both deeply touched by Ishigo's story as well as deeply troubled by their own symbolic shift from mere spectators of internment history to participants of it through the spectacle of this white woman in the camps. The disparity in student response raises complicated questions about the politics of racial representation and ownership of the historical gaze. To whom do historical representations of the internment camp experience "belong"? *Days of Waiting,* after all, reminds us that individuals with as little as one-sixteenth Japanese blood were subjected to relocation and internment.

34 Alan Parker, as quoted in Sara Frankel's "American Lesson, British Eyes: 'Paradise' Director Alan Parker Attacks the U.S. Social Problem through Love Story," in the *San Francisco Examiner,* December 23, 1990.

35 For an excellent discussion of the racial and gendered politics in *Come See the Paradise,* see Laura Hyun-Yi Kang's "The Desiring of Asian Female Bodies: Interracial Romance and Cinematic Subjection," in *Visual Anthropology Review* 9, no. 1 (Spring 1993): 5–21.

36 Ibid., 6.

37 It should be noted that *Come See the Paradise* appeared briefly at the box office during the Persian Gulf War. Perhaps as a result of this poor timing, this film (critical as it was of U.S. wartime policy in another era) lasted only a few weeks in the theaters before it was abruptly pulled from circulation and rushed straight to video.

38 Traise Yamamoto, *Masking Selves,* 68.

39 Kimberly Chun, "Snow Falls on Cold Hearts," *Asian Week* 21, no. 20 (January 19, 2000): 19.

40 The Media Action Network for Asian Americans (MANAA) criticized Scott Hicks for casting a native Japanese actress, Youki Kudoh, in the role of Japanese American nisei, Hatsue Miyamoto. The media group complained that the casting would reinforce the misconception that "people with Asian features must be foreign-born" and "therefore must have an Asian accent." For a full discussion of this controversy, see "Group Criti-

cizes Casting in 'Snow Falling on Cedars,'" in *North American Post* 17, no. 1 (January 1, 2000): 2.

41 Quotes are taken from the reviews of Stephen Holden, "Prejudice Lingers in a Land of Mists," *New York Times*, December 22, 1999, and Jay Carr, "Mysteries of 'Snow Falling' Unfold in Layers," *Boston Globe*, September 14, 1999.

42 David Guterson, *Snow Falling on Cedars* (San Diego: Harcourt Brace, 1994), 154.

43 Kang, "Desiring of Asian Female Bodies," 12.

44 Alan Parker manages to compress the internment history into a forty-minute sequence, while Scott Hicks squeezes this history into a mere twenty-minute interlude.

45 Holden, "Prejudice Lingers in a Land of Mists."

46 Bob Thomas, "At the Movies: 'Snow Falling on Cedars,'" Associated Press, December 20, 1999.

47 Chun, "Snow Falls on Cold Hearts."

NOTES TO CHAPTER FOUR

1 See Lisa Yoneyama's work on World War II memory and commemoration in her study of Japanese public and private remembering of the atomic bombing of Hiroshima in *Hiroshima Traces: Time, Space, and the Dialectics of Memory* (Berkeley: University of California Press, 1999).

2 Joan Myers and Gary Okihiro, *Whispered Silences: Japanese Americans and World War II* (Seattle: University of Washington Press, 1996), 9.

3 Ibid.

4 Ibid., 15.

5 Yoneyama, *Hiroshima Traces*, 4.

6 A 1998 Japanese American National Museum exhibit on the internment camps at Ellis Island's immigrant museum made headlines for the exhibit's use of the term "concentration camp." See Somini Sengupta, "What Is a Concentration Camp? Ellis Island Exhibit Prompts a Debate," *New York Times*, March 8, 1998.

7 Lecture by John Dower, "Contemporary Japan Bashing," at Wellesley College, March 1, 1995.

8 This information is based on a personal interview with the exhibit's senior curator, Thomas Crouch," on April 30, 1999, at the Smithsonian Institution's National Air and Space Museum, Washington, D.C.

9 See my discussion of this famous photograph in chapter 1.

10 Both Hector Bywater's *The Great Pacific War* (1925) and Homer Lea's *The Valor of Ignorance* (1909) are exhibited as examples of racist anti-Japanese "yellow peril" literature of the early twentieth century.

11 See my discussion in chapter 1 of how the Smithsonian has used Dorothea Lange's photographs in this exhibit.

12 Actress Nikki Harada, a yonsei Japanese American born in 1976, plays the role of the daughter. Sansei actor and former internee Sab Shimono plays the father. Shimono was interned at Amache, Colorado, at age four.

13 For a fascinating history of the arts and crafts created in the internment camps, see Allen H. Eaton's *Beauty Behind Barbed Wire: The Arts of the Japanese in Our War Relocation Camps* (New York: Harper and Bros., 1952).

14 See Crouch interview.

15 Quoted in Michael Milstein, "Japanese Americans Revisit Their Painful Past History: World War II Internees Dismantle Barracks at Wyoming Prison Camp and Send It Back to L.A.'s Little Tokyo as a Permanent Reminder," *Los Angeles Times,* October 3, 1994.

16 From Tina Nguyen, "Preserving a Dark Remnant of National History: Barracks from a World War II Japanese American Internment Camp Is Transported to Los Angeles," *Los Angeles Times,* November 10, 1994, San Gabriel Valley section, part J, 6.

17 Sharon Yamato, *Moving Walls: Preserving the Barracks of America's Concentration Camps* (Los Angeles: Sharon Yamato, 1998), 6.

18 *Japanese American National Museum Quarterly* 9, no. 3 (October–December 1994): 2.

19 Darrell Hamamoto included a discussion of how contemporary Asian American documentary filmmakers have engaged in such a self-reflexive creative and critical process in his paper on the Asian American Caucus panel at the Society for Cinema Studies, Dallas, Texas, March 1996.

20 Annual pilgrimages of remembrance are also held at the other sites of former internment camps. Like Manzanar, they too are desolate places that together comprise a culture of camp ruins. Manzanar was singled out by an act of Congress to become a national historic site that would represent the history of all ten former camps.

21 James D. Houston, "Another Kind of Western" (with Jeanne Wakatsuki Houston), *One Can Think about Life When the Fish Are in the Canoe* (Santa Barbara: Capra Press, 1985), 58.

22 Carl Nolte, in *San Francisco Chronicle,* April 13, 1997. Nolte cites this description from a December 1946 *Los Angeles Times* article. The wooden barracks and administration buildings were torn down after the war and

sold at auction, much of it to the local residents of the nearby towns of Lone Pine and Independence. The Manzanar exhibit at the nearby Eastern California Museum posts several photographs of local homes that were built out of former barracks, such as the Willow Motel in Lone Pine that is constructed out of a former barracks.

23 National Park Service archaeologists have found numerous graffiti at Manzanar, including writing from the "Zero Boys" (a Los Angeles gang) and various statements scratched into the concrete of the camp reservoir.

24 Bill Michael, director of the Eastern California Museum, has estimated this number of annual visitors to Manzanar National Historic Site. A National Park Service planning book on the site estimates that the number could grow to 300,000 by the year 2000. For more information on the little-known history of Manzanar's Children's Village, see Arthur A. Hansen's oral history project on former orphan internees, which is being conducted at California State University, Fullerton. See also Satsuki Ina's documentary on this subject, "Children of the Camps" (San Francisco: National Asian American Telecommunications Association, 1999).

25 From the program to the 24th Annual Manzanar Pilgrimage.

26 These quotations are taken from the July 1993 "Summary of Scoping Comments" on the general management plan for Manzanar National Historic Site, published in a report printed and distributed by Stanley T. Albright, regional director of the United States Department of the Interior, National Park Service.

27 Robert Kinoshita quoted in Houston's "A Different Kind of Western," in *One Can Think about Life When the Fish Are in the Canoe,* 51.

28 In Paul Rogers's "W.W. II Internment Camp Survivors Upset by Lack of Progress on Memorial," *San Jose Mercury News,* March 10, 1997.

29 Ibid.

30 It took over one year of debate before consensus could be reached on the wording on the Manzanar memorial plaque that is attached to one of the stone sentry buildings. In part, the final wording says, "May the injustices and humiliation suffered here as a result of hysteria, racism and economic exploitation never emerge again." Since it was erected on April 14, 1973, the plaque has been the site of desecration and vandalism.

31 Hastings's quote is taken from an interview in William Booth's "A Lonely Patch of History: Japanese Americans Were Forced to Live Here. They Don't Want It to Be Forgotten," *Washington Post,* April 15, 1997, 1.

32 Hastings is also quoted by journalist Carl Nolte in his story, "Lonesome Monument to a National Heartache," *San Francisco Chronicle,* April 13, 1997. The debate Hastings has raised concerns whether there were eight or

one watch towers installed at Manzanar. A National Park Service historian has conducted a three-year historic resource study on Manzanar that documents that there are toppled stone foundations for eight original towers.

33 Booth, "Lonely Patch of History," 1.

34 See Associated Press reporter Michael Fleeman's "Japanese-American Internment Camp in California Opening as Historic Site," published in the *Chicago Tribune,* July 28, 1997.

35 See ibid.

36 I am indebted to Richard Stewart for sharing his insights with me in a telephone conversation on August 26, 1999.

37 Filmmaker Rea Tajiri does a particularly excellent job of contextualizing Poston's Native American history in her film, *History and Memory: For Akiko and Takashige* (1991). The land on which the camp was built was seized from the native community and used by the War Relocation Authority during the war.

38 Phone conversation with Stewart, August 26, 1999.

39 The above quote is from Adams, *Born Free and Equal,* 25, 29.

40 The National Park Service Website for Manzanar National Historic Site is http://www.nps.gov/manz/.

41 At the beginning of the twenty-first century, plans are also now underway to build an internment sculpture in Washington, D.C. Also, in February 2000, Vice-President Al Gore proposed a $4.8 million dollar initiative to preserve all of our nation's World War II–era internment camps.

NOTES TO CHAPTER FIVE

1 David Leiwei Li, *Imagining the Nation: Asian American Literature and Cultural Consent* (Stanford, CA: Stanford University Press, 1998), 3–4.

2 John Okada, *No No Boy—a Novel* (Rutland, VT: Charles E. Tuttle, 1957), 1.

3 See *Time,* "How to Tell Your Friends Apart from the Japs," December 22, 1941, 33, and *Life,* "How to Tell the Japs from the Chinese," December 22, 1941, 81–82.

4 Nellie Wong, from *Dreams in Harrison Railroad Park* (Berkeley: Kelsey St. Press, 1977), 16.

5 See Ron Takaki's more extensive discussion of this subject in his book, *Strangers from a Different Shore: A History of Asian Americans* (Boston: Little, Brown, 1989), 370–371. According to Charles Kikuchi's diary entries, some Japanese Americans also took to wearing "I am Chinese" buttons for their own sense of safety.

6 *Time,* "How to Tell Your Friends Apart," 33.

7   Ibid.

8   During the Persian Gulf War in 1991, Renny Christopher brought a certain cartoon to my attention depicting Saddam Hussein's head attached to the body of a spider under the slogan, "Iraqnophobia." While this depiction obviously played off the then-popular sci-fi film, "Arachnophobia," it was also uncanny in its resemblance to a well-known World War II cartoon (documented in John Dower's book) of "Louseous Japanicus"—depicting a bucktooth Tojo head on the body of a louse with a caption declaring that the Tokyo area "must be completely annihilated" in a final solution or "complete cure" of the Japanese vermin.

9   See John Dower's *War without Mercy: Race and Power in the Pacific War* (New York: Pantheon Books, 1986), 81, 84.

10 Ibid., 186.

11 Ibid., 10.

12 See James Moy's discussion of the fascinating history of Asian exhibition and performance in his *Marginal Sights: Staging the Chinese in America* (Iowa City: University of Iowa, 1993).

13 What makes "Tokyo Rose" especially unique—even problematic as a subject for study in Asian representation—is her status as a disembodied object of desire and horror. Or, as journalist Masayo Duus has put it, a contradictory blend of "vocal pin-up girl" and "female Fu Manchu." As a radio creation, she exists purely as "voice." I mention her here as a relevant Japanese American female figure while acknowledging that she is worthy of fuller treatment.

14 See Masayo Duus, *Tokyo Rose: Orphan of the Pacific,* translated by Peter Duus (Tokyo: Kodansha International, 1979), 9.

15 Other Japanese female radio personas were dubbed Madam Tojo and Radio Rose and were heard throughout the Pacific, especially in Alaska and the Aleutian Islands.

16 See Leslie Bow's discussion of Asian American women in narratives of betrayal and national allegiance in *Betrayal and Other Acts of Subversion* (Princeton, NJ: Princeton University Press, 2001). Her short discussion of the "Tokyo Rose" myth in her introduction offers an excellent place of departure for further critical and cultural investigation of Iva Toguri D'Aquino's victimization.

17 I would like to give special thanks to Leslie Bow, Claudia Castaneda, James Clifford, Angela Davis, Joe Dumit, Donna Haraway, Ellen Louise Hart, Laura Kang, Lorraine Kenny, Glen Mimura, and Teresia Teaiwa for their invaluable feedback, help, and inspiration in initially exploring my discussion of the media representation of Yamaguchi and Ito.

18 The 1988 Winter Olympic games posed a similar dilemma in the show-down between superstar and defending gold medalist Katarina Witt of East Germany and Debi Thomas of the United States. Thomas was the first African American woman to compete in this event. She won the silver medal in her competition against Witt, but she was virtually invisible if not erased from Olympic memory in 1992. Like Midori Ito, Thomas was constructed as the ultimate athletic powerhouse and sensation in women's figure skating at that time. As with Yamaguchi, her "ethnic heritage" was noticeably downplayed by the media.

19 See Takaki's *Strangers from a Different Shore* and Michael Omi and Howard Winant's updated 1994 edition of *Racial Formation in the United States: From the 1960s to the 1990s* (New York and London: Routledge, 1984, 1994), for their excellent discussion of the historical and political context of racism against Asian Americans in the last two decades.

20 See Omi and Winant, *Racial Formation*, 3.

21 See Dorinne K. Kondo's commentary on the problematic nature of the "hyphen" in *Crafting Selves* (Cambridge, MA: Harvard University Press, 1990). She discusses the politics of the hyphen as a signifier that locates "American" as the privileged term in Asian American identity formation.

22 Frank Deford, "The Jewel of the Winter Games," *Newsweek*, February 10, 1992, 53.

23 Ibid., 46–47. Italics are mine.

24 Ibid., 52.

25 Takaki, *Strangers from a Different Shore*, 214–215.

26 Monica Sone, *Nisei Daughter* (Seattle: University of Washington Press, 1953), 19.

27 John Armour and Peter Wright, eds., *Manzanar* (New York: Times Books, 1988), 56.

28 Mike Downy, "Going Beyond the All-American Story," *Los Angeles Times*, February 21, 1992.

29 *Newsweek*, February 10, 1992, 51. Italics are mine.

30 Martha Duffy, "Spinning Gold," *Time*, February 10, 1992, 56.

31 I am indebted to Leslie Bow for first articulating this observation in our conversations on the topic.

32 This debate centered over what direction the future of women's figure skating would take: A sport where artistry would be privileged? Or an event dominated by "jump mania" rendering it more like a kind of gymnastics on ice?

33 The Japanese media dubbed Ito the "Tsunami Girl" and the "Japanese Jumping Bean" in honor of her amazing athletic abilities.

34 Duffy, "Spinning Gold," 55, and E. M. Swift, "Next Stop, Albertville," *Sports Illustrated,* March 2, 1992, 20.

35 Duffy, "Spinning Gold," 55.

36 Swift, "Next Stop," 20.

37 There is no question that Midori Ito's silver medal performance in the 1992 Olympics has forever changed the nature of the sport. She is without a doubt the most powerful athletic jumper the women's event has ever had. And she now holds the honor of being the first woman in history to land the difficult triple-axel jump in Olympic competition.

38 Deford, "Jewel," 51, and Duffy, "Spinning Gold," 56.

39 Duffy, "Spinning Gold," 55, and Frank Deford and Mark Starr, "American Beauty," *Newsweek,* March 2, 1992, 52.

40 Duffy, "Spinning Gold," 55.

41 For a provocative reading of the sexual representation of women figure skaters, see Cynthia Baughman's excellent anthology, *Women on Ice: Feminist Essays on the Tonya Harding/Nancy Kerrigan Spectacle* (New York and London: Routledge, 1995).

42 When Ito is shown doing the classic spins in other photographs, she too has an elegant look, one that is virtually indistinguishable from the longer lines allowed Yamaguchi's photographs.

43 Duffy, "Spinning Gold," 55.

44 Deford, "Jewel," 50.

45 Ibid.

46 Ibid., 46.

47 Tonya Harding is the only other woman skater besides Midori Ito who has successfully performed the difficult triple axel jump in an official competition. Harding has been and continues to be represented by the media as the working-class bad girl of figure skating who shoots pool, runs drag races, and was once thoroughly capable of achieving Olympic greatness if only she had been able to shake her bad attitude and turbulent past: as a survivor of a broken family, sexual assault, asthma, a propensity for weight gaining, an on-again, off-again marriage. In similar fashion, the 1992 American pairs figure-skating duo of Calla Urbanski and Rocky Marvel (dubbed by the media as the "aging waitress and truck driver" team) were also constructed as the working-class would-be Olympic heroes of every "dreamer and working stiff." Enormous media attention was focused on their class background, but as soon as it was apparent that they would not actually win their competition, the team all but disappeared from media view.

48 A former gymnast and two-time European figure-skating champion from

France, Bonaly leaped into notoriety and the public gaze on the basis of her provocative costumes, her strong Olympic performance, and the fact that she executed an illegal back flip during practice, which cut into Midori Ito's rehearsal space, thus foiling the latter's concentration. It is worth noting that Bonaly is the only woman of African descent since Debi Thomas and Tai Babilonia of the United States who has had such a visible Olympic presence in women's figure skating. Bonaly was born in Africa and adopted by white French parents, but there was virtually no mention of race in the U.S. media coverage of her. Instead, media attention was focused almost exclusively on her *natural* physical abilities, her wardrobe, and her "abhorrent behavior" during practice. According to Olympic journalists, other women may glide effortlessly, but Bonaly *pumps, tears,* and *stalks* the ice in the programs as if her body were somehow more naturally inclined for athletic aggression and performance. Furthermore, while skaters like Katarina Witt win praise and recognition for their sexual charms and Western-style beauty, Bonaly was unduly punished for what the press unanimously condemned as her sexually charged skating costumes—personally designed by French couturier Christian Lacroix—and described by one journalist as "outfits that appeared to come from a garage sale at Hugh Hefner's."

49 Harding's vilification can be traced in virtually every editorial page of newspapers and magazines in the months following the 1994 attack on Kerrigan. Ironically, while Kerrigan may have earned upwards of $12 million in endorsement deals during the month before and after the 1994 Olympics, she was herself subjected to a media campaign of vilification based on her off-the-cuff comments overheard during the Olympic awards ceremony and afterwards at Disneyworld.

50 While Yamaguchi and Ito symbolically operated as the model minorities of figure skating, at the ensuing Summer Olympic games the entire Chinese women's swim team was represented as the bad girls of Barcelona. They were also constructed, not unproblematically, as particularly monstrous minorities as well. Virtually all of the televised coverage of the summer games included references to the illicit use of steroids on the part of the Chinese women's team, based on both fearful eyewitness locker-room allusions to "masculinized" bodies as well as the fact that the once obscure team dominated the event and outperformed their competitors from the West. It was also rumored that the trainers from what was previously the East German swim team had been invited to work with Chinese swimmers and were in fact the ones behind the alleged steroid use and new training technology; hence, with the official end of the Cold War, one

could say that the Chinese women's swim team here doubly operated as a new type of monstrous communist Other.

51 *Time* magazine reporter Martha Duffy seems to have gone out of her way not even to mention "race" in her special reports on Yamaguchi.

52 I am indebted to Ramona Fernandez, who brought Kristi Yamaguchi's audio-animatronic Disneyworld appearance to my attention in the spectacle of the American Adventure show.

53 While much of the Olympic representation of Yamaguchi would try to convince us that she is unambiguously all-American, persistent rumors have since abounded over how her Japanese heritage may have hurt her post-Olympic commodification. This has been an ongoing debate in the editorial pages of Kristi's hometown newspaper, the *San Jose Mercury News*, in the months after the Olympics. For further discussion of the rumors of her trouble in landing endorsements, see E. M. Swift's "A Golden Snub?" in *Sports Illustrated* 76, no. 11 (March 23, 1992): 7, and Mark Starr's and Todd Barrett's "What's the Value of Gold?" in *Newsweek*, October 26, 1992, 53–55.

54 See Laura Zinn, "To Marketers, Kristi Yamaguchi Isn't as Good as Gold," *Business Week*, March 9, 1992, and Jonathan Yardley, "The Sick Sense of Japan Bashing," *Toronto Star*, March 9, 1992, and "From Sports Star to Scapegoat," *Toronto Star*, March 11, 1992.

55 Jane Gottesman, "Kristi Yamaguchi's Coach Denies Her 'Ethnic Heritage' Has Limited Her Endorsement Range," *San Francisco Chronicle*, March 26, 1992.

56 Yamaguchi also appeared in a 1995 "Milk—What a Surprise!" ad by the National Fluid Milk Processor Promotions Board. To date she is the only Asian American female in this series of ads. In the photograph, a smiling, scantily clad Yamaguchi appears wearing a milk moustache, black leotard, and white skates. She is bent over, her arms clasped behind her back in a pose that suggests either a skating warm-up or sexual submission.

57 Darrell Y. Hamamoto comments on the strangeness of this ad in his excellent study of Japanese Americans in the media: *Monitored Peril: Asian Americans and the Politics of TV Representation* (Minneapolis: University of Minnesota Press, 1994), 243.

58 For more discussion of the offending MSNBC headline and Kwan's lucrative ability to profit from her Olympic silver and bronze medals, see Eric Sorensen, "Asian Groups Attack MSNBC Headline Reference to Kwan—News Web Site Apologizes for Controversial Wording," *Seattle Times*, March 5, 1998; "No Medal for Kwan," *San Francisco Chronicle*, March 4, 1998; Rachel Blount, "Silver Won't Cost Kwan a Lot of Green,"

Star Tribune, March 29, 1998; Dwight Perry, "Skater Kwan Could Sell Ice in Antarctica," *Seattle Times,* February 17, 2000; Bruce Horowitz, "Spins Silver into Gold," *USA Today,* February 9, 2000.

59 Kimiko Hahn, "Introduction," in Asian Women United, eds., *IKON #9: Without Ceremony* (Stuyvesant Station, NY: IKON, Inc., 1988), 7.

NOTES TO THE EPILOGUE

1 I cite these excerpts by Mike Moto and Amy Hill from Darby Li Po Price's excellent ethnographic essay on mixed-race Asian American standup comics, "Humorous Hapas, Performing Identities," *Amerasia Journal* 1, no. 23 (1997): 99–111. Also see Amy Hill's autobiographical performance piece, "Tokyo Bound," included in Brian Nelson, ed., *Asian American Drama: 9 Plays from the Multiethnic Landscape* (New York: Applause Theater Book Publishers, 1997).

2 Peggy Phelan, *Unmarked: The Politics of Performance* (New York and London: Routledge, 1993), 25–26.

3 For other Asian American performances dealing with multiracial identity, see Brenda Wong Aoki's autobiographical work drawing from her Japanese, Chinese, Spanish, and Scottish heritage, and Teja Arboleda's writing and performance work as "Ethnic Man"—documenting his heritage as an American of Chinese, African American, Filipino, Native American, German, and Dutch background who continually passes as Iraqi, Pakistani, and Latino.

4 See Traise Yamamoto, *Masking Selves, Making Subjects: Japanese American Women, Identity, and the Body* (Berkeley and Los Angeles: University of California Press, 1999).

5 I refer to the widespread violence targeting South Asians together with Middle Easterners in the aftermath of the terrorist attacks on September 11, 2001.

6 See Velina Hasu Houston's outstanding trilogy of plays dealing with the interracial marriages between Japanese war brides and American servicemen: "Tea," in *Unbroken Threads: An Anthology of Plays by Asian American Women,* Roberta Uno, ed. (Amherst: University of Massachusetts Press, 1993); and "Asa Ga Kimashita," in *The Politics of Life: Four Plays by Asian American Women,* Velina Houston, ed. (Philadelphia: Temple University Press, 1993), and "American Dreams" (unpublished).

7 Velina Hasu Houston, "On Being Mixed Japanese in Modern Times," *Pacific Citizen,* December 20–27, 1985.

8 This poem was originally published in the text of ibid.

9　Velina Hasu Houston, "Green Tea Girl in Orange Pekoe Country" was reprinted in *Caffeine* (Woodland Hills, CA: n.p., 1993).

10　Ai, "On Being 1/2 Japanese, 1/8 Choctaw, 1/4 Black, and 1/16 Irish," *Ms,* May, 1978, 58. It is ironic that Ai's representation of her racial lineage privileges the "1/2 Japanese and 1/8 Choctaw" over the "1/4 African American" line of descent in her ancestry.

11　Ibid., 58.

12　Ibid.

13　Thelma Seto, "The Archipelago of My Bones," *Amerasia Journal* 23, no. 1 (1997): 157–159. In her biographical notes, Seto tells us that she is a mixed-race, multicultured sansei who was born and raised in the Middle East.

14　For other brief discussions of the *Time* magazine cyber cover girl, see Donna Haraway, *Modest-Witness@Second-Millennium.FemaleMan-Meets-OncoMouse: Feminism and Technoscience* (New York: Routledge, 1997); Jennifer Gonzales, "The Appended Subject: Race and Identity as Digital Assemblage," in *Race in Cyberspace,* Beth E. Kolko, Lisa Nakamura, and Gilbert B. Rodman, eds. (New York and London: Routledge, 2000); Evelyn Hammond, "New Technologies of Race," in *Processed Lives: Gender and Technology in Everday Life,* Jennifer Terry and Melodie Calvert, eds. (New York: Routledge, 1997); and Lauren Berlant, *The Queen of America Goes to Washington City: Essays on Sex and Citizenship* (Durham, NC: Duke University Press, 1997).

15　This quote is taken directly from the notes of the managing editor of *Time* magazine, James R. Gaines, in the fall 1993 special issue: vol. 142, no. 21, 2.

16　See Donna Haraway's discussion of Varley's story in her essay, "The Promise of Monsters," in *Simians, Cyborgs, and Women: The Reinvention of Nature* (New York: Routledge, 1991).

17　John Varley, "Press Enter," in *Blue Champagne* (New York: A Berkley Book, 1986), 241.

18　Ibid., 275.

19　Haraway herself admits to a visceral response to the horrible death of Lisa Foo at the story's end by torture and mutilation, and opts as a "resistant" reading to rewrite the ending of the narrative with "fanzine" poetic license by extracting her body from such a finale and elevating her to the status of a cyborg woman-of-color guide.

20　From "A Cyborg Manifesto," in *Simians, Cyborgs, and Women,* 149.

21　Ibid., 154.

22　Haraway alludes here to the work of Chela Sandoval, who has theorized this "new political voice," designated "woman of color," in her extensive work on "oppositional consciousness" in *Methodology of the Oppressed* (Minneapolis: University of Minnesota Press, 2000).

23 See Audre Lorde, *Sister/Outside: Essays and Speeches* (Trumansburg, NY: Crossing Press, 1984); Patricia Hill Collins, *Black Feminist Thought: Knowledge, Consciousness, and the Politics of Empowerment* (Boston: Unwin Hyman, 1990); Trinh T. Minh-ha, "Not You/Like You: Post-Colonial Women and the Interlocking Questions of Identity and Differencee," *Inscriptions* nos. 3/4 (1988): 71–77; Gayatri Spivak, *In Other Words: Essays in Cultural Politics* (New York: Methuen, 1987); and Gloria Anzaldúa, *Borderlands: The New Mestiza/La Frontera* (San Francisco: Spinsters/Aunt Lute, 1987).

24 See Jessica Hagedorn's "On Theater and Performance," in the special issue on ethnic theater in *Melus* 16, no. 3 (Fall 1989): 13–15.

25 "Cyborg Manifesto," 174.

26 Haraway, *Simians, Cyborgs, and Women.*

27 According to Haraway, Randolph painted her "Cyborg" while at the Bunting Institute in 1989 and exhibited it there in a spring 1990 solo exhibition titled "A Return to Alien Roots." The show incorporated, from many sources, "traditional religious imagery with a postmodern secularized context."

28 See Haraway's interview with Constance Penley and Andrew Ross in "Cyborgs at Large: Interview with Donna Haraway," in *Technoculture* (Minneapolis: University of Minnesota Press, 1991).

29 See Laura Hyun Yi Kang's *Compositional Subjects: Enfiguring Asian/American Women* (Durham, NC: Duke University Press, 2002).

30 I am indebted to Jennifer Gonzalez, who has brought to my attention another rare image of the Asian woman warrior as a combat model cyborg conjured from the fashion pages of *Mondo 2000*. In this representation of what I identify as the "cyborg masquerade," the body of the Asian woman is literally strapped into prosthetic cyborg armor (not unike Sigourney Weaver in her robotic forklift suit of armor in *Aliens*) and stands armed and ready for battle against an infernal backdrop of death's heads, shadows, and flames. Another visually arresting image of the Asian woman as cyborg can be found in Nick Knight's photograph in *Visionaire* magazine of multiracial Japanese American model Devon Aoki, dressed up in Alexander McQueen haute couture like a monstrous one-eyed cyborg punk geisha. With a safety pin and cherry blossom stick pushed through her forehead, Aoki returns the camera's gaze with a rather menacing one of her own.

31 From Kia Asamaya's *Silent Mobius*, no. 6 (San Francisco: Viz Comics, 1991).

32 Jennifer Gonzales, "Envisioning Cyborg Bodies: Notes from Current Research," in *The Cyborg Handbook*, Chris Hables Gray, Heidi J. Figueroa-Sarriera, and Steven Mentor, eds. (New York and London: Routledge, 1995), 277.

33 Ibid.

34 Ibid.

35 Pratibha Parmar, "That Moment of Emergence," in *Queer Looks: Perspectives on Lesbian and Gay Film and Video*, Martha Gever, John Greyson, and Pratibha Parmar, eds. (New York and London: Routledge, 1993), 10.

36 For intriguing discussions of Asian American pornography, see James S. Moy, *Marginal Sights: Staging the Chinese in America* (Iowa City: University of Iowa Press, 1993), and Darrell Y. Hamamoto, "The Joy Fuck Club: Prolegomenon to an Asian American Porno Practice," in *Countervisions: Asian American Film Criticism*, Darrell Y. Hamamoto and Sandra Liu, eds. (Philadelphia: Temple University Press, 2000). A sampling of some of Carrera's parodic, self-Orientalizing performances includes *Samurai Pervert 2* (1999), *Thai Me Up* (1998), *Bangkok Boobarella* (1996), and *Hell on Heels* (1994).

37 All quotations and biographical background information are taken from her official Website: html://www.asiacarrera.com. Her "namesake," actress Tia Carrere, is a well-known multiracial Chinese-Filipino-Spanish American performer who is perhaps best known as the "babe" in the *Wayne's World* films.

38 On her Website, Carrera currently offers us a fascinating step-by-step documentation of the "glamorous make-up tricks" she deploys in order to transform her face for the camera.

39 Quote is taken from Carrera's Website: html://www.asiacarrera.com.

40 Yamamoto, *Masking Selves*, 101.

41 I am well aware that Asia Carrera operates as an exception to the rule of representation of Asian women in pornography, where there is a striking lack of empowering or resistant images of women in the American and international markets. Carrera is unique as an adult entertainment performer who manages her own Website, where she routinely posts her own critical articulations as a woman of color who works inside the industry.

42 Peggy Phelan, *Unmarked: The Politics of Performance* (New York and London: Routledge, 1993).

Adams, Ansel. *Born Free and Equal: Photographs of the Loyal Japanese-Americans at Manzanar Relocation Center, Inyo County, California.* New York: U.S. Camera, 1944.

———. *Born Free and Equal: Photographs of the Loyal Japanese Americans at Manzanar Relocation Center, Inyo County, California,* ed. Emily Medvec. Washington, DC: Echolight Corporation, 1984 [1944].

Aguilar-San Juan, Karin, ed. *The State of Asian America: Activism and Resistance in the 1990s.* Boston: South End Press, 1994.

Anzaldúa, Gloria. *Borderlands/La Frontera: The New Mestiza.* San Francisco: Aunt Lute Books, 1991.

Arboleda, Teja. *In the Shadow of Race: Growing Up as a Multiethnic, Multicultural, and "Multiracial" American.* Mahwah, NJ: Lawrence Erlbaum, 1998.

Armour, John, and Peter Wright, eds. *Manzanar.* New York: Times Books, 1988.

Asamiya, Kia. *Silent Mobius.* No. 6. San Francisco: Viz Comics, 1991.

Asia Society. *Asia America: Identities in Contemporary Asian American Art.* New York: New York Press and the Asia Society Galleries, 1994.

Asian Women United. *IKON #9: Without Ceremony.* Stuyvesant Station, NY: IKON, Inc., 1988.

Asian Women United. *Making Waves: An Anthology of Writings by and about Asian American Women.* Boston: Beacon Press, 1989.

Barthes, Roland. *The Empire of Signs.* Trans. Richard Howard. New York: Hill and Wang, 1982 [1970].

———. *Mythologies.* New York: Hill and Wang, 1957.

Baughman, Cynthia, ed. *Women on Ice: Feminist Essays on the Tonya Harding/Nancy Kerrigan Spectacle.* New York and London: Routledge, 1995.

Berlant, Lauren. *The Queen of America Goes to Washington City: Essays on Sex and Citizenship.* Durham, NC: Duke University Press, 1997.

Berson, Misha. *Between Worlds: Contemporary Asian American Playwrights.* New York: Theater Communications Group, 1990.

Blount, Rachel. "Silver Won't Cost Kwan a Lot of Green." *Star Tribune,* March 29, 1998.

Booth, William. "A Lonely Patch of History: Japanese Americans Were Forced to Live Here. They Don't Want It to Be Forgotten." *Washington Post,* April 15, 1997.

Bow, Leslie. *Betrayal and Other Acts of Subversion.* Princeton, NJ: Princeton University Press, 2001.

Bruchac, Joseph, ed. *Breaking Silence: An Anthology of Contemporary Asian American Poets*. Greenfield Center, NY: Greenfield Review Press, 1983.

Buck, Ray. *Tiffany Chin: A Dream on Ice*. Chicago: Children's Press, 1986.

Burton, Jefferey F., Mary M. Farrell, Florence B. Lord, and Richard W. Lord, eds. *Confinement and Ethnicity: An Overview of World War II Japanese American Relocation Sites*. Seattle: University of Washington Press, 2002.

Caldwell, Erskine, and Margaret Bourke-White. *You Have Seen Their Faces*. New York: Modern Age Books, 1937.

Carroll, Dennis, ed. *Kuma Kahua Plays*. Honolulu: University of Hawaii Press, 1980.

Chalfen, Richard. *Turning Leaves: The Photograph Collections of Two Japanese American Families*. Albuquerque: University of New Mexico Press, 1991.

Chan, Jeffery Paul, Frank Chin, Lawson Fusao Inada, and Shawn Wong, eds. *The Big Aiiieeeee! An Anthology of Chinese American and Japanese American Literature*. New York: Meridian, 1991.

Chan, Judy, Heeyon Chang, Michael Cho, et al. *Finding Family Stories: An Arts Partnership Project, 1995–1998*. Los Angeles: Japanese American National Museum, 1998.

Chan, Sucheng. *Asian Americans: An Interpretive History*. Boston: Twayne, 1991.

Chang, Irene. "Camp Barracks May Go on Display in Little Tokyo." *Los Angeles Times,* February 4, 1992.

Cheung, King-Kok. *Articulate Silences: Hisaye Yamamoto, Maxine Hong Kingston, Joy Kogawa*. Ithaca, NY, and London: Cornell University Press, 1993.

Chiang, Fay. "Mine Okubo." *Dialogue* (Asian American Arts Alliance). Fall 1998, 30–33.

Chow, Rey. *Writing Diaspora: Tactics of Intervention in Contemporary Cultural Studies*. Bloomington and Indianapolis: Indiana University Press, 1993.

Chun, Kimberly. "Snow Falls on Cold Hearts." *Asian Week,* January 19, 2000, 19.

Clifford, James. *The Predicament of Culture: Twentieth-Century Ethnography, Literature and Art*. Cambridge, MA: Harvard University Press, 1988.

———. *Routes: Travel and Translation in the Late Twentieth Century*. Cambridge, MA: Harvard University Press, 1997.

Conrat, Maisie, and Richard Conrat. *Executive Order*. Los Angeles: University of California, Los Angeles, Asian American Studies Center, 1992 [1972].

Constantine, Mark and Annie Nakai. "Executive Order 9066." *San Franscisco Examiner,* February 16, 1992.

Daniell, Fidel. "A Rewriting of History." *Artweek* 17 (May 1986): 10.

Daniels, Roger. *Asian America: Chinese and Japanese in the United States since 1850*. Seattle: University of Washington Press, 1988.

Daniels, Roger, Sandra C. Taylor, and Harry H. L. Kitano, eds. *Japanese Ameri-*

cans: From Relocation to Redress. Seattle: University of Washington Press, 1991.

Danovitch, Sylvia E. "The Past Recaptured? The Photographic Record of the Internment of Japanese-Americans." Prologue: The Journal of the National Archives 12, no. 2 (Summer 1980): 91–103.

Davidov, Judith Fryer. "'The Color of My Sin, the Shape of My Eyes': Photographs of the Japanese-American Internment by Dorothea Lange, Ansel Adams, and Toyo Miyatake." Yale Journal of Criticism 9.2 (1996): 223–244.

Davis, Keith F. The Photographs of Dorothea Lange. Kansas City, MO: Hallmark Cards in Association with H. N. Abrams, New York, 1995.

Deford, Frank. "The Jewel of the Winter Games." Newsweek, February 10, 1992.

Deford, Frank, and Mark Starr. "American Beauty." Newsweek, March 2, 1992.

Deleuze, Gilles, and Felix Guattari. "What Is a Minor Literature?" In Kafka: Toward a Minor Literature. Minneapolis: University of Minnesota Press, 1986.

Dower, John. War without Mercy: Race and Power in the Pacific War. New York: Pantheon Books, 1986.

Downy, Mike. "Going beyond the All-American Story." Los Angeles Times, February 21, 1992.

Du Bois, W. E. B. The Souls of Black Folk: Essays and Sketches. Chicago: A. G. McClurg, 1903.

Duffy, Martha. "Spinning Gold." Time, February 10, 1992.

Duus, Masayo. Tokyo Rose: Orphan of the Pacific. Trans. Peter Duus. Tokyo: Kodansha International, 1979.

Eaton, Allen H. Beauty behind Barbed Wire: The Arts of the Japanese in Our War Relocation Camps. New York: Harper and Bros., 1952.

Embrey, Sue. The Lost Years: 1942–1946. Los Angeles: Moonlight Publications, 1972.

Feng, Peter. Identities in Motion: Asian American Film and Video. Durham, NC: Duke University Press, 2002.

Fong, Katheryn M. "Feminism Is Fine, but What's It Done for Asia America?" Bridge 6 (1978): 21–22.

Friedlander, Saul, ed. Probing the Limits of Representation. Cambridge, MA: Harvard University Press, 1992.

Fung, Richard. "Seeing Yellow: Images of Asians in Film and Video." In The State of Asian America. Karin Aguilar-San Juan, ed. Philadelphia: Temple University Press, 1994.

Fusco, Coco. "The Other History of Intercultural Performance." The Drama Review, Spring 1994, 143–167.

Fuss, Diana, ed. Inside/Out: Lesbian Theories, Gay Theories. New York and London: Routledge, 1991.

Gee, Emma, ed. *Counterpoint Perspectives on Asian America.* Los Angeles: UCLA Asian American Studies, 1976.

Gesensway, Deborah, and Mindy Roseman. *Beyond Words: Images from America's Concentration Camps.* Ithaca, NY: Cornell University Press, 1987.

Gilligan, Carol. *In a Different Voice: Psychological Theory and Women's Development.* Cambridge, MA: Harvard University Press, 1982.

Gilman, Sander. *Difference and Pathology: Stereotypes of Sexuality, Race, and Madness.* Ithaca, NY: Cornell University Press, 1985.

Glenn, Evelyn Nakano. *Issei, Nisei, Warbride: Three Generations of Japanese American Women in Domestic Service.* Philadelphia: Temple University Press, 1986.

Gotanda, Philip Kan. "Yankee Dawg You Die." In *New American Plays 1.* Portsmith, NH: Heinemann, 1992.

———. "The Wash." In *Between Worlds: Contemporary Asian-American Plays.* Misha Berson, ed. New York: Theatre Communications Group, 1990.

Gottesman, Jane. "Kristi Yamaguchi Coach Denies Her 'Ethnic Heritage' Has Limited Her Endorsement Range." *San Francisco Chronicle,* March 26, 1992.

Gray, Chris Hables, Heidi J. Figueroa-Sarriera, and Steven Mentor, eds. *The Cyborg Handbook.* New York and London: Routledge, 1995.

Green, David. "Photography and Anthropology: The Technology of Power." *Ten 8,* no. 14.

Grossberg, Lawrence, Cary Nelson, and Paula Treichler, eds. *Cultural Studies.* New York and London: Routledge, 1992.

Grover, Jan Zita. "The Winner Names the Age." *AfterImage.* April 1988, 14–18.

Gunn, Rex B. *They Called Her Tokyo Rose.* Santa Monica, CA: Gunn, 1977.

Guterson, David. *Snow Falling on Cedars.* San Diego: Harcourt Brace, 1994.

Hagedorn, Jessica. *Charlie Chan Is Dead: An Anthology of Contemporary Asian American Fiction.* New York: Penguin Books, 1993.

———. "On Theater and Performance." *MELUS* 16, no. 3 (Fall 1989): 13–15.

Hall, Stuart. "Cultural Identity and Diaspora." In *Identity: Community, Cultural Difference.* Jonathan Rutherford, ed. London: Laurence and Wishart, 1990.

———. "Cultural Studies: Two Paradigms." In *Culture, Ideology, and Social Process: A Reader.* Tony Bennett, Graham Martin, Colin Mercer, and Janet Woollcott, eds. London: Open University, 1981.

———. "The Local and the Global: Globalization and Ethnicity." In *Culture, Globalization, and the World System.* Anthony King, ed. Binghamton, NY: Department of Art and Art History, SUNY Binghamton, 1991.

———. "Old and New Identities, Old and New Ethnicities." In *Culture, Globalization, and the World System.* Anthony King, ed. Binghamton, NY: Department of Art and Art History, SUNY Binghamton, 1991.

Hamamoto, Darrell Y. *Monitored Peril: Asian Americans and the Politics of TV Representation.* Minneapolis: University of Minnesota Press, 1994.

———. *Nervous Laughter.* New York: Praeger, 1989.

Hamamoto, Darrell Y., and Sandra Liu, eds. *Countervisions: Asian American Film Criticis.* Philadelphia: Temple University Press, 2000.

Hansen, Asael T. "My Two Years at Heart Mountain: The Difficult Role of an Applied Anthropologist." In *Japanese Americans: From Relocation to Redress.* Roger Daniels, Sandra C. Taylor, and Harry H. L. Kitano, eds. Seattle: University of Washington Press, 1986.

Haraway, Donna J. "The Actors Are Cyborg, Nature Is Coyote, and the Geography Is Elsewhere: Postscript to 'Cyborgs at Large.'" In *Technoculture.* Constance Penley and Andrew Ross, eds. Minneapolis: University of Minnesota Press, 1991.

———. "A Cyborg Manifesto: Science, Technology, and Socialist-Feminism in the Late Twentieth Century." In *Simians, Cyborgs, and Women: The Reinvention of Nature.* New York: Routledge, 1991.

———. *Modest-Witness@Second-Millennium.FemaleMan-Meets-OncoMouse: Feminism and Technoscience.* New York: Routledge, 1997.

———. "The Promises of Monsters: A Regenerative Politics for Inappropriate/d Others." In *Cultural Studies.* Lawrence Grossberg, Cary Nelson, and Paula Treichler, eds. New York and London: Routledge, 1992.

———. "Situated Knowledges: The Science Question in Feminism as a Site of Discourse on the Privilege of Partial Perspective." *Feminist Studies* 14:3 (Fall 1988).

Harris, Neil. "All the World a Melting Pot? Japan at American Fairs, 1876–1904." In *Mutual Images: Essays in American-Japanese Relations.* Akira Iriye, ed. Cambridge, MA: Harvard University Press, 1975.

Hart, Lynda, and Peggy Phelan, eds. *Acting Out: Feminist Performances.* Ann Arbor: University of Michigan Press, 1993.

Hartigan, Patti. "Digging Out the Secrets." *Boston Sunday Globe,* January 2, 2000.

Harwit, Martin. *An Exhibition Denied: Lobbying the History of Enola Gay.* New York: Copernicus, 1996.

Henderson, Amy, and Adrienne L. Kaeppler, eds. *Exhibiting Dilemmas: Issues of Representation at the Smithsonian.* Washington, DC: Smithsonian Institution Press, 1999.

Higa, Karin. *Bruce and Norman Yonemoto: Memory, Matter, and Modern Romance.* Los Angeles: Fellows of Contemporary Art: Japanese American National Museum, 1999.

Holborn, Mark. "Past and Present." *Aperture,* no. 102 (Spring 1986): 6–8.

Hongo, Garrett. *The Open Boat.* New York: Doubleday, 1993.

hooks, bell. "Critical Interrogation: Talking Race, Resisting Racism." *Inscriptions* 5 (1990).

———. *Feminist Theory: From Margin to Center.* Boston: South End Press, 1984.

———. *Talking Back: Thinking Feminist, Thinking Black.* Boston: South End Press, 1989.

———. *Yearning: Race, Gender, and Cultural Politics.* Boston: South End Press, 1990.

Horowitz, Bruce. "Michelle Kwan Spins Silver into Gold." *USA Today,* February 9, 2000.

Houston, James. *One Can Think about Life When the Fish Are in the Canoe.* Santa Barbara, CA: Capra Press, 1985.

Houston, Jeanne Wakatsuki. *Beyond Manzanar: Views of Asian-American Womanhood.* Santa Barbara, CA: Capra Press, 1985.

Houston, Jeanne Wakatsuki, and James Houston. *Farewell to Manzanar.* Boston: Houghton Mifflin, 1973.

Houston, Velina Hasu. "On Being Mixed Japanese in Modern Times." *Pacific Citizen,* December 20–27, 1985.

———. "The Past Meets the Future: A Cultural Essay." *Amerasia* 17:1 (1991): 53–56.

———, ed. *The Politics of Life: Four Plays by Asian American Women.* Philadelphia: Temple University Press, 1993.

———. "Tea." In *Unbroken Thread.* Roberta Uno, ed. Amherst: University of Massachusetts Press, 1994.

"How to Tell Your Friends Apart from the Japs." *Time,* December 22, 1941.

"How to Tell the Japs from the Chinese." *Life,* December 22, 1941.

Howe, Graham, Patrick Nagatani, and Scott Rankin, eds. *Two Views of Manzanar: An Exhibition of Photographs by Ansel Adams/Toyo Miyatake.* Los Angeles: Frederick S. Wight Art Gallery, University of California, Los Angeles, 1978.

Howe, Russell Warren. *The Hunt for Tokyo Rose.* Lanham, NY: Madison Books, 1990.

Hsu, Kai-yu, and Helene Palubinskas, eds. *Asian-American Authors.* Boston: Houghton Mifflin, 1972.

Hune, Shirley, Hyung-chang Kim, Stephen S. Fugita, and Amy Ling, eds. *Asian Americans: Comparative and Global Perspectives.* Pullman, WA: Washington State University Press, 1991.

Hwang, David Henry. *Broken Promises: Four Plays by David Henry Hwang.* New York: Avon Books, 1983.

———. *M. Butterfly.* New York: Penguin Books, 1986.

Ichioka, Yuji, ed. *Views from Within: The Japanese American Evacuation and Resettlement Study.* Los Angeles: Resource Development and Publication,

Asian American Studies Center, University of California, Los Angeles, 1989.

Inada, Lawson. *Legends from Camp.* Minneapolis: Coffee House Press, 1994.

Inoue, Todd. "Nihonjin Homeboy: Writer David Mura Explores the Tensions of Sansei Life." *Bay Area Metro,* April 8–14, 1993, 44.

Ishigo, Estelle Peck. *Lone Heart Mountain.* Los Angeles: Communicart, 1989 [1972].

Jameson, Frederic. *Signatures of the Visible.* New York: Routledge, 1990.

JanMohammed, Abdul R., and David Lloyd. "Introduction: Minority Discourse—What Is to Be Done?" *Cultural Critique* 7 (Fall 1987).

———, eds. "Introductions: Toward a Theory of Minority Discourse." *Cultural Critique* 6 (Spring 1987).

———, eds. *The Nature and Context of Minority Discourse.* New York: Oxford University Press, 1990.

Japanese American Citizens League. *Iva Toguri (d'Aquino): Victim of a Legend.* San Francisco: Committee for Iva Toguri/Japanese American Citizens League, September 1975.

Kang, Laura Hyun Yi. *Compositional Subjects: Enfiguring Asian/American Women.* Durham, NC: Duke University Press. 2002.

———. "The Desiring of Asian Female Bodies: Interracial Romance and Cinematic Subjection." *Visual Anthropology Review* 9, no. 1 (Spring 1993): 5–21.

Kaplan, Caren. "Deterritorializations: The Rewriting of Home and Exile in Western Feminist Discourse." *Cultural Critique* 6 (Spring 1987).

Kapp, Robert. "Introduction to the Review Symposium on Orientalism." *Journal of Asian Studies* 39, no. 3 (May 1980): 481–484.

Karp, Ivan, and Steven Lavine, eds. *Exhibiting Cultures: The Poetics and Politics of Museum Display.* Washington, DC, and London: Smithsonian Institution Press, 1991.

Kikuchi, Charles. *The Kikuchi Diary.* Urbana: University of Illinois Press, 1973.

Kikumura, Akemi. *Through Harsh Winters: The Life of a Japanese Immigrant Woman.* Novato, CA: Chandler and Sharp, 1981.

Kim, Elaine. *Asian American Literature: An Introduction to the Writings and Their Social Context.* Philadelphia: Temple University Press, 1982.

———. "Defining Asian American Reality through the Literature." *Cultural Critique* 6 (Spring 1987).

Kobayashi, Tamai, and Mona Oikawa. *All Names Spoken.* Toronto: Sister Vision Press, 1992.

Kogawa, Joy. *Obasan.* Boston: David R. Godine, 1981.

Kolko, Beth E., Lisa Nakamura, and Gilbert B. Rodman. *Race in Cyberspace.* New York and London: Routledge, 2000.

Kondo, Dorinne K. *Crafting Selves: Power, Gender, and Discourses of Identity in a Japanese Workplace.* Chicago: University of Chicago Press, 1990.

———. "Dissolution and Reconstruction of Self: Implications for Anthropological Epistemology." *Cultural Anthropology* 1, no. 1 (1986): 74–88.

Kuramitsu, Kristine C. "Internment and Identity in Japanese American Art." *American Quarterly* 47, no. 4 (December 1995): 619–658.

La Duke, Betty. *Women Artists: Multi-Cultural Visions.* Trenton, NJ: Red Sea Press, 1992.

Lange, Dorothea. *Dorothea Lange.* New York: Museum of Modern Art, 1966.

———. *Dorothea Lange: Photographs of a Lifetime.* Millerton, NY: Aperture, 1982.

Lange, Dorothea, and Paul Taylor. *An American Exodus: A Record of Human Erosion.* New York: Reynal and Hitchcock, 1939.

Leong, Russell, ed. *Moving the Image: Independent Asian Pacific American Media Arts.* Los Angeles: University of California Asian American Studies Center, 1991.

Li, David Leiwei. *Imagining the Nation: Asian American Literature and Cultural Consent.* Stanford, CA: Stanford University Press, 1998.

Li, Tommy. "Barracks Will Be Exhibited." *Los Angeles Times,* October 2, 1994.

Lim, Shirley Geok-lin, and Amy Ling, eds. *Reading the Literatures of Asian America.* Philadelphia: Temple University Press, 1993.

Lim, Shirley Geok-lin, Amy Ling, Margarita Donnelly, and Mayumi Tsutakawa, eds. *The Forbidden Stitch: An Asian American Women's Anthology.* Corvallis, OR: Calyx Books, 1989.

Lipton, Dean. "Wayne M. Collins and the Case of 'Tokyo Rose.'" *Journal of Contemporary Studies* 8, no. 4 (Fall/Winter 1985).

Lowe, Lisa. *Critical Terrains: French and British Orientalisms.* Ithaca, NY: Cornell University Press, 1991.

———. *Immigrant Acts: On Asian American Cultural Politics.* Durham, NC: Duke University Press, 1996.

———. "Heterogeneity, Hybridity, Multiplicity: Marking Asian American Differences." *Diaspora* 1, no. 1 (Spring) 1991: 24–44.

Mani, Lata, and Ruth Frankenberg. "The Challenge of *Orientalism.*" *Economy and Society* 14, no. 2 (May 1985): 174–192.

———. "Multiple Mediations: Feminist Scholarship in the Age of Multinational Reception." *Inscriptions* 5 (1989).

Marchetti, Gina. *Romance and the Yellow Peril: Race, Sex, and Discursive Strategies in Hollywood Fiction.* Berkeley and Los Angeles. University of California Press, 1993.

Matsuoka, Jack. *Camp II, Block 211: Daily Life in an Internment Camp.* San Francisco: Japan Publications, 1974.

McWilliams, Carey. "What About Our Japanese Americans?" New York: Public Affairs Committee, 1944.

Medvec, Emily. *Born Free and Equal: An Exhibition of Ansel Adams Photographs.* Fresno Metropolitan Museum of Art, History, and Science. Washington, DC: Echolight, 1984.

Meltzer, Milton. *Dorothea Lange: A Photographer's Life.* New York: Farrar, Straus and Giroux, 1978.

Miller, Randall M., ed. *The Kaleidoscopic Lens: How Hollywood Views Ethnic Groups.* Englewood, NJ: Ozer, 1980.

Milstein, Michael. "Japanese Americans Revisit Their Painful Past." *Los Angeles Times,* October 3, 1994.

Mirikitani, Janice. *Awake in the River.* San Francisco: Isthmus Press, 1978.

———. *Shedding Silence.* Berkeley, CA: Celestial Arts, 1987.

———, ed. *Ayumi: A Japanese American Anthology.* San Francisco: Japanese American Anthology Committee, 1980.

———. *Time to Greez! Incantations from the Third World.* San Francisco: Third World Communications, 1975 [1973].

Miyatake, Atsufumi, Taisuke Fujishima, and Eikoh Hosoe, eds. *Toyo Miyatake: The Man behind the Camera, 1923–1979.* Tokyo: Bungeishunju, 1984.

Miyoshi, Masao. *Off Center: Power and Culture between Japan and the United States.* Cambridge, MA: Harvard University Press, 1991.

Mori, Toshio. *Yokohama California.* Seattle: University of Washington Press, 1979 [1949].

Morioka, Lois. *The Long Road from White River.* New York: New Writers' Press, 1983.

Morrison, Toni. "The Site of Memory." In *Inventing the Truth: The Art and Craft of Memoir.* William Zinsser, ed. Boston: Houghton Mifflin, 1987.

Moy, James. *Marginal Sights: Staging the Chinese in America.* Iowa City: University of Iowa Press, 1993.

Mura, David. "Cultural Claims & Appropriations: (e.g. Who Owns the Internment Camps?)." *Art Papers* 21, issue 2 (March/April 1997): 6–11.

———. *Turning Japanese: Memoirs of a Sansei.* New York: Anchor Books, 1991.

———. *Where the Body Meets Memory: An Odyssey of Race, Sexuality, and Identity.* New York: Doubleday, 1996.

Murayama, Milton. *All I Asking for Is My Body.* San Francisco: Supa Press, 1975 [1959].

Mydans, Carl. "Coast Japs Are Interned in Mountain Camp." *Life,* April 6, 1942, 15–19.

———. *Carl Mydans, Photojournalist.* New York: Abrams, 1985.

————. "Tule Lake." *Life*, March 20, 1944, 25–35.

Nakamura, Hiroshi. *Treadmill: A Documentary Novel*. Oakville, Ontario, and Buffalo, NY: Mosaic Press, 1996.

Nakano, Mei. *Japanese American Women: Three Generations, 1890–1990*. San Francisco: National Japanese American Historical Society, 1990.

Nguyen, Tina. "Preserving a Dark Remnant of National History." *Los Angeles Times*, November 10, 1994.

"No Medal for Kwan." *San Francisco Chronicle*, March 4, 1998.

Oehling, Richard. "The Yellow Menace." In *The Kaleidoscopic Lens: How Hollywood Views Ethnic Groups*. Randall M. Miller, ed. Englewood, NJ: Ozer, 1980.

Ohrn, Karin Becker. *Dorothea Lange and the Documentary Tradition*. Baton Rouge: Louisiana State University Press, 1980.

————. "What You See Is What You Get: Dorothea Lange and Ansel Adams at Manzanar." *Journalism History* 4:1 (Spring 1977): 14–22, 32.

Okada, John. *No No Boy*. Seattle: University of Washington Press, 1979 [1957].

Okihiro, Gary Y., and Joan Myers. *Whispered Silences: Japanese Americans and World War II*. Seattle: University of Washington Press, 1996.

Okihiro, Gary Y., Shirley Hune, Arthur A. Hansen, and John M. Liu, eds. *Reflections on Shattered Windows: Promises and Prospects for Asian American Studies*. Pullman: Washington State University Press, 1988.

Okimoto, Daniel I. *American in Disguise*. New York and Tokyo: John Weatherhill, 1971.

Okubo, Mine. *Citizen 13660*. New York: Arno Press, 1978 [1946].

Omi, Michael, and Howard Winant. *Racial Formation in the United States: From the 1960s to the 1990s*. New York and London: Routledge, 1994 [1986].

Orvell, Miles. *The Real Thing: Imitation and Authenticity in American Culture, 1880–1940*. Chapel Hill, NC, and London: University of North Carolina Press, 1989.

Palumbo-Liu, David. *Asian/American: Historical Crossings of a Racial Frontier*. Stanford, CA: Stanford University Press, 1999.

Parmar, Pratibha. "That Moment of Emergence." In *Queer Looks: Perspectives on Lesbian and Gay Film and Video*. Martha Gever, Pratibha Parmar, and John Greyson, eds. New York and London: Routledge, 1993.

Partridge, Elizabeth, ed. *Dorothea Lange: A Visual Life*. Washington, DC, and London: Smithsonian Institution Press, 1994.

Pauly, Brett. "Relics Tell Sad Tale of American Internment Camp." *Star Tribune* (Minneapolis), August 16, 1994.

Penley, Constance, and Andrew Ross. "Cyborgs at Large: Interview with Donna Haraway." In *Technoculture*. Minneapolis: University of Minnesota Press, 1991.

Perry, Dwight. "Skater Kwan Could Sell Ice in Antartic." *Seattle Times,* February 17, 2000.

Phelan, Peggy. *Unmarked: The Politics of Performance.* New York and London: Routledge, 1993.

Price, Darby Li-Po. "Humorous Hapas, Performing Identities." *Amerasia Journal* 1, no. 23 (1997): 99–111.

Rogers, Paul. "W.W. II Internment Camp Survivors Upset by Lack of Progress on Memorial." *San Jose Mercury News,* March 10, 1997.

Rydell, Robert W. *All the World's a Fair: Visions of Empire at American International Expositions, 1876–1916.* Chicago: University of Chicago Press, 1984.

Said, Edward. *Orientalism.* New York: Pantheon, 1979.

Schodt, Frederick L. *Manga! Manga! The World of Japanese Comics.* Tokyo: Kodansha International, 1983.

Seguro, Ed. "Potpourri, Ed's Observations." *Northwest Nikkei* 9, no. 2 (January 14, 1997): 9–11.

Sengupta, Somini. "What Is a Concentration Camp? Ellis Island Exhibit Prompts a Debate." *New York Times,* May 8, 1998.

Several, Michael. "Photographic Memories: Miyatake at Manzanar." *Public Art Review,* Spring/Summer 1996, 22–24.

Simpson, Caroline Chung. *Absent Presence: Japanese Americans in Postwar American Culture, 1945–1960.* Durham, NC: Duke University Press, 2001.

Sone, Monica. *Nisei Daughter.* Seattle: University of Washington Press, 1979 [1953].

Sorenson, Eric. "Asian Groups Attack MSNBC: News Web Site Apologizes for Controversial Wording." *Seattle Times,* March 5, 1998.

Spiegelman, Art. *Maus: A Survivor's Tale.* New York: Pantheon Books, 1986.

Spivak, Gayatri Chakravorty. *In Other Worlds: Essays in Cultural Politics.* New York and London: Routledge, 1988.

Starr, Mark, and Todd Barrett. "What's the Value of Gold?" *Newsweek,* October 26, 1992.

Steele, Danielle. *Silent Honor.* New York: Delacorte Press, 1996.

Sturken, Marita. "Absent Images of Memory: Remembering and Reenacting the Japanese Internment." *Positions* 5:3 (1997): 687–707.

———. *Tangled Memories: The Vietnam War, the AIDS Epidemic, and the Politics of Remembering.* Berkeley: University of California Press, 1997.

Sun, Shirley. *Mine Okubo: An American Experience.* San Francisco: East Wind Printers, 1972

Suzuki, Peter T. "Anthropologists in the Wartime Camps for Japanese Americans: A Documentary Study." *Dialectical Anthropology* 6 (1981): 23–60.

————, "The University of California Japanese Evacuation and Resettlement Study: A Prolegomenon." In *The Big Aiiieeeee!* Jeffery Paul Chan, Frank Chin, Lawson Inada, and Shawn Wong, eds. New York: Meridian Books/Penguin Books, 1991.

Swift, E. M. "A Golden Snub?" *Sports Illustrated,* March 23, 1992.

————. "Next Stop, Albertville." *Sports Illustrated,* March 2, 1992.

Tajima, Renee. "Lotus Blossom Don't Bleed." In *The Forbidden Stitch: An Asian American Women's Anthology.* Shirley Geok-lin Lim, Margarita Donnelly, and Mayumi Tsutakawa, eds. Corvallis, OR: Calyx Books, 1989.

Takagi, Dana. *The Retreat from Race: Asian-American Admissions and Racial Politics.* New Brunswick, NJ: Rutgers University Press, 1992.

Takaki, Ron. *Strangers from a Different Shore: A History of Asian Americans.* Boston: Little, Brown, 1989.

Takano, Cynthia. "Manzanar: Life in an Internment Camp through a Photographer's Eyes." *Rice,* August 1987, 61–62.

Tanaka, Chester. *Go for Broke: A Pictorial History of the Japanese American 100th Infantry Battalion and the 442nd Regimental Combat Team.* Richmond and San Mateo, CA: Go for Broke, 1982.

Taylor, Paul S. "Our Stakes in the Japanese Exodux." *Survey Graphic* 31, no. 9 (September 1942): 373–378, 396–397.

Tchen, John Kuo Wei. "Believing Is Seeing: Transforming Orientalism and the Occidental Gaze." In *Asia/America: Identities in Contemporary Asian American Art.* New York: Asia Society Galleries and the New Press, 1994.

Terry, Jennifer, and Melodie Calverts, eds. *Processed Lives: Gender and Technology in Everday Life.* New York: Routledge, 1997.

Trinh T., Minh-ha. "Not You/Like You: Post-Colonial Women and the Interlocking Questions of Identity and Difference." *Inscriptions,* nos. 3 and 4 (1988).

————. *Woman, Native, Other: Writing Postcoloniality and Feminism.* Bloomington and Indianapolis: Indiana University Press, 1989.

Tsujimoto, Karen. *Dorothea Lange: Archive of an Artist.* Oakland: Oakland Museum of California, 1995.

Tsutakawa, Mary. *They Painted from Their Hearts: Pioneer Asian American Artists.* Seattle: Wing Luke Asian Museum, University of Washington Press, 1994.

Uno, Roberta. *Unbroken Thread: An Anthology of Plays by Asian American Women.* Amherst: University of Massachusetts Press, 1994.

Uyeda, Clifford I. *A Final Report and Review: The Japanese American Citizens League National Committee for Iva Toguri.* Seattle: University of Washington Asian American Studies Program, 1980.

Uyematsu, Amy. *30 Miles from J-Town.* Brownsville, OR: Story Line Press, 1992.

Varaday, Brian. *Persistent Women Artists: Pablita Velarde, Mine Okubo, Lois Mailou Jones.* Ashland: Southern Oregon State College Productions, 1996.

Varley, John. "Press Enter." In *Blue Champagne.* New York: A Berkley Book, 1986.

The View from Within: Japanese American Art from the Internment Camps, 1942–1945. Los Angeles: UCLA Wight Art Gallery, UCLA Asian American Studies Center, and Japanese American National Museum, 1992.

Visweswaran, Kamala. "Defining Feminist Ethnography." *Inscriptions* 3/4 (1988).

Watanabe, Sylvia, and Carol Bruchac, eds. *Home to Stay: Asian American Women's Fiction.* Greenfield Center, NY: Greenfield Review Press, 1990.

Weglyn, Michi. *Years of Infamy: The Untold Story of America's Concentration Camps.* New York: Morrow Quill Paperbacks, 1976.

Wei, William. *The Asian American Movement.* Philadelphia: Temple University Press, 1993.

Welchman, John C. "Turning Japanese (In)." *Artforum* 27 (April 1989): 152–156.

White-Parks, Annette, ed. *A Gathering of Voices on the Asian American Experience.* Ft. Atkinson, WI: Highsmith Press, 1994.

Wong, Eugene Franklin. *On Visual Media Racism: Asians in the American Motion Pictures.* New York: Arno Press, 1978.

Wong, Nellie. *Dreams in Harrison Railroad Park: Poems.* Berkeley, CA: Kelsey St. Press, 1977.

Wong, Sau-ling Cynthia. *Reading Asian American Literature.* Princeton, NJ: Princeton University Press, 1993.

Wright, Pamela Stennes. "'Hitting a Straight Lick with a Crooked Stick': Strategies of Negotiation in Women's Autobiographies from the U.S. 1940s: Zora Neale Hurston, Mine Okubo, and Amelia Grothe." Ph.D. diss., University of California, San Diego, 1993.

Xing, Jun. *Asian America through the Lens: History, Representations, and Identity.* Walnut Creek, CA: AltaMira Press. 1998.

Yamada, Mitsuye. *Camp Notes and Other Poems.* Latham, NY: Kitchen Table Press, 1976.

———. *Desert Run: Poems and Stories.* Latham, NY: Kitchen Table Press, 1988.

———. "Invisibility Is an Unnatural Disaster." In *This Bridge Called My Back.* Cherríe Moraga and Gloria Anzaldúa, eds. Latham, NY: Kitchen Table Press, 1981.

Yamaguchi, Jack. *This Was Minidoka.* Nagaoka, Japan: Nagai Printing Co., 1989.

Yamamoto, Hisaye. *Seventeen Syllables and Other Stories.* Latham, NY: Kitchen Table Press, 1988.

Yamamoto, Traise. *Masking Selves, Making Subjects: Japanese American Women, Identity, and the Body.* Berkeley and Los Angeles: University of California Press, 1999.

Yamato, Sharon. *Moving Walls: Preserving the Barracks of America's Concentration Camps.* Los Angeles: Sharon Yamato, 1998.

Yardley, Jonathan. "From Sports Star to Scapegoat." *Toronto Star,* March 11, 1992.

———. "The Sick Sense of Japan Bashing." *Toronto Star,* March 9, 1992.

Yoneda, Karl. *Ganbatte: Sixty Years of Struggle as a Kibei Worker.* Los Angeles: Resource Development and Publication, Asian American Studies Center, University of California, Los Angeles, 1983.

Yoneyama, Lisa. *Hiroshima Traces: Time, Space, and the Dialectics of Memory.* Berkeley: University of California Press, 1999.

Zich, Arthur. "Japanese Americans: Home at Last." *National Geographic* 169, no. 4 (April 1996): 512--538.

Zinn, Laura. "To Marketers, Kristi Yamaguchi Isn't as Good as Gold." *Business Week,* March 9, 1992.

INDEX

Adams, Ansel, 18–37, 46, 111, 117, 142; aestheticized images of Manzanar, 29; representation of internees to land, 33–36, 149

Ai, 178

American in Disguise (Okimoto), 14, 26

American Indian boarding schools, 200

Anzaldúa, Gloria, 26, 81–82, 185

Aoki, Devon, as punk cyborg geisha, 226

Archaeology of memory, 107, 120

Armour, John, 32–33

Aso, Jerry, 55–56, 116

Bad Day at Black Rock (film), 94–95, 111

Beyond Words: Images from America's Concentration Camps (Gesensway and Roseman), 72–76

Body: the abject Japanese American body, 22–23, 40; bestial wartime representations of the Japanese/American body, 150–151; depictions of obedient and disobedient Japanese American males in internment camps, 198, 202–203; disciplining and punishment of Japanese American body, 93; Japanese American bodies as targets of violence, 147; masculinized Chinese Olympic women's swim team, 222–223; media fascination with Kristi Yamaguchi's body, 156–159; media fascination with Midori Ito's body, 160–164; the multiracial Asian American body, 173–179; reading gestures of resistance, 203; reading the Japanese American face, 3, 13–16, 19; sexualized Olympic female athlete bodies, 165–166; as signifier of historical trauma, 100–104; the spectacle of Asian American women's bodies, 145; World War II ethnic identity buttons, 218;

Bonaly, Surya, racialized representation, 222

Born Free and Equal (Adams), 18

Bow, Leslie, 152

Caldwell, Erskine, 40

Carrera, Asia, 191–192, 194, 224; self-Orientalizing performances, 227

Chun, Kimberly, 116

Citizenship: visual politics of representation, 7, 145–146; stripping of, from Iva Toguri D'Aquino, 152

Civil Liberties Act, 93, 126

Come See the Paradise (film), 55, 105, 111–113; representation of the camps, 115–118

Concentration camp, debate over use of the term, 215

Conrat, Masie and Richard. See *Executive Order 9066*

Constantine, Mark, 43–44

Crouch, Thomas, 127

Culbert, Drew, 124

Culture of ruins, 107; internment camp sites, 120–121, politics of memory at Hiroshima, 121–122, 215

Cyborgs, Asian women as, 183–191, 226. *See also* Haraway, Donna

Daniels, Roger, 9, 74

Danovitch, Sylvia, 203

Days of Waiting (film), 105–110, 214. *See also* Okazaki, Steven

Deford, Frank, 154–155, 167–168

DeWitt, John L., 16

Ding, Loni, 53–55

Dower, John W., 95, 122, 150–151

Downy, Mike, 156–157, 167–168

Du Bois, W. E. B., double consciousness, 26, 82, 209

Enola Gay, controversial exhibition of, 122

Executive Order 9066, 38, 68

Farewell to Manzanar (Houston), 55, 57, 99–100

Farewell to Manzanar (TV film), 55, 111

Gaze, betrayal by the camera, 45; in *Citizen 13660*, 82, 85–86; Lange's tragic gaze, 201, panoptic surveillance, 62–64, 191

Gesensway, Deborah. See *Beyond Words: Images from America's Concentration Camps*

Go for Broke (film), 94–97, 111

Gonzalez, Jennifer, 190

Gotanda, Phillip Kan, 99, 102

Grover, Jan Zita, 19

ABOUT THE AUTHOR

ELENA TAJIMA CREEF is Associate Professor of Women's Studies at Wellesley College, where she specializes in Asian American cultural studies, feminist theory, visual culture, and theories of race and ethnicity. She has published widely in journals and edited volumes.